SALE
M25
£7-50

CW01476704

THE STRUGGLE FOR HUMAN RIGHTS

An International and South African Perspective

by

Lorenzo S Togni

B.Soc Sc (Hons), M. Pub Ad (UCT), D. Phil (UNISA)

Juta & Co, Ltd

Dedicated to my niece Lara Nadia Zazeraj
for the love and joy she brought into my life.

First edition 1994
© Juta & Co, Ltd 1994
PO Box 14373, Kenwyn 7790

This book is copyright under the Berne Convention.
In terms of the Copyright Act 98 of 1978 no part of this book may be
reproduced or transmitted in any form or by any means,
electronic or mechanical, including photocopying, recording or by any
information storage and retrieval system, without permission
in writing from the Publisher.

ISBN 0 7021 3072 9

RP—D2758

CONTENTS

PART 4

INTERNATIONAL HUMAN RIGHTS ACTIVISTS

PART 5

MAJOR HUMAN RIGHTS ABUSERS

PART 6

THE LEGAL SYSTEM AND HUMAN RIGHTS – EARLY POLITICAL ACTIVISTS

PART 7

MAJOR MOVEMENTS IN THE HUMAN RIGHTS STRUGGLE IN SOUTH AFRICA

PART 8

HUMAN RIGHTS ACTIVISTS: SOUTH AFRICA

APPENDICES

ACKNOWLEDGEMENTS

I wish to thank Chris Gardner for suggesting that I write this book; Tania Adriaanse for typing the manuscript and patiently assisting me; and my sister Bula for her invaluable help and support. I also thank Shawn Lawrence of South Newspaper for his invaluable assistance and Mr Johan Kriel of the Naspers library for his co-operation. I am also indebted to the Manuscripts and Archives division of Cape Town Library for making material available to me.

LORENZO S TOGNI

PREFACE

In writing a book about human rights an author faces many challenges. This is especially the case if the text deals with South African society, which to date has lacked a tradition or human rights culture. The ongoing democratisation process in South Africa has brought the human rights issue into the forefront of political and constitutional debate.

Indeed, nearly all South Africans will have to be socialised into a human rights culture, thereby internalising its precepts. The establishment of a new democratic order in South Africa necessitates the entrenchment of a strong human rights foundation. The lessons of the past are sufficient to bring human rights issues into sharp public focus.

With this in view, this book hopes to serve as a preliminary textbook in the field of human rights studies. That it is imperfect is readily admitted by the author, in the hope that other persons, jurists, social scientists and others in the humanities will continue to research and publish this much needed material.

The book is sub-divided into eight parts, including a substantial appendix in order to provide a wide scope of the field to prospective students, politicians, business leaders and academics. It deals with the history of the human rights movement, slavery in many parts of the world, human rights movements and personal biographies of human rights abusers and activists. Treaties, conventions, protocols and other agreements are highlighted to give a broad perspective of the subject matter. Uppermost in the mind of the author is to inform and provide a grounding in the field of human rights.

Despite an unavoidable international perspective, the book depicts a wide range of South African movements and individuals who have been and still are involved in the struggle for the inalienable rights of man. Several activists have not been dealt with in this book as a result of the scope of the study. However, their contribution is acknowledged and may be the subject of a future project. The author has made an attempt to provide the relevant information, while making the book user friendly, because it is not addressed to highbrows and academics only, but to all South Africans.

LORENZO S TOGNI

PART 1

A MACROCOSMIC PERSPECTIVE OF THE HUMAN RIGHTS MOVEMENT

CHAPTER 1

HUMAN RIGHTS:
AN HISTORICAL PERSPECTIVE

INTRODUCTION

Today the term 'human rights' is being used perhaps more than at any time in history. These rights and their codification in law have their origin in the expressions emanating from the American and French revolutions in particular. However, the ideas relating to the rights of man or human rights go much further back than the period in which these two revolutions took place, ie the last decades of the 18th Century.

The notion of human rights is much older and was discussed by philosophers, poets and thinkers in antiquity, especially in ancient Greece and in Europe generally during the Middle Ages. Throughout the history of man, the idea of natural law has always been closely linked with the 'natural rights of man'. The ancient Greeks and Romans were particularly interested in the notion of human rights. The medieval Christian philosophers, in particular Saint Thomas Aquinas, were also very interested in the role of man in society and the relations between the individual and the various political systems of the time. A number of Christian theologians took a great interest in human rights, but the three most prominent people to make a study of the subject were the Dutch jurist, Hugo Grotius, the father of international law, the poet and author John Milton and the philosopher John Locke in England.

In ancient times the legal codes did not deal specifically with the issue of human rights as we know it. One of the first documented 'human rights codes' was promulgated during the reign of King Alfonso IX in the year 1188. The Cortes (Parliament) of the Kingdom of Leon (part of what today is Spain) received a confirmation from the King, in which, *inter alia*, he conceded a series of rights, eg the right of an accused to a proper trial, the right to the inviolability of human life, the right to a home, the right to property and the right to be known and respected as a human being. A recognition of a similar character was promulgated by King Andrew II of Hungary in the year 1222. The king gave a number of guarantees, among which was that no nobleman would be punished unless he was first given a fair trial that conformed to accepted judicial procedure at the time. It must be made clear, however, that in both these cases, these 'rights' applied mainly to the nobility and not the peasantry or other classes in the society of the time.

3

The famous Magna Charta, signed in 1215 at Runnymede, England, between King John and the feudal barons, also fell short of being an all-inclusive charter of human rights covering all members of English society, but one of its clauses was significant. Clause 39 stated, *inter alia*, that 'no freeman shall be taken or imprisoned ... or exiled or in any way destroyed ... except by the lawful judgement of his peers and according to the law of the land'. This clause was one of the earliest documented references, however remote, to the idea of individual freedom.

Three important revolutions gave strong impetus to the development of human rights: the English, French and American revolutions. In England in the 17th Century, two documents were promulgated giving its citizens their rights. They were the English Petition of Rights of 1628 and the English Bill of Rights 1689. These two documents set out clearly the rights of Englishmen and they soon found favour in the colonies in North America. The English Bill of Rights of 1689 was the model upon which the other very important human rights documents were based. These were the American Declaration of Independence in 1776, the Virginia Declaration of Rights, also of 1776, and the American Bill of Rights of 1791. In fact the American Bill of Rights in many cases follows the exact text of the original English Bill of Rights. A number of French thinkers and philosophers of the enlightenment also had a great influence upon the construction of the now famous American Bill of Rights. However, the influence was reciprocal. Events in America gave the French great encouragement, and in 1789, France produced its own Declaration of Rights of Man and of the Citizen.

These documents had a profound effect on political events throughout the world in the 19th and 20th centuries. Most major constitutions in Europe, America, Asia, Africa and the Caribbean followed the example of both the United States and France by adopting bills of rights in their respective constitutions. The Russian Bolsheviks in 1917 also used the examples of France and the United States during the establishment of their revolutionary regime. However, in Russia's case, the emphasis was on social and economic rights, rather than on individual freedom.

The Russian (Soviet) view of human rights differed from the traditional Western understanding of what these rights were. A comparison of the constitution of the United States and that of the former Soviet Union will indicate a number of these differences of approach. The First Amendment to the Constitution of the United States guarantees freedom of speech and of the press, two cornerstones of Western thinking with regard to human rights. The Russian Constitution of 1918 did not specifically mention freedom of speech or freedom of the press. Instead it spoke of freedom of the 'masses' and was worded to the effect that capitalist publishers were to be divested of property, machinery and other means of newspaper production and these turned over

4

to the masses. The American Constitution guarantees people the fundamental right of assembly, while the Soviet Constitution stated that the working class (masses) would be guaranteed premises, heating, lighting and furniture for purposes of assembly. In 1936, the Soviet Constitution changed its wording to a degree, but did not go so far as to guarantee the masses the right to peaceful assembly. It merely reworded the other stipulation, promising technical and other facilities without guaranteeing people the right to assemble. With the recent collapse of the Soviet system and the fragmentation of the Soviet empire, new and more democratic procedures with regard to human rights have been instituted, and are in the process of evolving.

The issue of human rights is of such great importance that the international community has brought pressure to bear to ensure that these rights are protected.

Humanitarian attitudes towards human rights violations have forced the signing of a number of treaties to safeguard the rights of the individual against arbitrary action by the state or other political/administrative authority. Humanitarianism has had a strong influence in forcing those states that violated the rights of individuals and groups to change their attitudes and their actions. There have been many documented examples of arbitrary action by states against religious and ethnic minorities in particular, and such actions are still taking place at present.

There are many instances of international action against states that violated basic human rights. Among the first of these humanitarian interventions took place in 1827. In that year, the Ottoman Empire was the subject of intervention by the combined forces of France, Russia and Great Britain. This intervention was caused by the constant and cruel abuses of the Turks against the Greeks. Through this international action, Greece gained its independence from Turkey in 1830. Syria was another country where a number of European states intervened in 1860, because the Syrian government had been responsible for the massacre of Christians in that country. The island of Crete was the subject of intervention between 1866 and 1868, because of the persecution of Christians there. Generally, intervention forced Turkey to end its persecution of Christians in the Slavic countries which were under its rule. There have been a number of other occasions when intervention has been necessary to stop human rights violations against minorities. In the early part of the 20th Century, western powers put pressure on the government of Russia to stop the persecution of Jewish citizens in Romania.

However, intervention on humanitarian grounds could not continue to be undertaken on an arbitrary basis; it had to be put under some form of international control and acknowledged as a tenet of international law. With the advent of the United Nations, intervention has become even more difficult to effect. The Charter of the United Nations forbids the use of force in international affairs and as such, intervention on humanitarian grounds cannot be undertaken without the express approval of the UN Security Council. It was in the sphere of religion that international treaties were first used to guarantee freedom of worship. In the German state of Westphalia, a treaty was signed in which both Roman Catholics and Protestants were guaranteed equality of worship. Countries that were predominantly Catholic also guaranteed the freedom of worship for Protestants. Another great step forward was the undertaking by Turkey in 1774 to protect the Christian religion and its property in territories under its control.

However, one treaty of very far-reaching significance in the religious sphere was the Final Act of Vienna, signed at the Congress of Vienna in 1815. This agreement provided, *inter alia*, for denominational equality in a number of Swiss cantons and in Germany, and one of its highlights was that for the first time the condition and status of Jews was improved and given official recognition. During the latter part of the last century, Montenegro, Serbia and Romania became independent of Turkish rule and they all had to guarantee freedom of religion. In 1878, Turkey was also forced to guarantee religious freedom to all people under its rule.

A number of other major treaties were very important to the issue of human rights. In 1814 the Treaty of Paris prohibited the slave trade on a universal basis, but the task of enforcing such a treaty was not easy. Treaty arrangements, in 1815, 1822, 1862, 1885 and in 1890, were all attempts to fight the slave trade and to try and stop the practice of slavery. It was only in 1926 that the League of Nations approved an International Slavery Convention, in terms of which the contracting parties undertook to do all in their power to suppress the slave trade and bring about the total abolition of all forms of slavery. The fight against slavery continues to this day under the auspices of the United Nations.

Regarding labour relations, several important treaties were concluded during the course of the 19th Century. These came into effect partly as a result of pressure from individual philanthropists, respected reformers and other social scientists, who pressed the governments of their countries to introduce legislation to regulate working conditions. To this end, representatives of a number of European countries met in the German capital, Berlin, in 1890. The Congress of Berlin, as this meeting was called, did not come to any solid conclusions, but accepted a number of recommendations that were of great moral importance. The pressure groups did not relent and a number of governments met in the Swiss city of Berne in 1905 and 1906. Here two multilateral labour conventions were signed which are credited with being the first international conventions for the protection of the individual. The conventions reached important conclusions, such as the prohibition of night work for women in industry. The use of dangerous chemicals in industry also received attention: one of the conventions forbade the use of very dangerous yellow phosphorous in the manufacture of watches. While these two conventions realised little in terms of modern (present day) expectations, they were very significant steps in the development of labour legislation.

War was another field that received international attention. In the 19th Century, two Swiss citizens, Henri Dunant and General Dufour, were instrumental in bringing about the Geneva Convention of 1864, relating to acceptable practices in the conduct of war. They were also responsible for the creation of the International Committee of the Red Cross, which was established in Geneva in 1864. Among the provisions of the Red Cross agreement was one that the wounded and sick in time of war must be cared for regardless of their country of origin. It also stipulated that wounded or captured soldiers were to be sent home if they were no longer capable of fighting. Another important treaty dealing with war and the rights of individuals and groups was the Declaration of St Petersburg in 1868. This stated clearly that everything possible should be done to avert war, but that, should war be inevitable, it should be conducted within the constraints of civilised behaviour and be compatible with the laws of humanity. This was the start of a movement towards the establishment of a humanitarian law of war. Congresses to this effect took place in Brussels in 1874, The Hague in 1899 and 1907, and a further two in 1925 and 1929. After World War II, Conventions were signed in Geneva with a view to alleviating the suffering of war victims, particularly at the end of the war.

HUMAN RIGHTS AND THE LEAGUE OF NATIONS

The League of Nations began with the treaties drawn up at the Paris Conference (Treaty of Versailles) in 1919. During the establishment of the Covenant of the League of Nations, Japan, one of the countries on the side of the victors, suggested that provisions be included in the League's Covenant which would oblige members not to discriminate on the basis of race or nationality. The insertion of this clause was very strongly opposed, surprisingly, by Britain and the United States and was consequently dropped. Japan tried once more to have a provision of no discrimination on the grounds of race or nationality included in the preamble to the Covenant, but this was also not approved, despite support from countries such as Italy, France and China. This meant that the Covenant of the League of Nations did not contain any provisions against racial discrimination, nor did it give formal recognition to the rights of man. The Covenant did, however, give recognition to the welfare and rights of man at an international level, in that it

(a) accepted the responsibility for fair treatment of women and children in labour practices;

(b) agreed to treat subjects of their colonies fairly and humanely;

(c) gave the League of Nations a supervisory role in stamping out the traffic in women and children; and

(d) made the League responsible for preventing and controlling diseases on an international level.

A number of the League's members were given control of colonies that were formerly German or Turkish, with the proviso that they treat the inhabitants of such colonies fairly and take responsibility for the appropriate development of such colonies and their people. These countries were held accountable to the League of Nations for the wellbeing of the citizens of the mandated territories. The fact that the countries concerned were responsible to the international community was in itself very significant, as evidenced by the controversial mandate given to South Africa over the former German Colony of South West Africa, now Namibia.

Another positive consequence of the Treaty of Versailles and other treaties at the conclusion of World War I was the establishment of the International Labour Organisation (ILO). In fact, Part XIII of the Treaty of Versailles is the constitution of the ILO. One of the distinguishing features of the ILO was that it was not a purely governmental body, but included representatives from employer groups as well as workers. With a few exceptions, the structure and the goals of the ILO are the same now as they were at the time of its inception in 1919. The ILO has been a prominent promoter of human rights in the field of labour relations law and related rights, such as industrial health, safety and welfare, working hours, holidays and pay. In the post-World War II era, the ILO became a very powerful organ (agency) of the United Nations Organisation, working for the abolition of forced labour, the removal of discriminatory practices in employment and occupations, the freedom of association generally and more specifically in work-related action, and equal pay for equal work. To this day, the International Labour Organisation is a major factor in combating discriminatory practices in the workplace.

The treaties concluded after the end of World War I also dealt with the issue of the rights of minorities. There were a number of states in eastern Europe, as well as Iraq in the Middle East, which were obliged to sign undertakings with regard to the proper treatment of minorities. The minority groups in these countries were to be given equal treatment before the law, and their social and political rights guaranteed without prejudice on the basis of race, language, colour or creed. In addition to the normal rights of minorities, they were to be guaranteed adequate access to the use of their own languages before the legal systems in these countries. It must be made clear, however, that the proper treatment of minorities was not a general requirement, placing responsibility on all nations, but was restricted to the regions mentioned. Non-signatories did not, of course, have a legal duty to comply with the requirements of the treaties governing minorities.

HUMAN RIGHTS IN THE POST-WORLD WAR II PERIOD

Any positive effects attributable to the efforts of the League of Nations, the International Labour Organisation and other institutions were completely undone by the rise of Fascism, predominantly in Italy, and National Socialism (Nazism) in Germany. The actions of the totalitarian regimes introduced in their respective countries by Benito Mussolini and Adolf Hitler brought on World War II, a retrogressive period for human rights, particularly in war-ravaged Europe. During the course of World War II there were a series of important declarations, statements and proclamations issued by a number of Allied powers. For example, on 14 August 1941 the Atlantic Charter was signed by the United States and Britain, followed by the United Nations Declaration, to which all allied powers were signatories, on 1 January 1942. In this declaration, the Allies undertook to preserve human rights and justice, adding that these would be included in the major peace aims of the Allies.

When World War II ended, the main Allied powers, namely, the United States, Britain, France and the Soviet Union, created the International Military Tribunal for the trial of German war criminals. A significant factor in the establishment of this tribunal was the fact that it could try crimes against peace, crimes of war, and, most important, crimes against humanity. The category 'crimes against humanity' was particularly relevant to crimes against the civilian population despite what the law of the country may have stipulated. Many laws promulgated under Nazi rule were in themselves violations of the conventions held sacred to the dignity of man. In addition, the tribunal stated quite clearly that any accused could not use the argument that he or she was obeying orders of a higher authority. This laid down the important principle that no person is forced to obey a command that in itself violates civilised conduct and accepted values and morals common to all mankind. In fact, the principles according to which the Nuremberg Trials (1945-1946) were conducted were later accepted and underwritten by the General Assembly of the United Nations.

THE UN CHARTER AND HUMAN RIGHTS

The Charter of the United Nations, adopted in 1945 after the San Francisco Conference, contains a number of clauses which affirm the positive stance on the issue of human rights. Among other things, the charter states that it has

> 'faith in the fundamental human rights, in the dignity and worth of the human person, in the equal rights of men and women and of nations large and small ... promoting and encouraging respect for human rights and assisting in the realisation of human rights and fundamental freedoms'.

Two articles in the UN Charter requires that members pledge themselves to take joint or separate action in co-operation with the UN for the attainment of universal respect for human rights and other fundamental freedoms for all mankind without reference to race, colour or creed, religion, sex or language. However, despite agreement on fundamental human rights and freedoms, a proposal at the founding of the United Nations that members not only promote but also protect human rights was not accepted by the founding members. In addition to this drawback, a clause in the Charter referred to as the domestic jurisdiction clause, says that the UN cannot intervene in the domestic affairs of a member country. Problems have arisen with regard to this clause, which creates legal difficulties in dealing with a member country that is in violation of sections of the Charter dealing with human rights. Some legal authorities argue that the protection of human rights is the responsibility of the individual member states, and further, that signature of the UN Charter by individual members does not put them under any legal obligation to protect human rights. However, another view holds that members do in fact have a legal obligation to protect human rights and that the domestic jurisdiction clause is of no effect since human rights is an international issue and not the exclusive domain of domestic interests.

In the past 25 years, the issue of domestic jurisdiction as enshrined in the UN Charter has caused much controversy, especially among scholars attempting to interpret the clause and a number of members states whose governments refused to accept UN intervention. One such case was the conflict generated by South Africa's racial policies which, until recently, caused controversy on an international level. The vagueness of the domestic clause has not, however, prevented the United Nations from investigating, assessing and then taking action against human rights violations. One of the clearest examples of such action by the UN was, and in a number of cases still is, the imposition of economic, diplomatic, sport and other sanctions levelled at South Africa. The UN General Assembly and its agencies have from time to time acted against other violations of human rights. Apart from South Africa, several Eastern countries have been investigated for violations of human rights, for example for using forced labour and violating the right of peaceful assembly by trade union organisations. The increasing incidence of human rights violations has prompted several UN members to press for an international bill of human rights, to supplement or replace the human rights proviso in the Charter. However, one positive step has been the establishment of a Commission on Human Rights, which is entrusted with the task of preparing documentation and researching international treaties for dealing with problems related to human rights and the violation thereof.

UNITED NATIONS HUMAN RIGHTS ORGANISATIONS

The General Assembly of the United Nations is the institution responsible for guaranteeing human rights. This task is in turn vested in the UN Social and Economic Council. Trust territories (of which almost none exist today) are under the watchful eye of the UN Trustkeeping Council. Where human rights violations are of such a nature that peace and security in the world are threatened, the UN Security Council has jurisdiction and can move for effective intervention in the situation. However, the UN Economic and Social Council remains the body mainly responsible for the assessment of human rights situations. It has two sub-units under its jurisdiction: the Commission on Human Rights and the Commission on the Status of Women. Through these organisations a number of human rights issues have been studied and dealt with over the years. These will be examined individually below:

1 International Bill of Rights

The Commission on Human Rights at its inception was given the task of preparing an International Bill of Rights. In its original scope, the Bill was to consist of three important sections. They included documents dealing with

(a) Declaration;

(b) Covenant; and

(c) The process of Implementation.

The Declaration, which was debated and issued in 1948 by the General Assembly, was and still is known as the Universal Declaration of Human Rights. This was, however, only a partial declaration and it was not until 1966 that the International Bill of Human Rights was ready for publication in its entirety. Three additional international treaties were submitted in 1966. These were:

(a) the International Covenant on Economic, Social and Cultural Rights;

(b) the International Covenant on Civil and Political Rights; and

(c) an optional protocol to *(b)* above, giving the right of communication or alternatively the right of petition.

2 Universal Declaration of Human Rights

These rights consist, for the most part, of the rights already existing in many countries' constitutions and legal systems, and include

(a) equality before the law;

(b) protection against arbitrary arrest;

(c) the right to a fair trial;

(d) freedom from *ex post facto* legislation;

(e) freedom of thought;

(f) freedom of religion;

(g) freedom of conscience;

11

(h) freedom of opinion and expression;

(i) freedom to assemble peacefully; and

(j) freedom of Association.

The Universal Declaration of Human Rights is not enforceable legally as it is not an international treaty, but simply an agreed-upon standard opinion of what constitutes human rights and how they should be applied. In addition to the abovementioned rights, the declaration also lists economic, social and cultural rights. Examples of these are the right to work and the freedom to choose one's work, equal pay for equal work, and the right to acquire sufficient education for personal betterment. Some may argue that because it imposes no legal treaty obligations, the Declaration is of little value. Against this it may be argued that at least members of the UN do have some standard to strive for in the field of human rights. In addition, a vast number of organisations, governments, political parties and other bodies have a standard against which to measure their performance with regard to human rights.

3 International Covenant on Civil and Political Rights and the Optional Protocol

In this Covenant, each member state undertakes to treat the individuals under its jurisdiction equally, without distinction on the basis of race, colour, creed, sex, language, political or other opinions, national or social origins, property, status or birth. The International Covenant and the Universal Declaration do differ slightly; for example, the right to own property and the right to political asylum are not included as rights in the Covenant. The Covenant in turn includes a number of rights not listed in the Declaration. These include more macro-economic rights, such as the right of all people to self-determination and the right of ethnic, linguistic or religious minorities to speak their own language and practise their own religions.

In addition to the above, the Covenant makes provision for the estab-lishment of a Human Rights Committee, consisting of 18 individual members. One of its main tasks is to study reports submitted by states indicating their progress, if any, in giving effect to the rights promulgated in the Covenant on Civil and Political Rights. The committee also has the power to assess grievances submitted by any state that another member state is not complying with the provisions of the Covenant. An attempt is then made to resolve the issue, failing which it is handed over to an *ad hoc* conciliation commission, which tries to find an amicable solution. Those states that become parties to the Optional Protocol give the Human Rights Committee the right to investi-gate allegations from individual people of violations of conditions or stipulations contained in the Covenant.

4   International Covenant on Economic, Social and Cultural Rights
The parties to this Covenant are obliged to take steps to achieve the realisation
of the rights it recognises. These include the economic, social and cultural
rights listed in the Universal Declaration. Signatories to the Convention on
Economic, Social and Cultural rights are obliged to put it into practice
immediately. That is, they must prohibit discrimination on the basis of sex,
race, colour, creed, language, political and other opinions, national or social
origins, property, birth status or any other status. The signatories are also
obliged to report their progress in implementing the provisions of the Covenant in the states under their jurisdiction. However, these conditions have to
be notified and become effective three months after the date of ratification or
when 35 members have notified the conditions of the Covenant.

CONVENTIONS UNDER UNITED NATIONS AUSPICES
There are several other conventions dealing with a variety of issues critical
to life and limb and to the maintenance of standards relating to human rights
and the violation thereof. One of the more important is the *Convention on the
Prevention and Punishment of the Crime of Genocide*. This Convention is
based largely upon the principles enunciated by the International Military
Tribunal that tried major German war criminals after World War II. The
Genocide Convention of 1948 is significant in that the contracting parties
accept and confirm that genocide is punishable whether it is committed in
time of peace or war and that this principle is accepted in International Law.

Genocide is defined as an act, or a number of acts, undertaken with the
specific intention of destroying a national, religious, ethnic, racial or other
group. The convention also specifically prohibits the killing of the members
of these groups or causing them bodily harm of a serious nature or causing
mental harm or generally inflicting any form of unlawful action that would
bring about the destruction of the group in whole or in part. The purposeful
curtailment in one form or another of the birth of members of such groups is
also an offence in terms of the convention. Children of such groups may also
not be forcibly removed and placed in another group, thereby bringing
detrimental consequences to such children. One of the most important provisions contained in this convention is that the domestic jurisdiction normally
applicable to states does not apply in the case of genocide perpetrated by a
government on its people. Genocide in any form is considered a matter so
grave that it warrants international concern and attention.

Another convention under the auspices of the United Nations is the
International Slavery Convention of 1926. The full title of the convention is
the *Supplementary Convention on the Abolition of Slavery, the Slave Trade,
and Institutions and Practices similar to Slavery*.

The 1926 convention was under the auspices of the League of Nations, forerunner to the United Nations Organisation. However, in 1956, a conference of Plenipotentiaries was convened by the influential Economic and Social Council of the UN. During this crucial conference, a supplementary meeting was suggested and prepared for, at which the attending members would sign a treaty document outlawing practices that were akin to slavery. These included such practices as debt bondage, where individuals and sometimes groups of individuals are bonded to work for a creditor, sometimes including women and children. The practice of bride purchase was also disallowed in terms of this supplementary convention. This practice, however, is still practiced widely in Africa and certain parts of Asia, where such practices are considered to be part of the marriage process. The exploitation of children for purposes of work was also deemed to be illegal in terms of this convention.

The International Labour Conference of 1957 adopted the *Convention concerning the Abolition of Forced Labour*. This conference made it compulsory for the signatories to attempt to suppress any form of forced labour, compulsory labour or any other form of enforced work which would force the victims to be 'politically educated' or 're-educated'. It was aimed particularly at making it illegal to punish an individual or group for holding political viewpoints or ideologies contrary to those of the governing or dominant party. Other clauses in the convention forbade the use of forced labour with the purpose of instituting and practising programmes of economic development. The convention, moreover, made the process of forced labour on the basis of racial, religious and national origin completely illegal and unacceptable.

Still in the field of work, ie employment, another convention deserves specific mention. This is the *Discrimination (Employment and Occupation) Convention*. In 1958, the convention concerning discrimination in respect of work and occupation was accepted by the International Labour Conference. This Conference stressed the importance of bringing equality of opportunity to all in the workplace and with regard to choice and maintenance of occupation. It also, like a number of other conventions sponsored by the UN, called for the elimination of discrimination on the basis of colour, race, sex, religious affiliation, political ideology, nation, social status or origin.

In the important sphere of education, a special convention was adopted by the United Nations Educational, Scientific and Cultural Organisation (UNESCO) in 1960. This was the *Convention against Discrimination in Education*, and called upon its members to assess their statutory systems and in so doing to eliminate any discriminatory practices relevant to education. A previous convention in 1958 had made a similar call. Note must be made here that the provisions of this convention did not prevent separate education for males and females, provided (*inter alia*) that the educational institutions provides adequately trained teachers, appropriate facilities and the presentation of courses whose standards are at best equal to the education being offered the other (gender) party.

The signatories are obliged to examine their educational systems periodically and to report to the UN on progress being made to eliminate discrimination. During 1962, the General Conference of UNESCO adopted a special process whereby a sub-organisation known as the Conciliation and Good Offices Commission would act as a dispute-resolving body in differences which might arise between parties from time to time.

One of the most important conventions in the history of the United Nations is the *International Convention on the Elimination of all Forms of Racial Discrimination*, which the General Assembly adopted during 1965. This called for the total elimination of all discrimination specifically based on race, colour, nation and/or ethnic descent. It came into effect in 1969 and differed from two other conventions held in 1958 and 1960 respectively. These two conventions included other discriminatory characteristics to be avoided, such as political ideology. The International Convention on the Elimination of all Forms of Racial Discrimination is more effective for being more comprehensive, and forbids all discrimination with regard to human rights and fundamental freedoms in all spheres of cultural, political, economic and social life in all member countries. The provisions of this convention have a more effective process built into them, since the member states undertake not to engage or otherwise be involved in acts or practices of discrimination based on race.

The provisions of the convention also force the member states to review their own legal institutions and government agencies at all levels in order to make quite certain the racially orientated discriminatory practices are not being carried on by some means that is not easily detected. Any propaganda for, or any organised attempt to in any way promote discrimination based on race or ethnic origin is made a punishable offence. These provisions have been difficult to enforce, both by the UN and its agencies, because a number of governments impose serious limitations on the right of free speech and freedom of the press and dissemination of information generally. A monitoring group of 18 members, known as the Committee on the Elimination of Racial Discrimination, is empowered to examine allegations of discriminatory practices made by one state against another. This committee in turn makes provision for the establishment of a conciliation commission which is empowered to settle disputes between two or more parties. Should any or all of the above procedures fail to provide a solution, the convention, through the conciliation committee, may refer the matter to the International Court of Justice. The convention further allows individuals or non-governmental groups to present or communicate their grievances directly to the convention. Petitions of grievances may also be presented by territories that are not independent or self-governing, as was the case with Namibia, or South West Africa as it was then called.

The status of women in the world has also come in for special attention by the United Nations, through the *Conventions on the Status of Women*. One of the more significant of these was the convention on the Political Rights of Women of 1952, whereby women were given equal status to men in the political processes of their countries. They were guaranteed the vote and could themselves stand for election to any public office. Another very important convention with regard to women's rights is the Convention on Consent to Marriage, Minimum Age for Marriages and Registration of Marriages, whose provisions stipulate that no marriage may be entered into or otherwise contracted without the full and free consent of the parties to a marriage. In order to avoid undue subtle pressure from parents or other parties, participants in a marriage must be in a position to publicly state their free intention to marry in the presence of competent legal or other official authority. A minimum legal age for marriage must be stipulated and an appropriate and acceptable process of registration of the marriage must be instituted.

The UN has also considered the rights of refugees and stateless persons. Two conventions govern these categories of people. One is the *Convention Relating to the Status of Refugees of 1951*, supplemented by the *Protocol of 1967*; the other is the *Convention on the Status of Stateless Persons of 1954*. Among the principal provisions of the 1951 convention is one that states that there should be as little discrimination as possible between refugees and nationals of the state in which they are resident. Another calls for no discrimination whatsoever on the grounds of race, religion or country of origin. This means that refugees are to be accorded freedom of religion, access to and freedom before the courts and other judicial processes, at least some elementary form of education, and public relief to alleviate their condition. With regard to employment, the right to association and wages, refugees must be given the same favourable treatment as the nationals of the member state concerned. The same goes for higher education, self-employment and other facets relating to the refugee problem. The Convention on Stateless Persons is subject to the same provisions as those in the Convention on Refugees.

Although the United Nations Organisation has promulgated several conventions or treaties relating to human rights, these are not binding upon members and they cannot under normal circumstances be forced to comply. However, the moral force behind such conventions, and especially the Universal Declaration of Human Rights of 1948, is such that members who do not comply are subject to some form of negative sanction. One other such declaration, passed by the General Assembly in 1960, was the Declaration on the Granting of Independence to Colonial Countries and Peoples. This declaration was responsible for the succession of African countries being granted independent status in the years following 1960. A number of other important conventions dealing with the status of children and the removal of discrimination against women (1967) have been passed by the UN.

Another convention emerging from the UN Declaration of Human Rights was the *European Convention on Human Rights*. In 1950, members of the Council of Europe agreed upon a European Convention for the Protection of Human Rights and Fundamental Freedoms, and five other European protocols relating to human rights followed in quick succession. These brought into being the European Commission on Human Rights, the Human Rights Committee and the Committee on the Elimination of Racial Discrimination. Like the UN bodies, the European Commission is entitled to hear evidence from individuals and groups on human rights violations, but similarly, its decisions against the offending parties are not binding. By 1971 there were 17 parties to the European Convention, of which only 11 accepted the right and competence of the European Commission to listen to petitions and make comments thereon.

Also brought into being by European Convention was the European Court of Human Rights. Once again, only 11 parties to the convention agreed that the findings of the court would be binding upon them and that the decisions handed down by the European Court of Human Rights are final. Should a matter not be heard by this court, or should it be of such a nature as to be outside the competence of the court, the matter is dealt with by a committee of Ministers of the Court of Europe. Quite a number of decisions in human rights cases heard by the European Court of Human Rights have been accepted and embodied in the constitutions of member states. The Americans have also made substantial progress in this field, culminating in the American Convention on Human Rights, drawn up within the framework of the Organisation of American States. One of the major outcomes of human rights activism in the Americas was the establishment of the Inter-American Commission on Human Rights in 1959. Ten years later, in 1969, at a meeting in San José, Costa Rica, the Inter-American Specialised Conference adopted the American Convention on Human Rights, which made provision for the establishment of the Inter-American Court of Human Rights. The American Conventions, although they flow from both the UN programme and human rights developments in Europe, differ from their European and UN counterparts in that individuals have direct access to them. They require neither the approval of their governments nor any other intervention in order to bring human right violations to the notice of the relevant committee. In Part 3, a number of these conventions will be dealt with in more detail.

PART 2

THE ISSUE OF SLAVERY

FORMS OF SLAVERY

INTRODUCTION

There are a number of definitions of what constitutes slavery. Basically, slavery is a social institution that permits a person or a group of persons to force others to perform a service or services by compulsion. A slave, of whatever nature, is forced to perform work or some other form of servitude for his or her master, normally for no payment save the basic essentials of life.

The slave's freedom of action is normally restricted and other conventions of a social nature make the slave inferior to his owner or master. From the historical point of view there are a number of forms of slavery, which will be analysed individually.

WHAT IS SLAVERY?

A slave is a human being who is owned by another person, and who has been deprived of his rights and freedom without his consent. In fact, during the days when slavery was an accepted institution in some societies, the slave was often the legal property of his master. Slaves had no freedom of choice and were subject to the whim of the owner, who often had power of life or death over his slave.

From the historical point of view, it is interesting to note that slavery involved, in some societies, degrees of status. Ancient Rome permitted slaves to be educated and allowed them property rights which could permit them to buy their freedom. In contrast to this view, slaves on the plantations in the pre-Civil War years (prior to 1860) in the United States, were legally forbidden to own property or to receive an education, hence they could not buy their freedom. One of the most brutal forms of slavery existed in Nazi Germany. There slaves, known as Sklavenarbeiter (slave labourers), were mostly Jews, Slavs, Gypsies and other people who had been subdued as a result of war. The status of these slaves was so miserable that one survivor described it in the following terms:

'We were not slaves; our status was much lower. True, we were deprived of freedom and became a piece of property which our masters put to work. But here the similarity with any form ends, for we were a completely expendable piece of property ... The equipment in the shop was well maintained. It was operated with ease, oiled, greased and allowed to rest; its longevity was protected. We, on the other hand, were like a piece of sandpaper, which, rubbed once or twice, became useless and is thrown away to be burned with the waste.'

MANCHESTER, W: *The Arms of Krupp* (1968)

This is indeed a sad reflection on the brutality that man will inflict on his fellow men. The history of the world is full of such horrific developments and modern man is attempting by various means to stamp out this evil practice, whatever form it may take. One of the reasons for the United States Civil War of 1860 to 1865 was to eradicate the practice of slavery in America.

It is not easy to determine at what stage of human development slavery came into existence as a common practice. If one assesses the history of Europe, slavery seems to have taken root when the roaming pastoral tribes settled down to an agricultural existence. While this simple agricultural society existed, the form of slavery remained patriarchal, that is, slaves did domestic and other chores and were often indistinguishable from the slave-owner's wives or children.

The introduction of a market economy had a dramatic effect on the nature and status of slavery. These included slaves who worked in the household and slaves who worked in large groups on plantations or large tracts of land owned by a few persons of wealth. Working in gangs made the slaves anonymous and they were treated in a far harsher manner than household slaves. When urban areas developed, slaves were used in all kinds of labour or service, ranging from teaching the children of the slave owner to such functions as being industrial and commercial workers. Women slaves were often made to work in brothels and many an attractive female slave was taken into the harems of wealthy owners.

People became slaves through a number of processes, but chief among these was by capture. Others were born slaves because their parents were slaves. Yet others were sold into bondage as a result of debts incurred by parents or guardians. The capture of individuals was, and in some cases still is, the main way of being made a slave. Slave raiding became a common practice and has been practised since antiquity. As recently as the 19th Century, slave raiding and trading was a common practice in many parts of the world, especially in Africa.

Another form of slavery was initiated as a result of punishment inflicted upon individuals who violated some law or social norm. Galley slaves on ships were an example of publicly owned slaves who had been condemned as criminals. In more recent colonial times, forced servitude was also used as a means of getting cheap, often free, labour. Political opponents have often been made to serve in penal colonies. Often the persons concerned were subjected to hard labour as a mode of punishment.

Ascription by birth was another way of getting slaves or increasing the number of slaves. The logic behind this form of slavery was that a child born of slave parents had no rights and was therefore automatically the property of the slave owner. This was the case in both ancient Rome and on the plantations in the Southern United States before the American Civil War.

Slaves could also be bought. As mere property they could be bought and sold as property and not as human beings. The brutality of this process is exemplified very well in the slave raiding that took place in Africa, from where the slaves were then transported to the United States or the Middle East and sold by the slave traders. Slave owners in the US and other places did not consider it unusual to buy the slaves, since they believed the slaves had already been captured, kidnapped or otherwise forced into servitude.

In a number of societies, parents have been known to sell their children as slaves to wealthy individuals through extreme poverty. In other societies, chiefs and clan leaders have sometimes sold families, groups of individuals and others under their traditional jurisdiction. In South-East Asia, Latin America and China, the practice of selling children into servitude has been known to take place until quite recently, and may still occur. This was called the *mui tsai* or 'little sister' system and involved children being 'adopted' by wealthy persons.

Another form of servitude which resembles true slavery is where the individual surrenders his freedom to another person for a period of time. In this form of servitude individuals choose to bind themselves to a work contract in order to receive some form of benefit, such as a free passage to another country. There are also cases where criminals have chosen to work on contract labour as a means of having their sentences commuted. In these forms of servitude the main similarity with slavery per se is that the contracted individual is not free to leave until the terms of his servitude are completed.

There are also known cases where insolvent debtors become slaves to the creditor, who can, in some instances, sell the persons to defray the debt. However, as is often the case, the person remains in service for the rest of his life, and often his offspring, if there are any, will also be pressed into slavery. Sadly this type of servitude still exists in a number of societies today, despite human rights groups' attempts to end the practice.

At the height of the colonial period, indentured service became a common form of acquiring cheap contract labour. From the middle of the 19th Century, Indian and Chinese labour was used in a number of regions of the world. Often these indentured labourers were recruited in underhand ways and deception and coercion were commonly used as means of acquiring their labour. Most of the indentured labourers were unskilled, had little or no education and were the poorest of the poor.

In colonial North America, ie before the American Revolution, indentured labour was brought in from Europe and Britain in particular. These labourers worked on the plantations and other agricultural establishments under very harsh conditions. However, there were instances where these labourers were able to negotiate better terms based on the accepted standards of the British Apprenticeship System. They normally completed a work period of between five and seven years and were then free to leave or continue working for the persons or the establishment.

There were various ways in which labour could be recruited and then misused by those in authority, for example, the *peonage* form of contract labour, in which labourers were forced to work for their creditors in order to pay off a debt. These labourers were compelled to pay their creditors through the medium of work done for no remuneration, except the most basic necessities of life.

The slave-holding states in the American South devised a means of circumventing the 13th Amendment to the constitution of the United States, which prohibited involuntary servitude. They passed state laws under which they were able to make ignorant persons sign documents to the effect that they were working to pay off debts. Persons found guilty of offences by courts and fined often could not afford to pay and signed themselves into servitude. One of the most brutal forms of enforced labour was the chain gang system, under which criminal offenders were forced into servitude. Short-term prisoners were also leased out to the plantations for periods of time in the Southern States prior to 1860.

Serfdom was another way in which control was exercised over others. Serfs were normally people who were attached to a piece of land for which they paid certain dues. Serfs were a little better off than slaves as they could not be killed or maimed, whereas slaves could be treated as mere chattels. Serfs were in fact peasant clans who derived their living from the land. In other words, a slave was provided with food by his master, while serfs provided their own sustenance. Serfs could in certain instances keep any surplus produce, after the overlord had been paid a portion of the fruits of the land. The freedom of movement of the serfs was, however, restricted. In other words, they could not move from one piece of land to another, nor dispose of their property at will, but were dependent upon the whims of the overlord.

Another way of forcing people into involuntary work situations was statute labour. This practice arose when people were forced by the state to work on public projects, especially the building of roads, when there was insufficient money to undertake or complete the project. This form of enforced labour existed until 1945 in French West Africa. Workers were obliged to work for at least five days per year on a public project. This applied to all African able-bodied men. By the same token, civilians in the People's

Republic of China were obliged to work on public projects for a period of between ten days and a year.

CHAPTER 2

AN HISTORICAL PERSPECTIVE
OF SLAVERY

INTRODUCTION

The institution of slavery seems to be as old as man himself. Some of the earliest records of the institution of slavery go back to the third dynasty of Ur in Babylon, approximately 2100 BC: Egyptian records go even further back, to between *circa* 2686-2160 BC.

These records indicate that one of the biggest sources of slaves was through warfare; slaves were one of the spoils of war. In ancient Egypt slaves became the property of the Pharaohs and hence of the state. They were used as labourers on public works such as the building of roads, pyramids, temples and so on. Apart from acquisition through war, slaves were also bought from neighbouring societies and often passed from the jurisdiction of the Pharaohs to private owners. The biblical account of the slavery of the people of Israel and their subsequent liberation by Moses is a good example of a story of human bondage.

However, there were instances in ancient Babylon, Israel and Egypt where slaves could and did receive their freedom. In ancient Babylon decrees were issued liberating slaves. In the Hebraic (Jewish) tradition of early Israel, the sabbatical year, ie the seventh year, was a period in which debt slaves were liberated. The famous code of Hammurabi also made provision for slaves to be freed after a period of three years' work for their creditor. In fact, the liberation of these slaves was held to be so important that the Prophet Jeremiah in the Old Testament, (Jeremiah XXXIV, 8-17) castigated slave owners for not abiding by this biblical injunction. Another example is given in the Book of Nehemiah the Prophet, where poverty-stricken Jews were forced to sell their children into slavery (Nehemiah V, 1-5).

At the time, a slave was not considered a human being and was numbered by head count in the same manner as one numbers livestock. Slaves could not leave their masters, and harsh treatment, even death, was prescribed as a penalty for runaway slaves.

In the Graeco-Roman period, one of the most important references to slavery was in the famous legal code of Justinian (AD 527-565). For a period of 15 centuries, the institution of slavery existed in Greek and Roman society. In fact, such men as the Greek philosopher Aristotle argued in favour of slavery, saying that it provided the slave owner with a good livelihood, while slaves derived benefit too. The Stoics and Cynics, however, held that slavery was evil and contrary to the natural order, but they stopped short of calling for its abolition.

The early Christians held the belief that as long as individuals believed in Christ, there was neither slave nor free man. However, the New Testament does tell masters to be kind to their slaves and slaves who were believers to obey their masters. The Justinian (Roman) Law stated with regard to slavery, 'slavery is an institution of the *jus gentium* (law of nations), whereby a man is, contrary to nature, subject to the ownership of another'. This laid the foundation for rules governing the institution of slavery in both Rome and Greece.

In Graeco-Roman times most slaves were acquired by conquest. The vast number of wars fought by Rome against nations the Romans regarded as barbarians brought in numerous slaves. However, in the latter years of the Roman Empire, there were fewer wars and with relative peace came a decline in the number of slaves being captured. The high point of slavery in the Roman Empire was during the second and first centuries BC. Wars, piracy and other forms of human conflict made slavery common and popular among the Roman upper classes and landed gentry in particular. These landowners built up huge agricultural establishments on which slaves were put to work. Apart from agricultural work, large numbers of slaves were made to work in mines and one authority suggests that there were as many as forty thousand slaves on the silver mines of New Carthage, in Roman-controlled Spain.

However, the lot of slaves in the Roman Empire was not altogether bad. As one authority put it (En. Br. 857):

'In the early principate in Rome, a curious anomaly arose. The Emperors, principal secretaries and accountants, who were slaves or freemen, inevitably became politically influential and important and came to do the work of secretaries of state and ministers of finance ...'.

Nevertheless, those who rose to ranks of importance were the exception rather than the rule. Slaves who were less fortunate and worked in mines were treated dismally and often ruthlessly worked to death. Those who worked in Roman mines or agricultural establishments had little opportunity of being freed.

SLAVERY IN THE EAST: INDIA AND CHINA

Slavery in early India was governed by a special code called the Laws of Manu. These laws are India's oldest legal documents, dating to the 12th Century BC. In terms of these laws, six types of servants or slaves were identified, namely: captives taken in the course of war; domestic personnel who became servants in order to be maintained (livelihood); those born in the master's household from a female slave; individuals bought in a transaction or won; persons inherited as part of the estate of a deceased relative; and servants who became enslaved as a result of not being able to pay fines imposed on them by a civil authority.

Despite all these categories of servants or slaves, the Laws of Manu stated that they were held on three basic conditions and could be freed in terms of these directives.

(a) A slave could get his freedom if he found another person to leave in his place. This applied only to the category of war captives.

(b) An individual who was enslaved for debt could repay his master the debt and be freed as a result.

(c) A slave could be freed if he was responsible for saving his master's life.

However, in all three cases, the master had to give his consent in addition to the slave fulfilling the other conditions of freedom.

But India had another form of slavery or serfdom, founded on social conventions. India had an extremely rigid caste system, with a strictly enforced hierarchical social structure, and those belonging to the Sudra caste had to serve other castes considered superior to it in the caste hierarchy. These superior castes include the Ksatriya or warrior caste, the Brahmins or priestly caste and the Vaisyas, comprising farmers, cattle-raisers and merchants. Although the Sudra caste had a low status there was yet another caste which was of even lower status – the 'pariahs' or untouchables who live by begging.

The pariah caste had to keep itself very strictly away from the other castes and the daily lives of the pariahs were marked by a number of humiliating rituals. No pariah could even approach a person in a higher caste, even during the course of begging. A certain distance had to be maintained, even from the Sudra caste, low as the Sudras were on the social scale. The Laws of Manu dictated relationships between castes and took a dim view of any Sudra attempting to better his position in life. Although he could improve his condition financially, there was no way in which a Sudra could elevate himself above his ascriptive position. Caste level was decided not by wealth, but by birth. The laws of servitude in relation to caste in ancient India were very rigid, as is indicated by the following declaration from the Laws of Manu:

'A man of low caste who dares to contest a man of higher caste must be branded below the hip and exiled. If he raises a hand or a stick to a superior, the hand shall be cut off; and if in a moment of rage he kicks him, that foot shall then be cut off. Should he inflict injuries upon a man of a higher caste, a hot dagger shall be put into his mouth.'

Slavery in China up to the 16th Century was based on a number of conditions. A poor person could voluntarily submit himself or herself for slavery if he or she were found guilty of high treason. Normally, this category of slave served the state either as a public servant or worked in the royal household. One brutal practice was the castration of the male children of those found guilty of treason. Once the castration had taken place, these unfortunates were made to tend the harems of the rich and royal. Women who committed adultery were usually thrown out of their homes and had no option but to offer themselves up as slaves in order to survive. Creditors who could not pay their debts could be taken into slavery. However, slavery was not a very practical proposition for the Chinese, who had a sophisticated system of serfdom, making it unnecessary to press people into slavery.

CHAPTER 3

SLAVERY IN THE ISLAMIC AND EUROPEAN SPHERES

During the period of the Eastern Roman Empire and subsequent Byzantine Empire, slavery continued, though with a number of variations. Slavery also existed in the Muslim world, and there are early records to indicate this. One of the most prominent records is found in the Muslim holy book, the Koran, written during the 7th Century. The prophet Muhammad was acquainted with slavery and, like the Christian teachings, he admonished his followers to treat slaves with humanity and compassion. To allow a slave his freedom was an act that was in keeping with the dictates of Islamic piety.

With the establishment of the religion of Islam, a number of wars ensued in which more slaves were taken as part of the spoils of war. The wars of conquest undertaken by Arabs covered a vast area, including North Africa, Asia, eastern and southern Europe. Apart from the Arab conquests of these regions, there came other Islamic powers, such as the Turkish Ottoman Empire.

When the Crusades took place, Christians also took Muslim prisoners and thus increased slavery in both the Muslim countries and in Europe. The church at the time attempted to put a stop to the practice of trading in slaves, but without much success. There are records of Venetian and Genoese slave traders buying slaves in the Middle East, Serbia, Bulgaria and Armenia and selling them in other regions. Muslim slave traders operated in the Mediterranean Sea, capturing numerous slaves through piracy on the high seas. Arab slavers also penetrated other parts of Africa and bought slaves from chieftains and other sources. Arab slavers sold most of their slaves.

However, slavery in the Islamic world and culture took a different form from that of Greece, Rome or other countries. Slaves in the Islamic world were very seldom made to toil in mines or on agricultural projects. They were mainly used in households of the wealthy and were treated in terms of the dictates of the Koran. One practice that was particularly cruel, however, was the practice of castrating male slaves and putting them in charge of harems. Female slaves, on the other hand, either became concubines or were taken as legitimate wives of the master of the household.

In addition, Muslim slave owners were not racially prejudiced and freed slaves often achieved positions of prominence. The best example of slaves achieving powerful political status is found in the Mumluk Slave Dynasty, which ruled Egypt for more than two hundred years.

Spain and Portugal also dealt in slaves. When the Moors were defeated in the 15th Century, the Spaniards took numerous slaves from the defeated Muslims. The Portuguese also became slave traders, establishing slave trading stations on the African coast. Portuguese slave trading was begun as early as 1444 by seamen working under the orders of Prince Henry the Navigator. The Portuguese had a number of slave trading posts along the coast of Guinea. Black slaves were imported increasingly into both Spain and Portugal and in due course integrated into a number of economic activities. As a result of the lack of race consciousness by both the Portuguese and Spanish, the slaves mixed quite freely with the rest of the population, eventually merging with it.

In the rest of Europe, slavery as such diminished over the centuries, but serfdom became predominant, with peasants often surrendering their personal lands to overlords in return for their protection. Often the surrendering of the land was accompanied by an act of swearing fealty to the overlord. During the Middle Ages, this act of fealty protected the peasants from invaders and from unfair taxes and other dues extracted by the political authorities of the region concerned. The serfs in Europe were bound to their land and could not move around freely.

Although serfdom existed for many years and in many forms over the centuries in Europe, it began to decline with the process of industrialisation. Other factors also led to the decline of serfdom, especially in the Italian Peninsula. Between 1256 and 1257, the city state of Bologna enfranchised the serfs in the region under its authority. This was the result of a moral debate among Bologna's city fathers, who said that man was born free and that slavery came into existence as a result of the fall of man. The Black Death plague also decreased the European population dramatically, altering population ratios and making tenant ownership of land possible. There were also a number of peasant revolts in England, France, Italy and Spain in the 14th and 15th Centuries, and a German peasant war in the early 16th Century.

In Eastern Europe, slavery in the form of serfdom diminished at a much slower rate. There were a number of reasons for this, including the fact that in the eastern portion of Germany, Poland, Bohemia, Moravia and Hungary, there were huge free peasant communities occupying vast tracts of forest land.

Other parts of Eastern Europe, in the Baltic and the Balkans, had a number of severe wars during the 14th and 15th Centuries. This almost decimated the serf (peasant) population. Huge tracts of land were laid waste and were taken over by a powerful landed nobility. They took over peasants' lands and made heavy demands on the peasants themselves for labour. It was only towards the end of the 18th Century that serfs in the Austro-Hungarian Empire were freed from their subordinate conditions. The Emperor, Joseph II, was reputed to have referred to serfdom as the absence of freedom of movement, of the freedom to marry, the freedom to learn a profession as one chose it and generally the lack of freedom to be in control of one's life.

CHAPTER 4

AN ASSESSMENT OF PLANTATION SLAVERY

In the Americas prior to the European occupation, slavery was not a common institution, although it existed in what is today Mexico. Cortes, the Spanish explorer and coloniser, described a slave market he saw in operation in the region of Tenochtitlan, now Mexico City, where he witnessed a large number of male and female slaves being bought and sold.

When Spain subdued the indigenous population of the Americas, it did not introduce outright slavery. However, the local population was made to work hard in the agricultural estates. But work in the Spanish-controlled mines was difficult and conditions there were similar to slavery. The Indian population of the Americas was not docile, however, and rebelled against being forced into hard labour. Many ran away and disappeared into other forest regions of the hinterland. The Indians were also not strong enough physically to undertake the hard labour on the estates and in the mines.

Missionaries also affected the induction of slaves into the estates and other forced labour conditions. They were there to convert the local population to Catholicism and thus demanded that the indigenous population be treated gently. This request was echoed by the Spanish monarch, Ferdinand II. He ruled that Indians could be forced to work, but they had to be humanely treated and paid for their labour.

In order to overcome the problem with indigenous labour, it was suggested that black (African) slaves be imported. In fact, the Roman Catholic Bishop of Chiapas, Bartolomé de Las Casas, petitioned King Charles I of Spain to allow Spanish settlers in the New World to import a limited number of black slaves from Africa. In 1517, the Spanish monarchy granted a permit to a nobleman to bring Africans into the Spanish American territories as slaves. The only condition was that duties had to be paid to the treasury.

No sooner had the Spanish monarchy granted the permission than thousands of African slaves were brought to the New World, first to the Caribbean islands and later to the mainland. From the beginning of the 19th Century, huge sugar plantations necessitated the labour of thousands upon thousands of plantation slaves. Black plantation slavery was thus institutionalised in the New World.

It was during the colonial period in North America that slavery was first introduced into the region. Slaves were first landed in Virginia in 1619 by the Dutch, but it was not a regular trade; by the year 1681, there were only about two thousand black slaves in the plantations of Virginia. However, tobacco and rice production was on the increase and with it the demand for slave labour, which reached a population of 59 000 by 1714 and 263 000 by 1754. With the introduction of cotton as a crop in the southern states of the USA, and particularly after the invention of the cotton gin in 1793, the number of slaves rose to about 4,5 million in 1860, on the eve of the American Civil War.

Gradually, the slave trade grew in Central and South America and, as shown, in the southern states of the US. Black slaves were first used for such work as stevedoring in the harbours, as domestic servants and in a number of trades. However, it was the large-scale production of sugar, tobacco and cotton that established slavery as an institution in North America. Enormous numbers of slaves were brought to the Americas from the west coast of Africa. Slave trading, with all its cruelties, became an extremely lucrative industry.

A number of European nations became prominent in the slave trade. These included England, which became one of the most important slave traders of that period. The French, Dutch and Portuguese also traded in slaves, either selling them to the southern US or taking them into service in their own colonies or spheres of influence. The Portuguese had a virtual monopoly of the slave trade between Africa and its own possessions, particularly Brazil.

This horrendous trade in human beings was being conducted along what came to be known as the 'triangular route'. That is, slave ships left their European port of origin, for instance Liverpool, Bristol or Lisbon, and made for the west African coast. They brought with them a number of items which were used as a medium of exchange in the bartering process for the slaves. Slave trading ports were set up along the west coast of Africa, and slaves from the interior kept there. This section of the African coastline was known as the slave coast and was mainly along the Gulf of Guinea. The next stage of the 'triangular route' consisted of the trip from the African coast to the West Indies or the mainland of the Americas.

This part of the trip was, by any standard, the most brutal and inhumane. Slaves were packed in the unsanitary hull of ships and normally chained together to avoid any uprisings or rebellion during the tortuous journey, and also to stop the slaves from jumping into the sea. They were given a minimal amount of food and water and it is said that about 20 % of the slaves died during the voyage. Once the ship arrived at its destination, slaves were either sold directly to their new masters or held under strict conditions until a buyer was found. The slave ships then loaded products from the American plantations to sell in Europe. These included molasses, which, after being distilled into rum, was used for buying more slaves on the next journey.

The treatment of slaves in the Americas varied from region to region. However, their treatment was a little better in the Catholic regions under the control of Spain, Portugal and France. Under Louis XIV, the French in 1685 promulgated the Code Noire (The Black Code) which defined conditions under which slaves had to be held. The Spaniards had a similar code, known as the Spanish Slave Code of 1789. Those in the British sphere of influence, such as the colonies and former British North American colonies, were not treated so well. White settler colonies were granted self-governing status or outright independence, as in the case of the former North American colonies. These regions often applied their own rules to the treatment of slaves.

In regions where there was a strong presence of Roman Catholic missionaries, pressure was brought to bear on the authorities to be lenient in the treatment of slaves. The clergy encouraged slaves to become Christians and as such required that their marriages be formalised by the church. The clergy also fought for the retention of family unity, thus at least keeping the family as a cohesive institution. However, Anglican clergy were not as sympathetic with the manner in which slaves were treated. In fact, in a number of British dependencies, including the US, the marriage of slaves was forbidden by law.

In the Portuguese and Spanish American possessions, slaves were generally treated with a little more compassion. In the first instance, the two European nations harboured little if any feelings of racial superiority. There was far less racial discrimination and many of the female slaves had sexual relationships with their masters. The children born of such unions were given their freedom, and often this was extended to the mother as well. In Haiti, under French rule, slaves of mixed blood became prominent citizens in the affairs of the colony. Brazil was another region where tolerance towards people of mixed blood and full blacks was exercised. As a result, quite a number of people of African descent reached prominent positions in society before the liberation of slaves in 1888. This attitude reinforced an attitude of non-discrimination between black slaves and their masters and eventually led to the integration of both population groups into the single entity that is Brazil today. In the southern United States, any person having even the slightest strain of African blood was considered a 'negro'.

Thus 'plantation slavery' took root, in the Americas in particular, and the evil of this system was as such that it became the cause of the fiercest civil war in history. In other parts of the Americas, such as Brazil and Haiti, slaves rebelled against the authorities and in the case of Haiti, gained independence from France.

CHAPTER 5

SLAVERY IN SOUTH AFRICA

Slavery in South Africa is closely linked to the history of the Cape of Good Hope. When the Dutch East India Company established itself at the Cape in 1652, slavery was already an accepted institution inherited from the other Dutch colonies.

As the Dutch East India Company was in the process of establishing itself at the Cape of Good Hope, and in the surrounding districts, a shortage of labour became an immediate problem. The local population, nomadic Khoisan, were opposed to anything that interfered with their need to be on the move constantly. In addition, the few Dutch workers attached to the garrison at the Cape did not like manual labour, either avoiding it when possible or stowing away on ships when the opportunity presented itself.

The first Commander of the Cape, Jan van Riebeeck, made recommendations for the introduction of slaves into the Colony. However, the Dutch East India Company had to comply with the Statutes of India, which forbade the use of the local population as slaves. Consequently in 1658, the first group of slaves, about 250 in all, were brought in from Dahomey and Angola. This group of slaves was in fact part of the cargo of two ships which were captured by the Dutch.

Large numbers of slaves were subsequently brought in from Madagascar, Mozambique, Ceylon, India, the East Indies, the Phillippines, south east Asia and even a number from Japan. The number of slaves in the Cape rose dramatically in the ensuing years. According to some statistics (Watson 1990), there were 16 839 slaves at the Cape by 1795, of which about 16 200 were in private ownership. The balance were owned by the Dutch East India Company. By the late 1700s, there were more slaves than free white persons in the Cape, indicating the extent to which slavery had grown.

Slavery was abolished in the British Empire in the year 1834 and this had an effect on conditions at the Cape. In that year there were about 34 000 slaves in the Cape. They were often treated badly, had no rights and their lives were controlled by a number of strict dictates. The following indicates how slaves fared at the Cape at the time (Watson, 1990):

'Until the 1820s, slaves could not marry, make wills, sell produce, or own a business or property. They required a note from their owner to travel, and were ordered to carry a lantern when out after dark. They were punished, often with extreme brutality, for transgressions of law and custom. Discipline was usually severe: there are on the public record numerous cases of slave holders charged with grievous mistreatment. Only rarely, however, were masters punished for mistreating their slaves; slaves who assaulted owners, on the other hand, could be tortured, then killed in the earlier years of slavery.'

Slaves in South Africa did not always remain timid towards their often harsh owners. In fact, they organised two rebellions, in 1808 and 1825.

The first 'rebellion' or revolt took place at Cape Town in 1808. A march of 300 slaves on Cape Town was led by three people, a Mauritian slave by the name of Louis, and two Irishmen, James Hooper and Michael Kelly. The slaves demanded that since slavery had been abolished as a trade, the Governor of the Colony, the Earl of Caledon, should put an end to the evil practice. During the march, there were some disturbances in which some farmers were beaten up and one white woman was raped. There was also some looting of property. The Governor ordered troops to subdue the rebellion, which they did with relative ease. Four of the leaders, including Louis the Mauritian slave and Kelly, were hanged for their part in it. More than 50 others were given severe prison sentences ranging from 15 years to life imprisonment and the rest were handed back to their owners.

The 1825 revolt by slaves was also a significant development. The revolt took place on a privately owned farm in the Worcester district, known as the Bokkeveld, about 150 kilometres from Cape Town. The farm was owned by a Willem van der Merwe. According to an historical account of the event, Van der Merwe owned eight slaves, among them one named Galant. Galant had complained to the authorities on a number of occasions about his treatment at the hands of his owner, but nothing was done. In retaliation for the complaints lodged against him, Van der Merwe inflicted further injury on Galant. Another slave who took part in this revolt was a man named Abel, owned by Van der Merwe's brother on a nearby farm.

Only 12 people participated in the revolt, hoping that it would lead to another march on Cape Town. Three whites, namely Willem van der Merwe himself, a visitor to the farm, J H van Rensburg, and a school teacher on the farm at the time, Johannes Verlee, were killed. A number of others, including Van der Merwe's wife, were injured. The revolt was stopped by the authorities, and Galant, Abel and a certain Isaac Thys were hanged on 15 April 1825 for their part in the uprising.

These unfortunate slaves were not only charged with murder, but also with 'the most heinous species of treason' (Watson 1990). The Crown's case was presented, with the prosecutor stating that slaves' obedience to their masters was a necessary prerequisite for the good order and wellbeing of the state. He asked for the death sentence to be imposed. During the trial, it was also stated that the slaves had revolted because they misinterpreted a decree, the 1823 Amelioration Act, as an act freeing slaves. After this small revolt, slave owners became insecure, fearing murder, rape and assault.

On 27 June 1828, a society was founded in Cape Town in the hope of eradicating the practice of slavery from the Colony altogether. This society was known as the *Cape of Good Hope Philantropic Society for Aiding Deserving Slaves to Purchase their Freedom.* The society was founded by whites and, according to historical records, this seems to be the only attempt by local people to free slaves. They were active members of the Cape liberal community acting in conscience. In addition, humanitarians in Britain were calling for an end to slavery all over the world.

The Society undertook a number of other activities in addition to their anti-slavery activities. However, they also believed in the preservation of the principle of private property and were hesitant to interfere with property rights even if the property happened to be human beings. Only 102 slaves were set free as a result of the society's activities, although one authority puts the figure at 126. In 1833, an Act of the British Parliament abolished slavery throughout the British Empire.

The impending end of slavery as an institution in the Cape was also partly responsible for the movement of at least 15 000 Dutch-speaking persons into the interior. The Great Trek was not solely motivated by the impending freedom of the slaves. It was an important factor, but it was mainly the threat to the farmers' lifestyle under the British Crown that led to the Trek. The freeing of the slaves had the effect of changing relations in the social order. In addition, when eventually the slaves were freed (1 December 1834), the Dutch-speaking farming community was dissatisfied with the mode of compensation undertaken by the British Government.

CHAPTER 6

THE RISE OF ANTI-SLAVERY
MOVEMENTS

By the beginning of the 19th Century, more than 15 million slaves had been removed from the African continent and transported across the Atlantic to the Americas. There was very little protest against this evil practice until the 18th Century, when a number of Christian groups, including evangelical organisations, began to view the slave trade as not only contrary to scripture, but also an injury to the dignity of man.

The Quakers, a religious group, were among the very first to protest against the inhuman practice; one of the earliest Quaker protests against slavery took place in 1671. However, religious movements as a whole were more concerned with condemning the sinfulness of slavery, rather than with finding an appropriate social policy to deal with it. In 1788, an organisation was formed in France, the Société Des Amis De Noir (The Society of the Friends of Blacks). This organisation used rational arguments to fight the slave trade, rather than religious pontifications.

By the late 1700s, anti-slavery sentiment was beginning to take root in several spheres. One tireless worker for the abolition of slavery was Granville Shap, in Britain. Shap, working almost without assistance, managed to get a court decision in 1772 which forbade West Indian planters from holding slaves in Britain, where it was not allowed by law. In North America, at least two of the founding fathers made their anti-slavery viewpoints quite clear to all. They were Benjamin Franklin and Thomas Jefferson. In the fledgeling United States, all slavery was abolished north of the state of Maryland between 1777 and 1804. The abolition of slavery took place either on a gradual basis, or in some cases, instantly. At this time too, quite a number of Abolitionist Societies sprang up and attempted vigorously to remove the evil of slavery. These societies were successful in some regions, but in the deep south, the owners of huge plantations still refused to relinquish the system.

The first two countries to make a concerted effort to abolish slavery were Britain and the United States. That is, they were the first nations to prohibit the importation of slaves to any British colony or the United States. In 1783, the English Quakers began an active campaign calling for the prohibition of slavery all over the world. In 1787 an Abolitionist Society was established, consisting mainly of Quakers. One name that stands out in the history of the struggle against slavery is that of William Wilberforce, who worked tirelessly in the British Parliament, drumming up support for the Abolitionist cause. Another devoted anti-slave trade worker was a man named Thomas Clarkson, who collected a vast amount of information on the trade. Despite opposition from the pro-slavery lobby, the trading of slaves to and from the British Colonies was abolished in 1807.

In the United States, the issue of slavery was brought up at the constitutional convention of 1787. Anti-slavery numbers suggested that slavery as an institution or in any other form, should be prohibited by the constitution. This was strongly opposed by the southern states, and in order to establish the Union, the issue of slavery was postponed for 20 years. That is, the provision included in the founding Constitution stipulated that slavery could be abolished after 20 years. The 20-year grace period elapsed in 1807 and slavery was prohibited from then on.

The anti-slavery campaigners hoped that once the slave trade became illegal, the practice would also stop. As the trade diminished, these organisations and individuals began concentrating on the emancipation of slaves already in captivity. With the exception of Puerto Rico and Cuba, slavery was abolished in the Spanish Colonies once they became independent. Once again, the British led the anti-slavery movement, establishing an anti-slavery society in 1823. By this time, Wilberforce was an old man, but Thomas Fowell Buxton took his place in Parliament to continue the struggle. Buxton's activities in Parliament, coupled with strong public support, finally brought the 1833 Act which freed all slaves in British Colonies. The freedom of the slaves was not unconditional, however. The slaves were to be freed over a five to seven-year period of apprenticeships to the owners and often compensation was paid.

The French followed suit and freed their slaves in the West Indies in 1848. It was not the first time the French had freed their slaves. The first release took place in 1794 when the revolutionaries had proclaimed the emancipation of all slaves. However, in 1802 Napoleon re-established slavery in an attempt to control a revolt on the Island of Haiti. Consequently, the slave trade in the French sphere of influence continued until the 1848 Decree of Emancipation.

As the cotton industry in the United States continued to prosper, so the slave owners dug in their heels against the prompting of the abolitionists. The anti-slavery lobby in the United States was becoming ever strong, and more militant, demanding immediate abolition and initiating the founding and the re-colonisation of Liberia with former slaves. One such abolitionist was the editor of the *Liberator Gazette*, William Lloyd Garrison. It was Garrison who also founded the American Anti-Slavery Society in 1833, the year that slavery was abolished in the British Colonies.

Another individual to exert a strong influence on the conscience of the

American nation at the time was the evangelist, Theodore Dwight Weld. He had a small following, but his zeal for the abolition of slavery led him to a number of pulpits in the northern states of America. There were others too who fought for abolition, among them Frederick Douglass, a freed slave, and the now famous John Brown.

The slave question in the United States was further complicated by the fact that in terms of the constitution, the issue of slavery was left to each state in the union to decide for itself. There was also much complacency in the northern states with regard to abolitonism. These states were more concerned with stopping the spread of slavery to their states than with calling for outright abolition. When Abraham Lincoln was elected president, the southern states seceded from the Union in 1860, which led to the American Civil War of 1861 to 1865. In 1863, during the course of the war, Lincoln emancipated the slaves in all states which were in rebellion, ie secession. In terms of the 13th Amendment to the United States Constitution in 1865, all slaves were freed.

Despite the abolition of slavery in most countries, including Britain, France, the United States and the Spanish sphere of influence, slave trading continued, though on a much smaller scale. In Cuba and Brazil slave trading continued very much as before. In 1839, a new organisation, known as the British and Foreign Anti-Slavery Society, was founded. The British authorities attempted to get an international agreement effectively permitting the Royal Navy to stop and board suspected slavers in order to stop the trade. During 1862, such a treaty was signed by the United States and this did bring the slave trade down considerably. There was a worldwide anti-slavery reaction which eventually forced abolition by Cuba between 1880 and 1886, and by Brazil between 1883 and 1888. After three centuries of slave trading this inhuman practice eventually came to a halt. However, different forms of slavery of a more sophisticated nature still continued into the 20th Century, necessitating the intervention of such bodies as the United Nations and its agencies such as the International Labour Organisation.

PART 3

HUMAN RIGHTS AND SOME INTERNATIONAL CONVENTIONS

CHAPTER 1

HUMAN RIGHTS: A DESCRIPTIVE INTRODUCTION AND THE UNIVERSAL DECLARATION OF HUMAN RIGHTS (1948)

Both the term 'human rights' and the philosophical principles behind it have come to us through two important historical events. The first was the *American Declaration of Independence* of 1776 and the second was the French Revolution of 1789. The seminal document of the French Revolution was the *Declaration of the Rights of Man and of the Citizen.* Human rights were espoused by the US Constitution and these rights were extended by the 16th Amendment in 1913. The US Constitution influenced a number of subsequent developments in the sphere of human rights conventions, charters and agreements.

One of the first documents relating to human rights in this century was the *Declaration of Human Rights and Duties* of 1929. This was the result of work done by the New York Institute of International Law for submission to the Inter-American Legal Committee. It stated, *inter alia*, that it was the duty of 'every state to recognise equal rights of an individual to life, freedom and property and to fully grant and protect these rights on its entire territory regardless of nationality, sex, race, language or religion' (Osmanczyk 1990). Article II of the Declaration called for the state to guarantee or recognise the equal rights of the individual to practice his or her religion, faith and worship, on condition such activities did not violate public order and the accepted norms of the society concerned.

The 1929 Declaration, together with the Inter-American Conference held in Chapultepec on 8 May 1945, laid the foundation for the international protection of human rights upon which the Universal Declaration of Human Rights of 1948 was constructed. The preparation of the Universal Declaration of Human Rights took place concurrently in the UN Human Rights Commission and the *International Legal Commission* between 1946 and 1948. In March 1948, the work done by these commissions was accepted by the 9th Inter-American Conference, held in Bogota, Colombia, dealing with the Declaration of American Human Rights and Duties. It also served as the basis upon which the Inter-American Convention based its debates in the subsequent conventions of 1950, 1953, 1954 and 1959. The Human Rights

Commission of the Organisation of American States also used and elaborated upon the work of the two commissions.

In December 1948, the UN Human Rights Commission introduced the Universal Declaration of Human Rights. The contents of the Declaration revolved around the rights of man and only one article, viz Article 29, deals with the duties of man, stating that the individual has 'duties to the community in which alone the free and full development of his personality is possible'.

The Universal Declaration of Human Rights is not an international treaty, but was adopted by a Resolution of the UN General Assembly. However, it is accepted as an international document which all nations are required to adhere to, although it does not have the force of law.

Many other Conventions, Declarations and Pacts were based on the 1948 Declaration, among which are the following (Osmanczyk 1990):

❑ The Convention on the Prevention and Prosecution of the Crime of Genocide, 1948.
❑ The European Convention on the Protection of Human Rights and the Fundamental Freedoms, adopted by the members of the European Council, 5 November 1950.
❑ The Convention on the Status of Refugees, 1951.
❑ The Convention on International Rights for Rectification, 1952.
❑ The Protocol on the Modification of the 1926 Convention on Slavery.
❑ The Convention on the Status of Stateless Persons, 1954.
❑ The Supplementary Convention on Elimination of Slavery, 1956.
❑ The Convention on Citizenship of the Married Women, 1957.
❑ The Convention on the Reduction of the Numbers of Stateless Persons, 1961.
❑ The Convention on Marriage (terms, minimum age, registry), 1962.
❑ The Convention on Elimination of all Forms of Racial Discrimination, 1965.
❑ The International Pacts on Human Rights: Civil and Political Rights and Economic, Social and Cultural Rights, 1966.
❑ The Protocol on the Status of Refugees, 1966.

There are a number of other resolutions and declarations by the UN referring to human rights of one kind and another. The Universal Declaration of Human Rights of 1948 is reproduced below (Osmanczyk 1990). It is one of the most important human rights documents in history. Each article deserves attention and assessment.

UNIVERSAL DECLARATION OF HUMAN RIGHTS (1948)
PREAMBLE

Whereas recognition of the inherent dignity and of the equal and inalienable rights of all members of the human family is the foundation of freedom, justice and peace in the world,

Whereas disregard and contempt for human rights have resulted in barbarous acts which have outraged the conscience of mankind, and the advent of a world in which human beings shall enjoy freedom of speech and belief and freedom from fear and want has been proclaimed as the highest aspiration of the common people,

Whereas it is essential, if man is not to be compelled to have recourse, as a last resort, to rebellion against tyranny and oppression, that human rights should be protected by the rule of law,

Whereas it is essential to promote the development of friendly relations between nations,

Whereas the peoples of the United Nations have in the Charter reaffirmed their faith in fundamental human rights, in the dignity and worth of the human person and in the equal rights of men and women and have determined to promote social progress and better standards of life in larger freedom,

Whereas Member States have pledged themselves to achieve, in co-operation with the United Nations, the promotion of universal respect for and observance of human rights and fundamental freedoms,

Whereas a common understanding of these rights and freedoms is of the greatest importance for the full realisation of this pledge,

Now, therefore,

THE GENERAL ASSEMBLY

Proclaims this Universal Declaration of Human Rights as a common standard of achievement for all peoples and all nations to the end that every individual and every organ of society, keeping this Declaration constantly in mind, shall strive by teaching and education to promote respect for these rights and freedoms and by progressive measures, national and international, to secure their universal and effective recognition and observance, both among the peoples of Member States themselves and among the peoples of territories under their jurisdiction.

Article 1

All human beings are born free and equal in dignity and rights. They are endowed with reason and conscience and should act towards one another in a spirit of brotherhood.

Article 2

Everyone is entitled to all the rights and freedoms set forth in this Declaration, without distinction of any kind, such as race, colour, sex, language, religion, political or other opinion, national or social origin, property, birth or other status.

Furthermore, no distinction shall be made on the basis of the political, jurisdictional or international status of the country or territory to which a person belongs, whether it be independent, trust, non-self-governing or under any other limitation of sovereignty.

Article 3
Everyone has the right to life, liberty and security of person.

Article 4
No one shall be held in slavery or servitude; slavery and the slave trade shall be prohibited in all their forms.

Article 5
No one shall be subjected to torture or to cruel, inhuman or degrading treatment or punishment.

Article 6
Everyone has the right to recognition everywhere as a person before the law.

Article 7
All are equal before the law and are entitled without any discrimination to equal protection of the law. All are entitled to equal protection against any discrimination in violation of this Declaration and against any incitement to such discrimination.

Article 8
Everyone has the right to an effective remedy by the competent national tribunals for acts violating the fundamental rights granted him by the constitution or by law.

Article 9
No one shall be subjected to arbitrary arrest, detention or exile.

Article 10
Everyone is entitled in full equality to a fair and public hearing by an independent and impartial tribunal, in the determination of his rights and obligations and of any criminal charge against him.

Article 11
1. Everyone charged with a penal offence has the right to be presumed innocent until proved guilty according to law in a public trial at which he has had all the guarantees necessary for his defence.
2. No one shall be held guilty of any penal offence on account of any act or omission which did not constitute a penal offence, under national or international law, at the time when it was committed. Nor shall a heavier penalty be imposed than the one that was applicable at the time the penal offence was committed.

Article 12

No one shall be subjected to arbitrary interference with his privacy, family, home or correspondence, nor to attacks upon his honour and reputation. Everyone has the right to the protection of the law against such interference or attacks.

Article 13

1. Everyone has the right to freedom of movement and residence within the borders of each State.
2. Everyone has the right to leave any country, including his own, and to return to his country.

Article 14

1. Everyone has the right to seek and to enjoy in other countries asylum from persecution.
2. This right may not be invoked in the case of prosecutions genuinely arising from non-political crimes or from acts contrary to the purposes and principles of the United Nations.

Article 15

1. Everyone has the right to a nationality.
2. No one shall be arbitrarily deprived of his nationality nor denied the right to change his nationality.

Article 16

1. Men and women of full age, without any limitation due to race, nationality or religion, have the right to marry and to found a family. They are entitled to equal rights as to marriage, during marriage and at its dissolution.
2. Marriage shall be entered into only with the free and full consent of the intending spouses.
3. The family is the natural and fundamental group unit of society and is entitled to protection by society and the State.

Article 17

1. Everyone has the right to own property alone as well as in association with others.
2. No one shall be arbitrarily deprived of his property.

Article 18

Everyone has the right to freedom of thought, conscience and religion; this right includes freedom to change his religion or belief, and freedom, either alone or in community with others and in public or private, to manifest his religion or belief in teaching, practice, worship and observance.

Article 19
Everyone has the right to freedom of opinion and expression; this right includes freedom to hold opinions without interference and to seek, receive and impart information and ideas through any media and regardless of frontiers.

Article 20
1. Everyone has the right to freedom of peaceful assembly and association.
2. No one may be compelled to an association.

Article 21
1. Everyone has the right to take part in the government of his country, directly or through freely chosen representatives.
2. Everyone has the right of equal access to public service in his country.
3. The will of the people shall be the basis of the authority of government; this will shall be expressed in periodic and genuine elections which shall be by universal and equal suffrage and shall be held by secret vote or by equivalent free voting procedures.

Article 22
Everyone, as a member of society, has the right to social security and is entitled to realisation, through national effort and international co-operation and in accordance with the organisation and resources of each State, of the economic, social and cultural rights indispensable for his dignity and the free development of his personality.

Article 23
1. Everyone has the right to work, to free choice of employment, to just and favourable conditions of work and to protection against unemployment.
2. Everyone, without any discrimination, has the right to equal pay for equal work.
3. Everyone who works has the right to just and favourable remuneration ensuring for himself and his family an existence worthy of human dignity, and supplemented, if necessary by other means of social protection.
4. Everyone has the right to form and to join trade unions for the protection of his interests.

Article 24
Everyone has the right to rest and leisure, including reasonable limitation of working hours and periodic holidays with pay.

Article 25
1. Everyone has the right to a standard of living adequate for the health and well-being of himself and of his family, including food, clothing, housing and medical care and necessary social services, and the right to security

in the event of unemployment, sickness, disability, widowhood, old age or other lack of livelihood in circumstances beyond his control.

2. Motherhood and childhood are entitled to special care and assistance. All children, whether born in or out of wedlock, shall enjoy the same social protection.

Article 26

1. Everyone has the right to education. Education shall be free, at least in the elementary and fundamental stages. Elementary education shall be compulsory. Technical and professional education shall be made generally available and higher education shall be equally accessible to all on the basis of merit.

2. Education shall be directed to the full development of the human personality and to the strengthening of respect for human rights and fundamental freedoms. It shall promote understanding, tolerance and friendship among all nations, racial or religious groups, and shall further the activities of the United Nations for the maintenance of peace.

3. Parents have a prior right to choose the kind of education that shall be given to their children.

Article 27

1. Everyone has the right freely to participate in the cultural life of the community, to enjoy the arts and to share in scientific advancement and its benefits.

2. Everyone has the right to the protection of the moral and material interests resulting from any scientific, literary or artistic production of which he is the author.

Article 28

Everyone is entitled to a social and international order in which the rights and freedoms set forth in this Declaration can be fully realised.

Article 29

1. Everyone has duties to the community in which alone the free and full development of his personality is possible.

2. In the exercise of his rights and freedoms, everyone shall be subject only to such limitations as are determined by law solely for the purpose of securing due recognition and respect for the rights and freedoms of others and of meeting the just requirements of morality, public order and the general welfare in a democratic society.

3. These rights and freedoms may in no case be exercised contrary to the purposes and principles of the United Nations.

Article 30

Nothing in this Declaration may be interpreted as implying for any State, group or person any right to engage in any activity or to perform any act aimed at the destruction of any of the rights and freedoms set forth herein.

[G A Res. 217A(111), 3(1) U.N. GAOR Resolutions 71, U.N. Doc. A/810 (1948)]

CHAPTER 2

INTERNATIONAL ORGANISATIONS INVOLVED IN THE IMPLEMENTATION OF HUMAN RIGHTS TREATIES

INTRODUCTION

In the international sphere, there are two basic forms of organisations dealing with human rights issues. They are Intergovernmental Organisations (IGOs) and Non-Governmental Organisations (NGOs). Each of these shall be dealt with separately.

INTERGOVERNMENTAL ORGANISATIONS (IGOs)

These comprise governments and other such structures. They include the United Nations Organisation, the Organisation of African Unity (OAU), the Organisation of American States and the Council of Europe.

Under this category may also be included any UN agency dealing with human rights, individuals appointed by their governments, members of Parliament collectively or individually and such organisations as the Inter-Parliamentary Union. These organisations and individuals may be found in Africa, Europe, Asia or the Americas.

A close look at an Intergovernmental organisation such as the Inter-Parliamentary Union will give a reasonable insight into the basic structure and functions of an IGO.

THE INTER-PARLIAMENTARY UNION (IPU)

This organisation has a membership of 110 countries (1989). The members are parliamentarians or other representatives of institutions such as congress or national assemblies. The main function of the Inter-Parliamentary Union is the maintenance of a special committee which examines violations of the human rights of members of Parliament. The IPU committee also seeks to redress any human rights violations against its members.

The committee meets up to four times a year and deals with any complaints made to it by parliamentarians from all over the world. Only members of national Parliaments or former members of Parliament may submit cases of violations to the IPU. In the case of former members, the violations of their rights would have had to occur during their elected term of office.

The normal procedure of the IPU is to deal with violations first on a bilateral basis, ie with the government concerned. Up to this stage, the proceedings are held confidentially. However, should the response not be positive or lead to a resolution of the problem, the matter may be taken to the Inter-Parliamentary Council, whose proceedings are held in public. The IPU has been quite successful in dealing with violations of the rights of Parliamentarians throughout the world. Submissions of alleged violations or further information may be had from the organisation's offices in Geneva, Switzerland (Am. Int. Report, AI index: 10R 30/01/89 Dist: SC/COPG).

Programme Officer for Questions Relating to Human Rights
Inter-Parliamentary Union
Place du Petit-Saconnex
C P 438
Ch – 1211 Geneva 19
SWITZERLAND
Telephone: (41) (22) 734 4150
Fax: (41) (22) 733 3141
Telex: 289784 I.P.U. C.H.

NON-GOVERNMENTAL ORGANISATIONS (NGOs)

As the name suggests, Non-Governmental Organisations are bodies, groups and institutions that are not part of a formal government. NGOs play a vital role in human rights issues at the international, national, regional and local levels of their respective societies. To compile a list of NGOs is not possible in a study of this nature as there are literally thousands of such organisations. Not all NGOs deal with the same problems; some deal specifically with one or two issues. These may include children's rights, freedom of expression, minority rights, peace, prisoners and criminal justice, refugees, religious freedom, torture or women's rights.

A number of non-governmental organisations deal with the promotion and protection of rights of persons or groups involved in a particular profession. These professions may include journalists, medical personnel, teachers and lecturers or trade unionists. NGOs may also be part of or linked to such social institutions as churches, exile groups, professional organisations, universities, colleges and other such institutions. Some deal with specific matters on a regional, national or international basis.

Non-governmental organisations may also deal with individual or family complaints. An individual or family may approach a local NGO for assistance if their human rights or civil liberties are violated. The NGO concerned may provide such assistance as it may deem fit in the situation. It may approach an Inter-Governmental Organisation to seek redress, failing which it may publicise the case in the hope of getting public support. NGOs may, for example, provide advice and assistance which may allow wronged parties access to the law, ie the protection of the courts. They may also help provide victims of human rights violations with advice and access to regional or international organisations. An example of such an organisation is the International Service for Human Rights. Through the offices of this organisation, NGOs, groups or individuals may be given the right to present their grievances to the United Nations. NGOs may, if they deem it necessary, raise matters of human rights violations with a government represented in the UN or any other inter-governmental organisations.

Non-Governmental Organisations may also play a vital role in assisting the United Nations or other inter-governmental organisations in relation to human rights violations. They may also help to raise public awareness of human rights, being a vital link in the chain of information relating to human rights, especially at local levels. This information is compiled in a publication, *Human Rights Internet Reporter*, which is available every quarter. It provides information on human rights developments at the United Nations and other inter-governmental organisations. The publication also provides a list known as a Master List of names and address of non-governmental organisations in the various regions where they function. The publication is available from:

Human Rights Internet
Harvard Law School
Pould Hall, Room 401
Cambridge, Massachusetts 02138
UNITED STATES OF AMERICA
Telephone: (1) (617) 495 9924
Fax: (1) (617) 495 1110
Telex: 510 601 4536
Cable: Internet

THE INTERNATIONAL COMMITTEE OF THE RED CROSS (ICRC)
This is one of the best-known non-governmental bodies in the world. It is a private organisation which over the years has provided invaluable services in the spheres of armed conflict, international disturbances, war situations generally and other humanitarian activities.
The major activities of the Red Cross include the following:
❑ The protection and material assistance to military and civilian victims of international conflicts, civil wars and internal disturbances.
❑ Implementation, development and dissemination of international humanitarian law, including the Geneva Conventions of 12 August 1949, and their additional protocols.

❑ Acting as a neutral intermediary in humanitarian matters.
❑ Relief operations in areas of conflict.
❑ Visits to prisoners of war and political detainees (eg security detainees), to assess the material and psychological conditions of detention and the treatment accorded prisoners.
❑ Tracing persons reported missing or whose relatives are without news.

(AI Index: 1OR 30/01/89, Distr: SC/CO/PG)

Persons who may need assistance from the International Committee of the Red Cross, may obtain relevant information from:

The International Committee of the Red Cross
Information Department
19 Avenue de la Paix
CH – 1202 Geneva
SWITZERLAND
Telephone: (41) (22) 734 6001
Fax: (41) (22) 348 280
Telex: 22263

CHAPTER 3

COMMITTEES SUPERVISING THE IMPLEMENTATION OF INTERNATIONAL TREATIES

INTRODUCTION

The Universal Declaration of Human Rights (1948) is the basis upon which governments all over the world enact legislation, formulate policy and otherwise promote human rights. As soon as a government in any part of the world ratifies or accepts the dictates of the Declaration or parts of it, it indicates that it respects human dignity and rights.

The mechanisms created for the protection of human rights, such as the special committees discussed below, are there for the use of governments which adhere to the treaties, protocols and conventions. However, should a government not ratify a particular treaty, then such mechanisms as exist are not available to that government, or the people of that state.

The member states of the United Nations have agreed and pledged themselves to promote respect for and observance of fundamental human rights through international co-operation. When member states of the UN accept the obligations contained in international treaties and conventions, they stimulate the real implementation of the rights and conventions. That such a large number of states have accepted, at least in principle, the Human Rights Declaration of 1948 and other treaties, further strengthens the desire to improve freedom and justice. As one authority has put it:

> 'For all these reasons, governments are urged to ratify and accede to these international and regional instruments if they have not yet done so, and to recognise fully the various recourse procedures and monitoring bodies which are provided in these treaties and which are crucial to their effective implementation.'

> (AI Index: IOR 30/01/89; Distr: SC/CO/PG)

THE HUMAN RIGHTS COMMITTEE

This is a UN body composed of 18 experts and has been established by the *International Covenant on Civil and Political Rights (ICCPR)*. The task of the Human Rights Committee is, *inter alia*, to monitor members states' implementation of the provisions of the ICCPR and an optional protocol appended to it. The ICCPR is a treaty that calls upon the signatories to ensure that specific human rights are accorded to their citizens. The optional protocol to this treaty is a separate agreement that establishes procedure by which individual complainants can submit their appeals to the ICCPR.

The Human Rights Committee may consider the complaints of individuals alleging violation of their rights only if the country in which they reside is a member or is a signatory to the **optional protocol**. Complaints may be submitted to the committee by the affected individual or by a nominee, who in most cases is a legal representative. Should the individual concerned be unable to present the complaint himself due to incarceration or disappearance, another person who has close links with the victim may make the submission for him. Such a person may be a spouse or other close member of the family. In order to be accepted by the HRC, the complainant or his nominee must indicate that all avenues on the domestic front have been explored or that effective procedures for remedies are non-existent in his or her particular society. For example, a complainant cannot plead his or her case at both the Human Rights Committee level and the regional level at he same time. There are, however, a number of exceptions to this rule in the case of at least nine signatories to the Protocol. There are other conditions under which complaints may be made to the HRC. They are:

'If the government concerned is party to both the Optional Protocol and to the relevant regional human rights treaty, and has made any required declarations accepting the regional treaty's individual complaints procedure, then one will need to decide whether to direct a complaint in the first instance to the Human Rights Committee or the regional body. In making this decision, the following should be taken into account:

❑ The nature of the violation, and whether the text of the international or regional treaty more effectively addresses the issue;

❑ The outcome of any previous cases before each body which raised similar issues;

❑ The chance of success before each body;

❑ Whether a decision by the regional treaty body would be legally binding under domestic law in contrast with the views of the Human Rights Committee;

❑ The comparative speed of the procedures;

❑ Whether the use of one of the procedures will preclude the use of the other (eg under the terms of the European Convention, the European Commission would be precluded from considering an individual complaint if it had already been submitted to the Human Rights Committee;

❑ The derived outcome and which body would be more likely to produce it (the outcome sought might include changing the government's practice; setting a legal precedent nationally, regionally or internationally; compensation, publicity, etc).

(AI Index: IOR 30/01/89; Distr. SC/CO/PG)

There are a number of difficulties facing any individual who may wish to lay a complaint at regional or HRC level. It would be advisable to consult expert advice available from a number of sources. Two important sources of consultation are given below:

Interights
Kingsway Chambers
46 Kingsway
No. 6831
London WC2B 6EN
UNITED KINGDOM
Telephone: (44) (1) 242 5581
Fax: (44) (1) 831 9489
Telex: 262 433 Ref.
OR
International Human Rights Law Group
1601 Connecticut Avenue
NW Suite 700
Washington DC 20009
UNITED STATES OF AMERICA
Telephone: (1) (202) 232 8500

In addition to complaints from individuals, the Human Rights Commission may receive complaints from state parties against another state party to the effect that it is not fulfilling its obligations under the ICCPR. However, both parties have to make a declaration recognising the competence of the HRC to review the situation and take appropriate action.

State parties to the ICCPR have to submit a report to the HRC at least one year after becoming a member of the ICCPR. After this initial report, the state party need submit a report only once every five years. The reports must indicate to what extent the treaty (ICCPR) or parts of it have been implemented by the state party concerned. These reports are public documents and state parties may be made to answer questions publicly with reference to reports submitted to the Human Rights Committee.

Non-Governmental Organisations (NGOs) do not have a formal relationship with the Human Rights Committee. They cannot present written or oral reports to the HRC. NGOs are permitted to observe open meetings of the

HRC, but not closed sessions.

THE UN CENTRE FOR HUMAN RIGHTS

The UN Centre for Human Rights is not to be confused with the Human Rights Committee (HRC). The Centre for Human Rights is a branch of the United Nations Secretariat and its specific task is to provide services to all bodies of the UN dealing with human rights and related matters. The Centre has two offices, one in the United Nations building in New York and the other, a liaison office, at UN Headquarters in Geneva. The New York office is headed by a person designated Under-Secretary-General for Human Rights. The Geneva office is situated at:

The UN Centre for Human Rights
United Nations Office in Geneva
Palais de Nations
Ch - 1211 Geneva 10
SWITZERLAND
Telephone: (41) (22) 734 6011
Fax: (41) (22) 733 9879
Telex: 289 696 UNO CH

THE COMMITTEE OF ECONOMIC, SOCIAL AND CULTURAL RIGHTS

The Committee of Economic, Social and Cultural Rights has 18 members who are nominated state parties. The Committee is responsible for the implementation of the International Covenant on Economic, Social and Cultural Rights (ICESCR).

In terms of the guidelines of the organisation, state parties to ECOSOC must submit a report to the committee within two years of their becoming members. After the first submission, reports on progress with the implementation of economic, social and cultural rights must be submitted every five years. The meetings are open to the public and Non-Governmental Organisations may submit written recommendations or other memoranda in consultation with the Committee.

THE COMMITTEE AGAINST TORTURE

The UN Committee Against Torture is made up of ten members, all experts, whose task is to monitor the Convention. In addition to torture, other cruelties, inhuman and degrading treatment and forms of punishment are monitored. The convention against torture and other forms of ill-treatment is called the *United Nations Convention Against Torture, and other Cruel, Inhuman and Degrading Treatment or Punishment.*

This Committee is entitled to examine complaints of individuals with the proviso that the state party to which he or she belongs recognises the competence of the Committee to consider the complaint. The Committee is also empowered to assess complaints by one state party against another, alleging violation of any article of the Convention. The state parties must, however, both be in agreement that the Committee is competent to review the complaints.

The Committee may also undertake investigations of torture against a state party or a particular state. The Committee's right to conduct systematic inquiries is applicable to all state parties who are signatories to the convention. States that are not signatories to this convention are not bound to submit to the Committee's investigations.

Like other UN committees, this one also requires state parties to submit a report to it not later than one year after becoming a signatory to the convention. Thereafter, a report need be submitted only once every four years. The hearings of the Committee are public.

Some NGOs may, in terms of the procedures of the Committee, be invited to submit information and written documentation and statements. However, others may have observer status at meetings of the Committee. This status is granted only when state parties are the subject of investigation. However, the NGOs are not permitted attendance when the committee deals with individuals' allegations of torture.

THE COMMITTEE ON THE ELIMINATION OF
RACIAL DISCRIMINATION

This Committee is made up of 18 members elected by the state parties. The main task of the Committee is to monitor the implementation of the *International Convention on the Elimination of Racial Discrimination*. The Committee meets twice a year for a period of three weeks per session at the United Nations in Geneva, Switzerland.

Individuals may submit allegations of violations of human rights. Groups of individuals may also make submissions to the Commission. However, these submissions may be made only if the relevant state party to the convention recognises the competence of the Committee to examine the complaints. State parties may also lay complaints against each other to the effect that the Convention on Human Rights is not being adhered to.

THE COMMITTEE ON THE ELIMINATION OF
DISCRIMINATION AGAINST WOMEN

The Committee comprises 23 members, who are experts in the field of Women's Rights. They are elected by the state parties which are signatories to the *International Convention on the Elimination of Discrimination Against*

Women. The Committee meets only once a year for a two-week period, either in New York or in Vienna, Austria.

Presently, the Committee does not have procedures to receive either individual complaints or inter-state complaints. Its meetings are open to the public and its main function is to review reports by State parties on any issue concerning the implementation of the Convention. Information about the committee is available from:

The Secretary
Committee on the Elimination of Discrimination Against Women
UN Vienna International Centre
PO Box 500
A – 1400 Vienna
AUSTRIA
Telephone: (43) (222) 21131
Fax: (43) (222) 32156
Telex: 135612 UNO A

CHAPTER 4

REGIONAL HUMAN RIGHTS ORGANISATIONS

THE AFRICAN COMMISSION ON HUMAN AND PEOPLES' RIGHTS

The Organisation of African Unity (OAU) is also active in the sphere of human rights on the Continent of Africa. The basis of human rights activities on the continent is the *African Charter on Human and Peoples' Rights*, originally known as the *Banjul Charter on Human and Peoples' Rights of 1981*. The OAU Human Rights Charter was adopted by the OAU on 27 June 1981 in Nairobi, Kenya, but came into effect only in 1986.

The African Commission on Human and Peoples' Rights consists of 11 members elected by the governments that are members of the OAU. These include island countries around Africa, such as the Comores, Madagascar and Seychelles. The Commission supervises the implementation of the OAU Human Rights Charter.

Complaints to the Commission or other allegations of violations of human rights may be made by individuals, groups or non-governmental organisations. The procedures are laid down in Articles 55 to 58 of the Human Rights Charter of the OAU (see Appendix). However, one of the main requirements is that domestic remedies on a local or national government level must have been exhausted or unduly hindered by official procrastination. Complaints may also be made to the Commission by state parties against another state party alleging violation of the Charter.

Information on the African Commission on Human and Peoples' Rights may be had by writing or otherwise communicating the request to:

The African Commission on Human and Peoples' Rights
c/o Organisation of African Unity
PO Box 3243
Addis Ababa
ETHIOPIA
Telephone: (251) (1) 517 700
Telex: 21046

OR

The Permanent Delegation of the Organisation of African Unity
13 Avenue De Budé
CH – 1202 Geneva
SWITZERLAND
Telephone: (41) (22) 733 8560
Telex: 28866

OR

Office of the Executive Secretary of the UN
346 East 50th Street
New York, NY 10017
UNITED STATES OF AMERICA
Telephone: (1) (212) 319 5490

INTER-AMERICAN COMMISSION AND COURT
OF HUMAN RIGHTS

This organisation came into existence in 1959. However, its status changed in 1978 when the American Convention on Human Rights was adopted. As a result of the Commission being formed prior to the adoption of the American Convention, the Commission retains its jurisdiction over all the member states of the Organisation of American States (OAS). The OAS is made up of 32 governments in Latin America, North America, the Caribbean and Cuba, which has been excluded since 1962. Canada, Belize and Guyana, although not members, have observer status. The Commission has seven members, elected by OAS member countries.

The Inter-American Commission can deal with complaints from individuals, groups or any other body. Non-governmental organisations (NGOs) which are legally recognised in member states are also entitled to petition the Committee with regard to human rights violations. These rights are entwined in two documents, namely the American Convention on Human Rights and the American Declaration of the Rights and Duties of Man (1948).

Before an individual or group petitions the Commission, they must have gone through channels at local and national levels. However, should the Commission be informed that persons or groups are in danger, to the extent that their lives are threatened, the Commission is empowered to intervene and petition the government concerned. There are a number of procedures of enquiry into human rights violations, but two are especially important. They are *(a)* an on-site investigation to assess an individual's case or a number of cases; and *(b)* a hearing on the case in special circumstances.

One state may also lay a complaint against another, with the proviso that the state parties involved both recognise the Inter-American Commission's right to review the complaint. Another process available only to governments and the Inter-American Commission is the Inter-American Court of Human Rights. Governments or the Commission may bring the matter to the court for assessment, and, in terms of article 62 of the American Convention, the court's jurisdiction is binding upon the parties.

Any party wanting more information on facts and procedures of the Inter-American Commission and the Court of Human Rights, may contact:

The Inter-American Commission on Human Rights
c/o The Organisation of American States
1889 F Street NW, 8th Floor
Washington DC 2006
UNITED STATES OF AMERICA
Telephone: (1) (202) 458 6002
Fax: (1) (202) 458 3992
Telex: 64128 OAS UW

THE EUROPEAN COMMISSION AND COURT
OF HUMAN RIGHTS

The Council of Europe of 1950 adopted the European Convention on Human Rights, which resulted in the establishment of the European Commission on Human Rights and the European Court of Human Rights, the members of which are elected by member states of the **Council of Europe**. The Council comprises 23 member countries: Austria, Belgium, Cyprus, Denmark, Germany, Finland, France, Greece, Iceland, Ireland, Italy, Liechtenstein, Luxemburg, Malta, the Netherlands, Norway, Portugal, San Marino, Spain, Sweden, Switzerland, Turkey and Britain.

Complaints of human rights violations in terms of conventions and protocols may be submitted by individuals, groups of individuals or non-governmental organisations. However, individual petitions to the Commission and the Court, may be accepted only if the state concerned recognises the right of that individual petition in respect of the relevant convention or protocol. Another requirement is that the individual or group concerned must have exhausted local remedies, or they must prove such remedies to be ineffective. State parties may also make allegations to the Commission or the Court with reference to another state party's violation of the convention or protocol. The Commission also provides information on processes and procedures relating to individuals or groups suffering human rights violations. Further information is available from:

The European Commission of Human Rights
Council of Europe
BP 431 R6
F – 67006 Strasbourg Cedex
FRANCE
Telephone: (33) (88) 614 961
Fax: (33) (88) 373 259
Telex: 870943

THE EUROPEAN COMMITTEE FOR THE PREVENTION OF TORTURE AND INHUMAN OR DEGRADING TREATMENTS OR PUNISHMENT

This is a committee of experts which functions in terms of the *European Convention for the Prevention of Torture and Inhuman or Degrading Treatment or Punishment.* In terms of the Convention the Committee may visit places of detention and prisons under the jurisdiction of state parties to the Convention. The Committee is free to visit such institutions at will and has the right to interview persons in private and gather any information it needs from any available source.

Persons who are in custody may request the Committee to suggest to the state party concerned changes to the penal institutions or improvement of conditions. When the Committee visits such institutions it must inform the state party of its intention to do so and state parties cannot refuse the Committee's request, though they may raise objections under certain circumstances. Should a state party refuse the Committee access to their detention facilities, the Committee may make a public statement on the issue which may serve as a form of pressure against the state concerned.

CHAPTER 5

AMNESTY INTERNATIONAL'S ROLE IN HUMAN RIGHTS PROTECTION

Amnesty International has its headquarters in London, where it was founded on 28 May 1961 by Peter Beneson, who was, among other things, a defence attorney for political prisoners in Hungary, a country then still under communist rule. The main functions of the organisation are to make the international public aware of human rights violations throughout the world.

Among the violations that Amnesty International keeps a watching brief on are those of basic human rights, freedom of speech and freedom of religion. It also takes a keen interest in the condition of prisoners, especially the torture of political dissidents. Amnesty International works in various ways to obtain the release of political prisoners and attempts to get relief for their families and dependents generally. The organisation has been instrumental in gaining freedom and relief for many prisoners in several countries. Its work is recognised by governments in most democratically orientated societies and in 1977 it was awarded the Nobel Prize for Peace.

Peter Beneson's efforts to secure human rights for all were also effective in bringing to the world's attention human rights violations in South Africa, and in Spain during the rule of General Francisco Franco. As a result of his efforts, Amnesty International was established as a collective agency for the advancement and propagation of human rights. Between 1961 and 1975, the Chairman of the Executive Committee of the organisation was Sean Mac-Bride, who received the Nobel Prize for Peace in 1974.

During the first five years of the organisation's existence, it operated on an annual budget of only £25 000, with a full-time staff complement of only eight people. By 1985, it had a budget in excess of £2 million, a Secretariat of 150 persons and offices in more than forty countries, with about 200 000 people involved as individual members in about 100 countries.

Amnesty International is involved in a number of activities in countries around the world. These include the publication of incidents of human rights violations, especially by offending governments, in publications such as its newsletters, its annual reports, the press and in research and background papers. It has a worldwide network of small groups, known as 'adoption groups', comprising between three and eight persons. The groups take responsibility for a number of 'prisoners of conscience', such as political prisoners.

The offending government is bombarded with letters, protest notes and other such activities until the prisoners are either released or charged in a legally constituted court that functions in terms of international juristic requirements.

Amnesty International has a research department at its London Head-quarters. Material relating to human rights violations in all parts of the world is collated and made available to human rights groups, individual human rights activists, governments, international agencies and in fact any group that may assist the process of eliminating human rights violations.

The organisation issues annual reports detailing violations of human rights by governments and other agencies linked to an offending government. In order to indicate the type of work taken on by Amnesty International, it is essential to assess at least one such report. The following is a shortened version of such a report (*Keesing's Record of World Events* pp 38366-38367, July 1991):

'AMNESTY INTERNATIONAL ANNUAL REPORT

In its 1991 annual report published on July 10, the human rights organi-sation Amnesty International claimed that human rights violations had occurred in 141 countries and had actually worsened in some cases.

Observing that ''governments of the world stand in danger of sabo-taging the hope of a new era of human rights'', it asserted that ''some are sabotaging it by the violations they commit directly, others by the selectivity with which they exert their influence''.

Human rights abuses in Iraq had received worldwide attention, but grave violations in countries such as Chad, China, Colombia, Mali, Syria and Turkey were accorded little publicity. In about half the countries in the world governments had imprisoned people for their beliefs, while more than 100 governments had resorted to torture or the maltreatment of prisoners; thousands of people had ''disappeared'' or were extra-judi-cially executed in 29 countries, most notably in Sri Lanka, Brazil, El Salvador, Guatemala and Peru.

Death sentences had been judicially imposed or carried out in 1990 in 90 countries; the death penalty was retained by every country in the Middle East, with Iran showing the region's highest number of death sentences (estimated at more than 700), while in China the report re-corded 750 executions, the highest number since 1983. Thousands of Chinese pro-democracy protesters arrested the previous year continued to be detailed without charge or trial. Numerous cases of arbitrary detention, often without trial, were recorded in Israel and the Israeli-oc-cupied territories where an estimated 25 000 Palestinians had been arrested since the start of the *intifada*, including 4 000 without charge or trial. In Syria and Iran thousands of political prisoners were unlawfully detained.

As in its 1990 report (see p 37630), Amnesty International again accused the United Kingdom government of seriously undermining human rights, especially in Northern Ireland. Detailing its allegations, which included the ill-treatment of suspects, unfair trials, killings of suspects without warning and the abuse of asylum seekers, the report concluded that the UK's record on many of these issues had actually worsened in recent years despite its stated commitment to international treaties.

Amnesty International has to have a well-run organisation in order to continue its work worldwide. This, as the above report may indicate, involves working for the release of prisoners of conscience, 'fair and prompt trials for political prisoners and the abolition of tortures and the death penalty' (Osmanczyk, 1990). In order to function efficiently, Amnesty International makes use of at least 42 national sections, 3 000 local groups and more than half a million individuals in about 150 countries.

Amnesty International's activities include the publication of bulletins, in-depth reports and international statements released to give insight into human rights violations all over the world. Its wide network of people at grassroots level makes it one of the best-informed human rights organisations today. In addition, Amnesty International has an excellent reputation for the fearless manner in which it pursues the truth in relation to human rights violations. Its reports are authentic and normally are first-hand accounts of events as they occured.

Reports issued by Amnesty International are substantial and the details contained therein contain statistics that substantiate its reports. Its constant updating and appraisal of situations make it one of the organisations in the forefront of the struggle for human rights the world over.

PART 4

INTERNATIONAL HUMAN RIGHTS ACTIVISTS

CHAPTER 1

ABRAHAM LINCOLN

'As I would not be a slave, so I would not be a master. This Expresses my idea of democracy. Whatever differs from this, to the extent of the difference, is no democracy'.

ABRAHAM LINCOLN

Abraham Lincoln, the 16th President of the United States, is one of the most remarkable men who ever lived. It was Lincoln's high ideals, his belief that all men are born equal before God, and a total commitment to the removal of slavery that prompted one of history's worst civil wars.

He was born on February 12, 1809 near the town of Hodgenville, in the American state of Kentucky. Lincoln's father, Thomas, was descended from an English family that had settled in Massachusetts from England as early as 1637. He was born in poverty and this factor was dominant throughout his life. Much of his humanitarian compassion is said to have taken root as a result of his humble beginnings. His father encountered difficulties with the title to his Kentucky farm, as a result of which he moved to south-western Indiana in 1816. Once in Indiana, the young Lincoln was shattered when his mother died. He was nine years old at the time, and her death made him uneasy and depressed. Soon after, his father remarried a kindly widow, Sarah Bush Johnson, who had three children of her own, two girls and a boy.

His stepmother had a profound effect on Lincoln and encouraged him to read, thereby increasing his love of knowledge. Lincoln's parents were both almost illiterate. In fact, Lincoln's own formal school attendance took place in short sporadic periods, resulting in only a year's formal schooling. In later years, he had this to say about his education: 'My environment provided absolutely nothing to excite ambition for education. Of course, when I came of age I did not know much. Still, somehow, I could read, write and cipher to the rule of three, but that was all.' One of the books that he was familiar with was the Bible, which was a constant companion to his family in their daily lives.

During March 1830, when Abraham was 21 years old, the Lincoln family moved again, this time to the state of Illinois. Once in Illinois, he made no secret of the fact that he disliked farming. Consequently he tried his hand at a variety of occupations. These included working as a rail splitter, later making a trip down the Mississippi River as a flat boatman, where he visited the city of New Orleans for the second time. He settled in the village of New Salem on his return upstream and worked as a storekeeper, a postmaster, and even tried his hand at surveying. Despite his many jobs, Lincoln's ambition was to become a legislator. He made an attempt to enter the State Legislature, but was defeated. He did not accept failure and on subsequent occasions he was repeatedly elected as a representative to the State Legislature. He developed an interest in law and began to study the law with determination. In 1836, he wrote and passed the bar examinations, which allowed him to practise.

It was during the presidency of Andrew Jackson that Abraham Lincoln first entered politics. He was a member of the Whig party in the Illinois State Legislature. He was a keen state representative, involving himself in economic development projects with enthusiasm. Lincoln opposed the practice of slavery, but was no outright abolitionist at the time. In 1837, resolutions were proposed in the State Legislature condemning abolitionist societies and stating that slavery as an institution in the southern states was 'sacred'. It was during this period that a mob lynched Elijah Lovejoy, a journalist, who was against slavery and made his views known through newspaper articles. Lincoln did not support the resolutions and together with a colleague in the Legislature, he drew up a protest against them. Lincoln was opposed to slavery and he made his views known. It was during his single term of office in Congress in Washington DC (1847-1849) that Lincoln put forward a bill which in effect would provide for the compensated emancipation of slavery in the District of Columbia. The bill, however, suggested that the white voters of the District of Columbia would have to approve it. As time went on, it seemed that by the age of forty, Lincoln's political career was ending.

Lincoln had a political rival in the person of Stephen A Douglas, who in 1854 managed to get a bill through Congress reopening the entire Louisiana Purchase to slavery, that is, it allowed settlers in Kansas and Nebraska to make their own decisions whether to permit slavery or not. The bill, passed as the Kansas-Nebraska Act, aroused strong opposition in Illinois and other northwestern states. The passing of this Act gave strong impetus to the new Republican Party, while the Whig party began to disintegrate. Lincoln became a Republican in 1856, and called on Congress to exclude the institution of slavery from the abovementioned territories. The United States was beginning to diverge into two separate camps, one against slavery and the other for retention of the institution. It was during this time (1858) while running for the Senate that Lincoln delivered one of his more important speeches, stating: 'A house divided against itself cannot stand. I believe the Government cannot endure permanently half slave and half free.' The country, he said, would become either one or the other.

Lincoln fought on, making every attempt to thwart slavery in the new territories, but the Dred Scott decision of 1857 dealt a significant blow to Lincoln's arguments against slavery. The US Supreme Court ruled that the Congress was not constitutionally empowered to exclude slavery from the territories concerned. Lincoln made an attempt in 1858 to get elected to the US Senate, but failed. However, his star was rising and he was becoming a household name in politics. In some quarters he was being suggested as a possible presidential candidate for the Republican Party. In fact, on 18 May 1860, after three ballots, he was nominated as the Republican candidate at the Republican Convention in Chicago. The opposition Democratic Party was not united as a result of a split between its Southern and Northern adherents. There were in fact four candidates contesting the presidency during the 1860 election. Despite having little support from the Southern states, Lincoln won the election with a clear and decisive majority in the electoral college.

Lincoln's election to the presidency caused the pro-slavery states in the south to fear the worst. South Carolina called a state convention soon after and announced that it was seceding from the Union. The split had started and early in 1861, Mississippi, Alabama, Florida, Georgia, Louisiana and Texas also left the Union, forming the Confederate States of America. On 4 March 1861 Lincoln made his inaugural speech, in which he said that no state had the right to secede from the Union. However, secession became a fact, with Unionist forces removing themselves from positions in the South (Confederate States) with the exception of Fort Sumter, in Charleston Harbour, South Carolina. The fort was commanded by Major Robert Anderson, who was completely besieged and very short of provisions. On 12 April 1861, the Confederate forces demanded the surrender of Fort Sumter, but Anderson refused, whereupon they opened fire on the fort and the American Civil War began in earnest. However, it is not the purpose of this study to discuss the military details of the war. It is sufficient to say that the North started the war with a number of distinct advantages. These included a population of 20 million as opposed to the Confederate states, which had a population of about five million whites and three million slaves. The North was also more highly industrialised, a fact that gave it the edge in weapons manufacture.

Lincoln's attitude to slavery had been established quite early in his life. In 1854, he made a comprehensive statement with regard to slavery: 'I hate it [slavery] because of the monstrous injustice of slavery itself. I hate it because it deprives our republican example of its just influence in the world; enables the enemies of free institutions with plausibility to taunt us as hypocrites....'

A year later, in a letter to a life-long friend, Lincoln described a number of other factors that made slavery repugnant to him. The letter recalled a trip he and the friend had taken down the Ohio River in their youth during which they had witnessed a scene that he never forgot. He said: 'You may remember, as well as I do, that from Louisville to the mouth of the Ohio there were, on board, ten or a dozen slaves, shackled together with irons. That sight was a continued torment to me; and I see something like it every time I touch the Ohio, or any other slave border'.

However difficult it was for Lincoln to accept slavery, during his early presidency he was reluctant to take strong action against slave states, hoping to bring them into line by encouragement and conviction. He devised a strategy known as the Lincoln Plan, whereby the slaves were to be set free by the states themselves, and the federal government was to pay partial compensation. The process of freeing the slaves was to be gradual, and once freed, the slaves were to be settled abroad. Although Congress in Washington was prepared to vote the funds for the plan, not a single state in which slavery existed agreed to the plan. In addition, many black leaders were also opposed to the plan because they did not wish to be sent abroad. Despite these difficulties, Lincoln issued his Emancipation Proclamation in two stages. The first stage was issued on 22 September 1862, and the second stage on 1 January 1863. He issued this proclamation with the belief that the President had special powers during a war: the Civil War was raging at the time. In fact, Lincoln himself was not sure that the proclamation was legal in terms of the US Constitution.

Something more concrete had to be done in order to guarantee that after the Civil War, the slaves could remain free and not be re-enslaved through lack of an appropriate legal mechanism to guarantee their liberty. With this in mind, the 13th Amendment was added to the Constitution of the United States. The adoption of this amendment was no easy task for Lincoln. When a new Congress was re-elected in 1865, with a Republican majority, Lincoln felt strong enough to put it through. With this amendment through and on the statute books, Lincoln's name went down in history as one of the great emancipators of the world. Apart from his political struggle to bring emancipation into force as law, Lincoln's personal interaction with all people was one of open-mindedness, respect for human worth and dignity regardless of race, colour or creed. He used every opportunity possible to get to know as many blacks as possible so as to get first-hand information on their view and vision of a future America, free of slavery or any other form of oppression. He befriended a former slave, Frederick Douglass, who later said of Lincoln: 'In all my interviews with Mr Lincoln, I was impressed with his entire freedom from prejudice against the coloured race.'

The Civil War continued into Lincoln's second term as President of the United States. His re-election campaign was more efficient than the first and he himself took a great interest in the day-to-day running of the campaign. He was elected with a popular majority of 55 %. By this time the Confederacy was making peace offers in the hope of ending one of history's most brutal civil wars. In an open letter, Lincoln states his views on peace terms quite clearly:

> 'Any proposition which embraces the restoration of peace, the integrity of the whole union, and the abandonment of slavery, and which comes by and with an authority that can control the armies now at war against the United States, will be received and considered by the Executive Government of the United States, and will be met by liberal terms on other substantial and collateral points.'

Lincoln attempted to please both the Republican radicals, who called for the total defeat of the Confederacy, and more lenient elements. On 3 February 1865, Lincoln met with Confederate delegates on a steamship at Hampton Road, promising to be lenient and liberal with presidential pardons. In his second inaugural address, on 4 March 1865, Lincoln spoke eloquently of his vision, saying that his administration would act 'with malice toward none; with charity for all'. When the war finally ended, Lincoln did not have a firm uniform policy with regard to the defeated Southern Confederacy. In the case of some states, he suggested that the state government of the day oversee the transition from war to peace. In other states, he suggested that the people themselves elect a new government, allowing for blacks on the voters' roll. In other words, Lincoln did not wish to impose any government on the Southern states, though insisting that these states return to the Union under one federal government in Washington DC. As time went on, Lincoln was being pressured by his radicals who were demanding that he alter his views on peace strategy and occupy the South by military force. They also demanded that the planter estates of the former slave masters be confiscated and divided among the freed slaves. However, fate decreed that Lincoln would not live to complete the task of peace. On the fateful evening of 14 April 1865, as he sat in Ford's Theatre in Washington DC, he was shot by John Wilkes Booth. He died on the morning of 15 April 1865.

To best sum up the life and the contributions of Abraham Lincoln to mankind, it is imperative that reference be made to his famous address, delivered on 19 November 1863, at the site of the battle of Gettysburg in the state of Pennsylvania. His famous speech, which he is reported to have written in pencil on the back of a brown envelope, has become almost sacred to freedom-loving people the world over. Edward Everett, the main speaker of the day at Gettysburg, wrote to Lincoln and paid him the following compliment: 'I should be glad if I could flatter myself that I came as near to the central idea of the occasion in two hours as you did in two minutes.' The text of his two-minute speech has stirred deep feelings in the United States, where most schoolboys are familiar with its memorable words:

'Four score and seven years ago, our fathers brought forth on this continent, a new nation, conceived in liberty, and dedicated to the proposition that all men are created equal.

Now we are engaged in a great civil war, testing whether that nation can long endure. We are met on a great battlefield of that war. We have come to dedicate a portion of that field, as a final resting place for those who have gave their lives that that nation might live. It is altogether fitting and proper that we should do this.

But, in a larger sense, we cannot dedicate – we cannot consecrate – we cannot hallow this ground. The brave men, living and dead, who struggled here, have consecrated it, far above our poor power to add or detract. The world will little note, nor long remember what we say here, but it can never forget what they did here. It is for us the living, rather, to be dedicated here to the unfinished work which they who fought here have thus far so nobly advanced. It is rather for us to be here dedicated to the great task remaining before us – that from these honoured dead we take increased devotion to that cause for which they gave the last full measure of devotion – that we here highly resolve that these dead shall not have died in vain – that his nation, under God, shall have a new birth of freedom – and that the government of the people, by the people, for the people, shall not perish from the earth.'

CHAPTER 2

MAHATMA GANDHI

'I would strain every nerve to make truth and non-violence accepted in all our national activities.'

GANDHI

One of the greatest leaders of the 20th Century, Mohandas Karamchand Gandhi, was born in the small provincial town of Porbandar, in western India. The town was the capital of a little Gujarat principality under the control of the British, as was the rest of India. Gandhi's father was the Chief Minister of the principality, for despite his lack of an appropriate education, he was particularly talented in political administration and managed to survive in a very turbulent political situation. Gandhi senior was particularly adept at balancing his approach to three main contenders in the principality's social fabric. These were the wealthy Indian princes, the people of the principality and the British Colonial authorities.

Mohandas Gandhi's mother was a quiet and saintly women who spent much of her time in prayer at the temple. She was completely dedicated to the welfare of her family and avoided such luxuries as jewellery or fine clothing. As a result of these influences, Gandhi grew up in a strongly religious environment where spiritual attendance and honour was paid to the Hindu god, Visnu. In addition to this religious tendency, Gandhi was intro-duced early in his life to Jainism, a powerful Indian religious philosophy steeped in traditions of non-violence and a strong adherence to the view that all things in the Universe are eternal in character. This led the young Gandhi to believe in Ahimsa, which held that all living beings were to be respected and treated with care so that no injury would come to them. These religious beliefs were expressed in vegetarianism and long periods of fasting for spiritual renewal and physical purification. One of the important tenets of the religion was its call on its adherents to be tolerant of others, despite the variety of creeds and beliefs.

Gandhi's primary education began under very poor and rudimentary conditions. It is said that he learned the alphabet by writing it in the dust on the ground. However, his politically active father became a leading figure (Dewan) in another principality where the educational system was a little better. Gandhi's educational record at this stage was not very good and a school report suggested that he was mediocre, good at such subjects as English and arithmetic, but weak in others, such as geography.

As was the custom in India, Gandhi married at the young age of thirteen, but continued his schooling after an absence of one year. At school, Gandhi showed no particular flair for learning, nor did he show any promise on the sports field. He enjoyed reading in solitude and often went on long walks in the country. While still young, he was very dedicated to his parents, helping his mother, Putlibai, and assisting her in looking after his father, who was ailing.

However, his early learning period had a negative effect on him for a short period. His strict upbringing made him a rebel in adolescence. Despite his strict upbringing in a Visnava family, he became an atheist in secret, took part in petty thieving, smoked secretly and ate meat, which his religion strictly forbade. His deviance during this difficult adolescent period was short-lived and he made a solemn promise never to return to unacceptable behaviour patterns. He made serious attempts to improve himself, both in the fields of knowledge and comportment. One of the results of his change of attitude was a dedication to the study of Hindu mythology. He studied such legendary figures as Prahlada and Hariscmandra, who, according to Hindu tradition, were embodiments of truth and sacrifice.

In 1887, Gandhi passed the matriculation exemption examination of the University of Bombay, allowing him to register at the Samaldas College in Bhavnagar. The process was quite traumatic for him as he had to switch from his native language of Gujarati to English as a medium of instruction. This subjected him to a number of serious difficulties, especially when attempting to follow the lectures which were in English. His future was not in his hands. He would have like to become a medical doctor, but the family's belief in the Visnava principles would have caused them to frown upon the practice of vivisection and he was thus excluded from this field of study. His family saw his future in political or public administration and in order to fulfil this role the young Gandhi was told that he would have to become a barrister. Since this would entail his having to study in Britain, he accepted the suggestion, as this would permit him to leave the Samaldas College which he did not particularly enjoy.

His decision to go to Britain was not easy to put into practice. The family's relative poverty and his mother's reluctance to allow him, as the youngest child, to be exposed to the dangers of Western civilisation in Britain were major obstacles. Gandhi, however, did not relent. He was determined to go to England and so promised his mother that while in Britain he would refrain from touching alcohol, women and particularly meat. He had to disregard the strictures of the Medh Bania Caste to which he belonged, which warned that his move to England was a violation of the Hindu religion, and he left for England by ship in September 1888. Upon his arrival in Britain, Gandhi joined the Inner Temple, one of London's law schools.

Gandhi's stay in Britain was, however, not an easy one. His transition from a provincial town in India to the metropolitan atmosphere in London had several obstacles. Besides having to adopt the western mode of dress, Gandhi had to deal with serious moral issues on a personal level. He was a vegetarian by religious conviction and this made it very difficult for him to assimilate into the cosmopolitan life of London. These factors nearly ruined his ability to study and also impaired his health to a certain extent. However, London did have one or two vegetarian restaurants at the time and he found this a great relief. Armed with his personal religious convictions and books and literature on vegetarianism, Gandhi was able to justify his way of life, a fact that gave him more self-confidence. One of the positive factors emerging from his vegetarianism was the fact that he became an executive committee member of the London Vegetarian Society. He was very active in the society's activities, attending many of its meetings and contributing articles to vegetarian publications.

It was as a member of the London Vegetarian Society that Gandhi became popular with a number of leading citizens of London, and it was through these members that he was introduced to the Holy Bible. During this period, also, he was able for the first time to read one of Hinduism's most important works, the Bhagavad-Gita, in English. The Vegetarian Society included a wide range of people who had some influence on Gandhi, both politically and morally, such as the Socialist humanitarian, Edward Carpenter, the Fabian Socialist and writer, George Bernard Shaw, and the theosophist, Annie Besant. These persons were mostly in the forefront of the quest for change and a number of them were anti-capitalists who denounced the prevailing values of the time. Many of them stressed the virtues of the simple life, steeped in moral values of co-operation and non-violence.

Gandhi returned to India in July 1891. Much had taken place during his absence, one of the sadder incidents being the death of his mother. He also found that his British legal degree did not open the doors to opportunity as he had hoped. He found it extremely difficult to enter the legal profession, because of competition from many other qualified legal people. One source suggests that he even had serious difficulties getting a job as a school teacher. Gandhi went to the town of Rajkot where he scraped a living by drafting legal petitions for litigants. In addition, he had difficulties with British officialdom and when he received an offer to join a legal firm in the province of Natal, South Africa, he had no hesitation in accepting.

His move to South Africa was a major turning point in his life. It was in South Africa that he developed his major philosophy of non-violent political action, which was to serve as the basis for his struggle to win independence for his native India from Britain. It was in South Africa that Gandhi got his first personal and direct experience of oppression and intolerance, of racial hatred and segregation. During one of his first appearances in a Durban court, the magistrate asked him to remove his turban while addressing the court. This he refused to do and left the courtroom. This was the start of a life-long process of action against all forms of segregation and racial and cultural intolerance.

Soon after the courtroom event, Gandhi was travelling by train from Durban to Pretoria, having bought a first-class ticket for the journey. A white conductor confronted him and threw him out of the first-class compartment. Refusing to accept the action, Gandhi was thrown off the train at the Pieter-maritzburg Station. He continued the journey, however, and once more came into conflict with racial prejudice. He received a beating from the white driver of a stage coach because he refused to be intimidated into travelling on the footboard of the coach in order to let a white passenger sit in his place. During this period, Gandhi, like his fellow Indians, was subjected to a number of other indignities, such as not being permitted to stay in hotels reserved for whites. The Durban to Pretoria journey was a landmark event in his life. Following this experience, Gandhi began to react to the humiliations heaped upon himself and his people. He made a firm decision to defend his rights as a human being and those of his fellow citizens who were subjected to the same prejudicial treatment in their daily lives in South Africa, particularly in Natal.

Gandhi studied the situation his countrymen were in, and all the injustices they had to bear under the socio-political conditions of the time. Despite his dedication to fighting these injustices, he decided to return to India when his contract expired in June 1894. While attending a function in his honour before leaving for India, Gandhi was shown a copy of the newspaper, the *Natal Mercury*, which reported that the Legislative Assembly of Natal was preparing to pass a bill which would remove Indians' right to vote. He was angered by this proposed legislation, and when he was asked to take up the fight against the proposed bill, his political career began in earnest. Despite a fear of appearing and speaking in public, Gandhi, who was now about 25 years old, began to show a marked ability as a politician.

He began his campaign by drafting petitions to the Natal Legislative Assembly and to the British Government. The petitions were signed by several hundred of his compatriots, but in spite of all his efforts, the bill was passed into law. However, his efforts were not all futile, for attention was drawn to the plight of his people in India, Natal and in Britain, where the British Government took note. One of the major outcomes of this issue was that Gandhi was persuaded by leaders of the Indian community to settle in Durban. This he did, practising law and dedicating himself to the fight for the rights of the Indian community. One of his major achievements was the founding of the Natal Indian Congress, of which he was the first secretary. The Natal Indian Congress was the instrument through which Gandhi was

able to create solidarity among his people and bring the community's grievances to the notice of the general public, the British Government and the Natal
Legislative Assembly. Through the press he was able to bring to the international community's notice the plight of Indians in Natal and the double
standards applied by Victorian Britain to its citizens of colour in the then
Colony of Natal. Gandhi was gaining such stature and reputation as a fighter
for human rights that such famous newspapers as *The Times* of London, *The
Statesman* and *The Englishman* of Calcutta made serious editorial comments
about the plight of Indians in Natal.

In 1896, Gandhi undertook a journey to India to fetch his devoted wife
Kasturbai and his children. While in India he made attempts to canvas public
opinion both in the country and outside for his fellow countrymen in Natal.
He addressed a number of public meetings in major centres in India, calling
on the international community to help alleviate the plight of his people.
However, news reaching Natal confused much of what Gandhi had said in
India and upon his arrival in Durban in January 1897 he was attacked by a
white mob and beaten. This vicious attack came to the notice of the British
authorities and the Colonial Secretary, Joseph Chamberlain, informed the
Natal Government that those responsible had to be prosecuted with the full
might of the law. Gandhi, however, refused to lay any charges against his
attackers, depending rather on the principle he believed in, that of not
returning violence with more violence of any nature.

When the Boer War broke out in 1899, Gandhi argued strongly for
Indians in Natal to support the British since Natal was a British Colony and
they as citizens were duty-bound to support Britain. He set about establishing
a principally Indian ambulance corps of more that 1 000 volunteers from the
Natal Indian community. Indians from all walks of life joined the corps,
including lawyers, ordinary labourers, artisans and others. This attitude of
loyalty to the British, whom Gandhi regarded as political enemies, was the
cause of much discussion both in Britain and South Africa. One newspaper
editorial described Gandhi's efforts in part in the following manner (*Pretoria
News*, 1899):

'After a night's work which had shattered men with much bigger frames,
I came across Gandhi in the early morning sitting by the roadside eating
a regulation army biscuit. Every man in General Buller's force was dull
and depressed, and damnation was heartily invoked on everything. But
Gandhi was stoical in his bearing, cheerful and confident in his conver-
sation and had a kindly eye.'

The ambulance corps distinguished itself in the war, but despite a British
victory, not much attention was paid to the plight of Indians in Natal. Boers
and British formed a partnership after the war, leading, in 1910, to the

formation of the Union of South Africa. The Natal administration's attitude changed little and in neighbouring Transvaal, the Government published an ordinance that humiliated Indians in the registration process for voting rights. In September 1906, Indians in the Transvaal converged on Johannesburg, where, under Gandhi's leadership, Indians of all persuasions took an oath to oppose the unjust ordinance and if necessary to go to jail for their beliefs. It was during this mass protest that his philosophy of Satyagraha took concrete form. This philosophy, 'firmness based on truth', was a novel way of resisting oppression, because it excluded the use of any form of violence. It was based on the principle of not hating your opponent ('enemy'), while disliking what he was doing. When violence against protesters was used, the recipients of the violence would bear the suffering while passively resisting the adversary. This campaign of passive resistance lasted nearly eight years.

Under Gandhi's leadership, the movement went through several difficult stages during these early years. Indians in South Africa, joined by a few members of the other races, made some tremendous sacrifices, often losing both property and livelihood in the process of resistance. Their strength and belief in the philosophy of passive resistance was such that they preferred to suffer physical and other abuse rather than give in on matters of conscience and human dignity. During the period from 1906 to late 1913, hundreds of Indians in South Africa chose to go to jail rather than subject themselves to humiliations. These included even women and children, poor wage-earning Indians and professional persons.

This mode of protest (satyagraha) had a profound effect on the South African Government as a result of publicity and consequent pressure, particularly from the governments of Britain and from Indians in India. As a result of his protest leadership, Gandhi was jailed on a number of occasions. During this period, he came face to face with another figure who would feature prominently not only in South Africa, but also in the international sphere – Jan Christiaan Smuts. When Gandhi left South Africa in 1914, Smuts observed 'I hope forever'. Smuts, despite his deep understanding of politics and of human nature, could not fathom the novel form of peaceful protest. During one of Gandhi's jail terms he made a pair of leather sandals and presented them to the bewildered General Smuts, who accepted them graciously. Several years later, when both Gandhi and Smuts were well-known figures on the international scene, Smuts said of his one-time political opponent: 'It was my fate to be the antagonist of a man for whom even then I had the utmost respect…. There was the atmosphere in which a decent peace could be concluded.' Although Gandhi did not achieve the goals he aspired to in South Africa, his time in the country formed his political character and taught him the process of political opposition, arming him with some important talents which were to prove useful in his campaign for the independence of India.

In South Africa, Gandhi also re-examined his religious convictions. He had a firm grounding in Hinduism as a result of his early religious socialisation in India. In South Africa he was associated with the Quakers (Society of Friends), but any attempt by them to convert him to Christianity failed. It was during this period that he read Tolstoy's works on Christianity. He also read and familiarised himself with the Qu'ran and continued to read Hindu religious scriptures and Hindu philosophy. He stated at the time that he felt all religions were true, but were misinterpreted by their adherents. 'My effort should never be to undermine another's faith, but to make him a better follower of his own', he said (Bush 1988). Through the influence of the Indian philosopher Rajchandra, Gandhi returned to his religious roots, embracing Hinduism with a new fervour. He studied the Bhagavad-Gita carefully and was particularly struck by two concepts that these Hindu scriptures expounded. They included the words Aparigraha and Samabhava. The first, Aparigraha, suggested that man should reject materialism, such as attachment to goods, money and property, which were detrimental to the development of the human spirit. The second word, Samabhava (principles), called on the faithful to remain aloof from such factors as pain or pleasure, victory or defeat, and other such physical conditions of man. This philosophy (Samabhava) called upon the adherent to 'work without hope of success or fear of failure'.

Gandhi tried hard to apply these religious scriptures to his daily life, including his legal practice. He often brought antagonists together by assisting them to settle matters outside court. He became a counsellor to his clients, helping them solve personal problems completely outside the scope of his legal practice. In short, he became a friend to all in need, often using money earned in the course of his duties to help people. His home became a meeting place for everyone, with his dedicated wife spending long days tending to the endless stream of visitors to their home. He put this philosophy of communal living into practice when, in 1904, he established a farm at Phoenix, outside Durban, where all those who lived there worked together for the good of all. This settlement exists to this day, although different activities are carried on there now. Once he moved to the Transvaal, Gandhi started another such settlement near Johannesburg, which he named Tolstoy Farm, in honour of this Russian novelist, philosopher and writer. These two communal farms in South Africa helped to form the basis for the Asramas, sometimes called Ashrams in India. South Africa thus moulded Gandhi into a strong political force and powerful moral protagonist. A student of Gandhi's life at the time, Gilbert Murray, said of him:

'Persons in power should be very careful how they deal with a man who cares nothing for sensual pleasure, nothing for riches, nothing for comfort or praise, or promotion, but is simply determined to do what he believes to be right. He is a dangerous and uncomfortable enemy, because his body which you can always conquer gives you so little purchase upon his soul.'

Hibberd Journal, 1918

His return to his native India in 1915 set Gandhi on another, far greater struggle. Between 1915 and 1918, he did not act strongly against the British colonial authorities in India. In fact, he was a peripheral political figure attending to the grievances of people in the Bihar and Gujarat areas occupied mostly by impoverished peasants. Gandhi still maintained a reasonably strong feeling for the British Empire, even helping to recruit Indians to serve the British in World War I. However, he was not politically dormant. In 1919, when the British authorities attempted to push through legislation (the Rowlatt Bills) that gave them the power to imprison people without trial for sedition, Gandhi rose to the occasion and announced that he would lead resistance to the bills using the Satyagraha form of opposition. The call for protest was well received by the general population. In fact, there was a virtual uprising, with outbreaks of violence throughout India. The British retaliated with a heavy hand, with soldiers killing about four hundred Indians at Armritsar in the Punjab. The British imposed martial law and Gandhi remained relatively aloof from activity for a period of about one year.

In 1920, he returned to the forefront of Indian politics, commanding an allegiance seldom achieved by any political leader in the country's history. He worked relentlessly, and in the process revitalised the 35-year-old Indian National Congress. The Congress gradually grew to be a powerful political force in India, becoming a mass movement with branches in villages throughout the rural regions of India. Gandhi did not blame the British for India's subservient status, but stated that it was inaction on the part of Indians themselves that was responsible. With this in mind, he introduced a non-co-operation programme against British courts, legislatures, schools, government offices and other institutions of British rule in India. Goods manufactured by the British were also the subject of boycott. This process gave India the impetus it needed to rise against British rule. Thousands of protesters, who did not respond to their arrest with anger, lined up peacefully, ready to face prison. However, violence flared up in the village of Chauri Chaura in eastern India. Gandhi would not accept violence and abruptly cancelled the mass civil disobedience campaign. On 10 March 1922, he was arrested, charged with sedition and sentenced to six years' imprisonment, but was released in 1924 after an operation.

While he was in prison the political allegiances in the Congress party had changed and the party split into two factions. One faction was headed by Motilal Nehru (the father of Jawaharlal Nehru, India's first post-independence Prime Minister) and Chitta Ranjan Das. The other faction was

headed by C Rajagopalachari and Vallabhbhai Jhaverbhai Patel. The faction
headed by Nehru and Das decided on a policy of 'co-operation', whereby they
would attempt to get elected to legislatures in order to get into the political
mainstream. The second faction opposed this policy. In addition to this
drawback, Gandhi was disappointed in the fact that the co-operation between
the two main religious groups, Hindus and Muslims (1920-1922) had all but
collapsed. The relationship between these two communities had deteriorated
so much that violent conflict had broken out between them. The inter-relig-
ious violence deeply disturbed Gandhi and during 1923 he undertook a
three-week fast in the hope of bringing the two groups together again. After
this major fast, in which Hindu and Muslim agreed to work together pea-
ceably, Gandhi moved out of the political limelight during the mid-twenties.

In 1927 the British appointed a constitutional reform committee to look
into the problems facing Indian politics. The commission was headed by a
prominent British jurist, Sir John Simon. However, not a single Indian
politician or jurist was appointed to the commission. This line of action
prompted Gandhi to return to the centre stage of Indian politics. In December
1928 a crucial meeting of the Congress took place in Calcutta, at which
Gandhi proposed a resolution demanding dominion status for India within a
year. He threatened that should the British not accede to the demand, he would
launch a non-violent campaign calling for total independence from Britain.
Soon a series of non-violent campaigns was undertaken by huge numbers of
people under the leadership of Gandhi, who by now was referred to as
Mahatma ('a great soul'), an endearing term implying almost saintly qualities.

During 1930, Gandhi led one of his most famous non-violent campaigns
against a tax on salt levied by the British authorities in India. This tax was
considered all the more unacceptable because it affected the poorest people
in India. The campaign began when he announced to his fellow Indians and
the British authorities that he would begin a mass walk to the coast, joined on
the way by hundreds of thousands of people, to protest against the salt tax.
The march took 24 days. Once there, Gandhi challenged the British monopoly
on salt production by picking up salt and having his followers do the same.
One of the consequences of this mass protest was the arrest of more than
60 000 people, including Gandhi himself. Despite the arrest of their leader, a
raid on the Dhaisana Salt Works was planned without Gandhi present. One
writer described the event as follows (Bush, 1988):

'The planned raid on the Dhaisana Salt Works that had led to Gandhi's
arrest went on without him. Twenty-five hundred satyagrahis marched
towards the great salt pans that stood surrounded by ditches and barbed
wire. Four hundred policemen armed with steel-covered clubs met them
and struck down row upon row of protesters. Those behind them never

faltered. Webb Miller, a reporter for United Press, recounted the horror to the western world. "Not one of the marchers even raised an arm to fend off the blows…. From where I stood, I heard the sickening whack of the club on unprotected skulls!'"

Soon after these terrible events, after negotiating a truce between Congress and the government, Gandhi was the sole Indian leader to represent the Indian National Congress at the London Round Table Conference on Indian constitutional reform in 1931. The Conference was a sad disappointment for Gandhi because little or no attention was paid to the transfer of power from the British to the Indians. The main point of discussion was the role of minorities in India. He returned to India in December 1931 and faced an even more difficult political foe in the person of Lord Willingdon, who took some very strong measures against the Congress movement, even imprisoning Gandhi. All attempts by the British to isolate Gandhi from his followers failed. In 1932, while still in prison, he undertook another fast to protest against the British authorities who wanted to isolate India's untouchables (the harijans) and place them on a separate voters' roll in a proposed new constitution. Gandhi's fast brought the plight of the untouchables into the forefront of Indian political discussion and resulted in an acceptable arrangement being worked out by the Hindu community and the untouchables. The agreement was endorsed by the British authorities. Gandhi had a special feeling for the untouchables, whom he renamed Harijans, meaning 'Children of God'.

Gandhi was to suffer further disappointment in his struggle for justice and a free India. In 1934 he resigned both as leader and member of the Congress, because he felt that other leaders in the movement had adopted non-violence as a means of achieving political goals, rather than because they believed in the philosophy. The Mahatma instead turned to educating his fellow Indians through a number of valuable programmes which included home industries such as weaving, hand-spinning and a number of other income-generating cottage industries. He also continued the struggle for the rights and upliftment of the untouchables. He moved to Sevagram in central India, from where he conducted his programmes for the general upliftment of India's rural and poor people.

The outbreak of World War II saw India in the throes of a concerted effort for independence from Britain. The Congress Party took a pro-British stance and supported the war effort, but despite this the gulf between the two groups widened. Gandhi once more entered the fray and demanded immediate independence, particularly after the breakdown of talks between Indian nationalists and Sir Stafford Cripps, a British cabinet minister who had been sent out in 1942 to undertake the negotiations. In addition, it was suggested that the British authorities were inclined to support those conservative Indian elements who felt that Hindus and Muslims could not live in a unitary Indian society. With the failure of this meeting, the British reacted with extreme harshness, arresting and imprisoning the entire executive of the Indian National Congress. When the war ended, the Labour Party victory in Britain changed the face of the government's relations with Indian nationalists. It was during this period that the future of India was planned seriously. With Earl Mountbatten as the new Viceroy of India, much progress was made. However, Hindus and Muslims could not come to an agreement on living in a united India and this resulted in a plan to partition this ancient land. The Mountbatten plan came out of discussions between the Muslim League, under the leadership of M A Jinnah, and the leaders of Congress. The result was the formation in 1947 of two dominions, that of Pakistan, a predominantly Muslim state, and Hindu India.

The separatist solution to the Hindu-Muslim conflict was one of Gandhi's greatest disappointments. While final constitutional details were being negotiated to establish the two separate states (an idea which Gandhi had never accepted), violence erupted in several parts of the country, resulting in the death of thousands of people and mass destruction of property. Gandhi appealed to both parties for reason and tolerance. He tried desperately to heal the wounds between the two communities, but both parties unfairly blamed Gandhi for many of the consequences of partition. He toured the areas where violence was most rampant and tried all in his power to still tempers and bring peace to these areas. In 1947, he went on a fast to the death in order to stop rioting and killing in Calcutta. The rioting and killings stopped. In January 1948, he managed to get a truce into operation in the city of Delhi. On 30 January 1948, Gandhi was on his way to a public prayer meeting in Delhi when a Hindu fanatic in the crowd drew a handgun and fired at him from only a few metres away. Gandhi died uttering the words: 'Oh God, Oh God', which in Hindu is 'Hai Rama, hai Rama'.

The voice of reason and non-violence was stilled. On 31 January 1948, Gandhi's body, covered with petals, was carried through a massive crowd of mourners to his cremation site where his son, Ramdas, lit the pyre. Mahatma Gandhi is considered one of the 20th Century's greatest men, who dedicated his life to justice and peace through non-violence.

In the words of the then US Secretary of State: 'Mahatma Gandhi was the spokesman for the conscience of all mankind.'

CHAPTER 3

MARTIN LUTHER KING JUNIOR

'I've been to the top of the mountain and I have seen the promised land of Justice and Freedom.'

MARTIN LUTHER KING JR

Martin Luther King Jr was born on Saturday, 15 January 1929 in the American city of Atlanta, Georgia. On that cold winter's day, few suspected that the almost-stillborn child would one day stand as a pillar of fire for civil and human liberties. His family consisted of his father, Martin (Mike) Luther King Sr, and mother Alberta, the daughter of the Reverend Adam Daniel Williams, Pastor of Atlanta's Ebenezer Baptist Church since 1894, his elder sister Millie Christine and his younger brother Alfred Daniel.

As a young man, Martin Luther King was small but healthy. He was very active and took part in sport. From an early age he learnt the scriptures and was influenced by his grandmother, a devout, warmhearted and sympathetic woman. He deeply respected his mother, who was described as being a quiet women who was the model of a preacher's wife. His father, the Reverend Martin Luther King, known as 'Mike', was an exemplary father who saw to it that his family was well provided for. He (Rev King Sr) had been brought up as a sharecropper on a plantation in the US State of Georgia. He had known suffering and discrimination and was very aware of the often vast discrepancies between the quality of life of American whites and those of his fellow blacks. During his youth, the Reverend King Sr had seen his mother toil as a domestic worker and his father dishonoured and cheated at the plantation where he worked. He was also witness to the hanging of a black man.

After some serious thought about his life, Mike King moved to Atlanta, where he came under the influence of a number of high-profile black American preachers, among them the Reverend Adam Daniel Williams, pastor of the Ebenezer Baptist Church. Mike King felt called to the ministry and after working as a mechanic and a fireman, he entered the ministry and became the pastor of two small churches. He continued his education on a part-time basis and earned a high school diploma which allowed him to enter Morehouse College to study for the degree of Bachelor of Divinity. He took part in a number of emancipation programmes, serving in the National Baptist Convention and the Regional Chapter of the National Association for the Advancement of Coloured People (NAACP), as its President. He was awarded an honorary doctor's degree by his alma mater for his services to the church and the community.

In 1926, the Reverend King Sr married Alberta, the well-educated daughter of the Reverend Adam Daniel Williams. He soon became assistant pastor of the Ebenezer Baptist Church, assisting his famous father-in-law. In 1931, Dr Williams had a massive heart attack and died, leaving Mike to take over as pastor of the Ebenezer Baptist Church, an institution that would become known throughout the world. He continued his studies on a part-time basis, earning the degree of Doctor of Divinity at Morris Brown College in Atlanta. Dr King Sr became, among other things, a bank director and served on the board of the civil rights movement, the NAACP.

In family matters, Rev Dr King Sr was a strict father and did not hesitate to chastise his children when necessity demanded it. He provided well for his family, making sure that his children did not want for anything, including a number of luxury items. It was under these conditions that Martin Luther King Jr was brought up. He was often the recipient of punishment, but bore it philosophically.

He was a keen student and had a number of exceptional qualities. He graduated from the Booker T Washington High School and in 1944 was admitted to Morehouse College at the remarkably young age of 15. The young student had a number of unhappy experiences while working as a tobacco farm worker during his holidays. His encounters with discrimination were plentiful, but one major incident was crucial in preparing the young Martin Luther King for his major role in the civil rights movements. He was on a train, returning from a pleasant trip to discrimination-free Connecticut. He went into the dining car and sat down at a table waiting to be served as he had done on trains in other Northern states, such as New York. A waiter asked him to move to a table at the rear section of the dining car and once there he drew a curtain, isolating him from the white passengers. This indignity was the foundation stone of his commitment to the civil rights struggle.

At Morehouse College, Martin Luther King decided to study Sociology as a major course, with English as the second course for his degree. From the start of his college studies he found that he was ill-equipped to deal with the study material as a result of a deficient high school educational system for blacks in the Southern United States. However, through sheer determination and hard work he earned distinctions in a number of courses, including Philosophy, History, English and his major, Sociology. However, he found sociology very abstract and was disappointed with the fact that it dealt with complicated theoretical precepts, often expressed as statistics. He felt that a study of human behaviour should evaluate human action that lay behind all sociological phenomena. Sociology, he felt, was too statistical.

While at Morehouse College, King was influenced by several professors and lecturers who helped build on the young man's natural abilities. During 1948, while still under 20 years of age, he graduated from Morehouse College with a Bachelor's Degree in Sociology. From there he moved to Chester, Pennsylvania, in the northern United States, where he entered the Crozier Seminary to read for the Bachelor's Degree in Divinity. This seminary was one of the finest in the United States and was a non-racial institution. After a life facing discrimination almost daily in Georgia, King felt that there he would be free from both parental authority and the degradation of segregation and all its negative consequences.

At Crozier Seminary, King learnt of the evils of capitalism, which he felt not only impoverished the working class but was also responsible in part for racism. As a potential minister of religion, King felt that the church had a broader function then just the spiritual. It was there to minister to all the needs of man and therefore had to serve both God and humanity. He read widely and undertook special studies of a number of philosophers such as Plato, Aristotle, Rousseau, Hobbes, Jeremy Bentham, Mill and Locke. However, the thinker who influenced him most was the theologian Walter Rausenbusch, who had lectured at the Rochester Theological Seminary during the turbulent social period of the 1890s. Rausenbusch moved away from traditional theological teaching, becoming a leading theorist of the new social gospel. He wrote a book entitled *Christianity and the Social Crisis*, in which he called on Christians to attempt to build a new social order based on moral law. According to Rausenbusch, theologians and other church leaders and functionaries had misunderstood Christ's teachings. Christ, he said, had instructed his disciples to form a kingdom and not a church. The church, he suggested, had become a propertied institution and thus developed interests of its own. Rausenbusch's interpretation of Christianity was that, with the advent of the industrial revolution, capitalism was born with all its concomitant ills, including exploitation of the poor (working class), prostitution and crime in general. The profit motive in capitalism, he added, eliminated the notion of human virtue. Human brotherhood, he claimed, was also denied by capitalism and hence Christians had a duty to eradicate capitalism. Rausenbusch suggested that in place of capitalism all economic resources should be socialised and God's Kingdom established on love, co-operation and social solidarity.

King became immersed in the study of Rausenbusch's teachings and came to disagree with the tradition that churches deal with matters of the soul only. The church, he felt, must deal with the total man. At the time, his feelings were clearly described by Stephen Oates (1982):

'A socially relevant faith must deal with the whole man – his body and soul, his material and spiritual well being. It must work for the Kingdom "down here" as well as "over yonder". Any religion that stressed only the souls of men and not their social and economic conditions was a spiritually moribund religion awaiting burial.'

King also undertook a study of Marx, reading both the Communist Manifesto and Das Kapital and other material relevant to Marxism. He came to the conclusion that communism was, in his words, 'a Christian heresy' that in both principle and practice no true christian could accept. King refuted the Marxist approach, which exalted materialism, and its suggestion that God does not exist. He also rejected the Marxist notion that man could perfect himself without the aid of a God or indeed Jesus. King felt that historical materialism lacked the most important element, namely the product of human warmth, the human heart and the deep feeling that it conjured. He disliked a number of the precepts of communism, calling it 'a grand illusion' wrapped in a 'crippling totalitarianism'. However, despite his aversion to the main tenets of communism, King felt that Marx's criticism of capitalism had some validity. He felt that capitalism inspired self-centredness and materialistic egoism and that this was not healthy for human society, which required social solidarity based on selflessness to function properly.

Another person who influenced King during his stay at Crozier Seminary was the pacifist Dr A J Muste. He attended a major lecture given by Dr Muste, but disagreed with his thesis that all war was evil. King felt that war could sometimes be justified if it was fought to combat such evils as Nazism or communist totalitarianism. However, King was profoundly influenced by a lecture he attended in Philadelphia, given by Dr Mordecai Johnson, who was then president of Howard University. The lecture dealt with the life and the teachings of Mahatma Gandhi, the Indian leader and spiritual philosopher. Gandhi, he heard, had used a phenomenon known as Satyagraha or soul-force, which is a form of 'power of God', as a means of achieving social change.

Through a study of Gandhi's life, King began to understand that Gandhi had undergone a personal change and had abandoned all violence and hatred, even for his 'enemies'. All resistance, in the Gandhian sense, was 'non-violent' and without hatred against the oppressor – in his case, the South African authorities and the British in India. Gandhi channeled his hatred and anger into the positive and creative power of love. This helped King relieve himself of any hatred he may have felt towards whites. Gandhi further applied the theory of passive resistance to all strikes, boycotts and protest marches, loving the opponent in the hope of winning him over, thus bringing together love and passive resistance as a powerful instrument for change. This gave an enthusiastic King the material he needed to forge a process of protest which he himself would use in the future. He learnt that reacting to hatred with hatred only aggravated the situation. Through a genuine love for all mankind, King felt, the Kingdom of God on earth could be created, bringing mankind together as a single entity under God.

King completed his studies at Crozier Seminary in mid-1951 and graduated with the Degree of Bachelor of Divinity. He came top of his class and won a scholarship enabling him to attend the graduate school of his choice. At Boston University, King registered for a PhD in Systematic Theology under Dr Edgan Sheffield Brightman, a prominent theologian and academic, who taught the philosophy of personalism. This philosophy held that a personal God operated within and on every human life. At this time (1953) he also rejected all forms of war, changing his original belief that some wars were justified. The Christian teaching that we must love our enemies was paramount in his philosophy. King felt that by opening the self to the fatherhood of Almighty God, individuals could deal with their own sinfulness. He also disagreed with his former teacher Rausenbusch, that sin was a social rather than a personal reality. Evil, he felt, was personal and it was at the personal level that it could be fought.

King was tired of his bachelor existence and in 1952 he met Coretta Scott, who had been brought up in Alabama. In 1953 the couple married in Marion, Alabama, the bride's home. Having graduated from Boston University with a PhD, he had an inclination to teach theology, but a number of churches expressed an interest in him and in 1954 he was invited to join the Dexter Avenue Baptist Church in Montgomery, Alabama. He joined the church in that year as its pastor, knowing that he was moving to an area where segregation was still rife.

In May 1954, the United States Supreme Court handed down a decision that was to change the course of history in the United States. In the case of *Brown v The Board of Education*, the court ruled that segregation in public schools was outlawed and that the 'separate-but-equal' system which had prevailed for nearly 60 years was nullified. Separate education, the court ruled, could not be equal. This momentous court decision knocked down 150 years of segregation and justification of it in the United States. However, this decision was not readily accepted in a number of Southern states and negative reaction came from Mississippi, Texas and Florida. In Alabama, where King was about to become pastor of the Dexter Avenue Baptist Church, the state legislature declared the US Supreme Court ruling unacceptable and continued to practise segregation.

King settled well into his vocation at the Baptist Church and spent much time ministering to his congregation on matters temporal as well as spiritual. Having a predominantly black congregation, King often had to calm down tempers and hatred towards whites, often cautioning individuals with violent impulses. King spoke with determination during his sermons and often resorted to oratory of the fire-and-brimstone kind, mixing deep emotion with a keen intellectual insight. The church became an instrument for King to fight for both the upliftment of the soul of the individual and the satisfaction of the needs that are common to the human condition. The following quotation clearly indicates his commitment to ministering to man as a totality (Oates, 1982):

> 'And I tell you that any religion that professes to be concerned with the souls of men and is not concerned with the slums that damn them and the social conditions that cripple them is a dry as dust religion. Religion deals with both heaven and earth, time and eternity, seeking not only to integrate man with God, but man with man.'

King was not satisfied with merely mouthing his philosophy. He began a social action programme which looked after the sick, the ailing and the aged, and administered funds for promising students for both school and university study. He also established a social and political action committee which strongly supported the local chapter of the National Association for the Advancement of Coloured People (NAACP). Before long, King's activism led to his election to the Executive Committee of the NAACP's regional Montgomery chapter. Most of the members of the NAACP were free of financial dependence on whites and therefore had no fear of any negative economic sanctions. During the same period, King was also elected to the Alabama Council on Human Relations, an interracial group in Montgomery. Montgomery was at the time still rigidly segregated to the extent that a local by-law was in force which made it illegal for blacks and whites to play such games as cards, dominoes, dice, etc together. Most blacks held menial jobs and could hardly expect to be able to move into business and social areas, which until then were monopolised by whites. King was made aware of the fact that blacks in that region were afraid to confront their white fellow citizens and accepted their condition with complacency, despite the fact that many of them were highly educated.

With such conditions prevalent, King's future in a leadership role in the civil rights movement was set. He soon saw that there was no unity among American blacks; the huge number of committees that existed often worked at cross-purposes and sometimes against each other, and he began to doubt that much could be done under such circumstances to win justice and equality of opportunity for all. It was during these dark days that King befriended a fellow pastor, the Reverend Ralph Abernathy of the First Baptist Church, who was gaining prominence as an activist, and these colleagues complemented each other's needs, even though Abernathy had come from a poor background and lacked King's forceful personality and powerful intellect. In that year (1955), King also completed his doctoral thesis at Boston University and his wife Coretta told him, much to his joy, that he was going to be a father.

However, on the social and political front, 1955 was a difficult year.

Whites in the South were reacting with vigour against the US Supreme Court decision *Brown v The Board of Education*. Almost throughout the southern states, whites were mobilising to counteract any attempt to integrate southern society. Whites were full of anxieties about integration and this was well understood by King. He knew that these fears were irrational and tried his level best to allay them. Meanwhile, white atrocities against black Americans took a steep rise, with a number of heinous actions making the national headlines and drawing attention to the conditions in which southern blacks lived. These ranged from crimes such as the rape and abuse of black women to the humiliation suffered by black commuters who were obliged to take the seats at the rear of buses. They were also not allowed to sit in seats reserved for whites on buses.

Martin Luther King Jr made a momentous decision: he would organise and lead a mass bus boycott in Montgomery. The opportunity presented itself when a prominent black citizen of Montgomery, Mrs Rosa Parks, refused to give up her seat in a bus to a white passenger and was arrested for disobeying Montgomery's segregation laws. The date was 1 December 1955. The Montgomery Improvement Association was formed, with Martin Luther King Jr as its leader. It was this incident that launched King into the forefront of the civil rights movement in the United States. One of his first statements in his new capacity was as follows (Enc Brit vol 10):

> 'We have no alternative but to protest. For many years we have shown an amazing patience, we have sometimes given our white brothers the feeling that we liked the way we were being treated. But we came here tonight to be saved from that patience that makes us patient with anything less than freedom and justice.'

Thus the Montgomery bus boycott began in earnest. All over the city buses ran empty of black passengers. Blacks from all walks of life used other means of transport, registering their protest in the strongest non-violent way possible. As the boycott continued, King and a delegation from the MIA met Montgomery's city fathers in the presence of the press, including television. King explained to the city fathers the indignities suffered by blacks, and asked that the segregation laws responsible for those indignities be scrapped. However, despite a noticeable shift in sentiment, the city fathers and representatives of the bus company refused to change their position. By this time, the bus company was operating at only 30% of its capacity.

The police commissioner of Montgomery stepped in and issued an order forbidding black taxis to charge the minimal rate of ten cents per passenger: they had to charge the normal rate of 45 cents. However, this move was countered by the MIA, which organised a car pool system operating from a number of pick-up points in the city. The boycott continued through December without results. A second meeting with the city fathers achieved nothing. However, the boycott had now reached such proportions that the nation focused its attention on the crisis. What was taking place in Montgomery, Alabama, would effect all other major US cities that practised segregation against their black citizens.

The differences continued and at times threatened law and order. The city authorities began to use strong-arm tactics, even arresting King for speeding and putting him in jail. This was the first time he was jailed for his beliefs. After some pressure from other civic leaders and a huge crowd which had gathered outside the prison, the police released him on his own recognisances and ordered him to appear in court. Persecution of King and other black leaders continued and on 30 January 1956, while he was addressing a mass meeting, he received news that his house had been bombed. A huge crowd of blacks gathered outside the devastated house, many carrying weapons and threatening the police on the scene. King sensed the potential for violence and stepped into the rubble of what was once the porch of the pastorage. In a voice filled with emotion, he made the following plea (Oates 1982):

> 'My wife and baby are alright. I want you to go home and put down your weapons. We cannot solve this problem with retaliatory violence. We must love our white brothers, no matter what they do to us. We must make them know that we love them. Jesus still cries out across the countries ''love your enemies''. This is what we must live by. We must meet hate with love. Remember, if I am stopped, this movement will not stop, because God is with this movement.'

Despite his persistence on non-violence, the city fathers did not give in and on 21 February 1956, an all-white grand jury found that blacks had violated an obscure state law which forbade boycotts. Nearly 90 black leaders were indicted. They did not wait to be arrested but gave themselves in to the authorities in true Gandhian style. King also handed himself in and his trial began in the old Montogomery County Court house. King was found guilty and fined $500, costs and 386 days hard labour. He immediately appealed. This brought him onto almost all the front pages of the national newspapers.

By mid-1956, there had been several court cases, but the most significant one took place in a federal court, which ruled that bus segregation violated the 14th Amendment to the Constitution of the United States and was therefore unconstitutional. This was a big victory for King and the MIA, but lawyers for the bus company lodged an appeal with the country's highest authority, the US Supreme Court. In October 1956, the city authorities once more attempted to stifle the boycott movement with yet another court action. But on the same day as the court action, during a recess in the proceedings, King noticed a commotion in the vicinity of the courtroom. A newspaper reporter handed him a slip of paper with the following news: 'The United States Supreme Court today affirmed a decision of a special three-judge US District Court in declaring Alabama's state and local laws requiring segregation on buses unconstitutional.' King's name was now in every household in the US and abroad.

During 1960 King found it necessary to move back to Atlanta, the city in which he was born. Once there, he became co-pastor with his father of the Ebenezer Baptist Church, where he played a prominent role in church affairs along with his dominant role in gaining civil rights for his fellow black Americans. In the same year (1960), King joined predominantly black college students in a demonstration against a segregated lunch counter in a department store in the city of Atlanta. He was arrested and on the pretext that he had violated a previous probation relating to a minor traffic offence, King was sent to the Reidsville State Prison Farm. This action against King caused a major uproar throughout the United States, especially since the then President, Dwight D Eisenhower, failed to act on behalf of the civil rights leader. John F Kennedy, the democratic contender for the presidency in that year's presidential election, intervened on behalf of King and he was released from prison. This fact may have swung millions of voters in Kennedy's favour which led to his victory over Eisenhower.

Between 1960 and 1965, King became even more involved in leading the civil rights movements in several states. In 1963, he attempted to desegregate lunch counters in the city of Birmingham, Alabama. During this action, city police used dogs and fire-hoses against the protesters, arousing nationwide attention. Once more King was put in jail, together with hundreds of school children. It was during this campaign that he conceived the idea of asking the nationwide civil rights movements for a mass march on the nation's capital, Washington DC. Hundreds of thousands of people, including members of every race, colour and creed, converged on Washington under his leadership on 28 March 1963. It was during this campaign that King, now a powerful voice for peaceful mass action, delivered his famous 'I have a dream' speech, in which he revealed his dream of all men being united in brotherhood throughout the world. It was a landmark speech.

One of the major results of the speech was the passing of the Civil Rights Act of 1964 by Congress. This Act gave the federal government the right to enforce desegregation in all public places, making it an offence to segregate any such place. Segregation in the sphere of employment was also made illegal. In December of 1960, Martin Luther King Jr was awarded the Nobel Peace Prize for his outstanding efforts at obtaining justice for all, non-violently. As well as his victories, however, King suffered a number of defeats and was criticised for his non-violence by young radicals. In 1965, he led a march in Selma, Alabama, to demand voting rights and a voting rights law.

He was confronted by state troopers, but reacted by asking his followers to kneel in prayer on the road, and after the prayers were said, he led his followers back, avoiding a confrontation. This action did not endear him to the more militant blacks. Despite the setbacks, victory once more came with the passage of the Voting Rights Act of 1965. He continued to preach non-violent action, but in some major cities across the US, militant blacks opposed him and a number of riots broke out. In August 1965, the Watts district of Los Angeles, California, broke out in rioting. The consequences were disastrous for the non-violent process advocated by King. In Chicago, Illinois, he led marches and protest demonstrations aimed at ending discrimination in housing and other spheres. However, despite an agreement being signed between the city authorities of Chicago and a coalition of black groups, nothing positive materialised. Militant black power leaders began a campaign to discredit King's non-violent process. King responded by announcing that he was to make an effort to deal with a broader spectrum of ills besetting the black American community.

In April 1967, at a peace rally in New York City, King called for an end to the Vietnam War, but his call aroused strong opposition from the US government and a number of black American groups. King then turned his attention to dealing with poverty and the problem of rising unemployment in the US. At a special meeting, he called for the 'reconstruction of the entire society, a revolution of values'. He received little support in these endeavours.

On 4 April 1968 King was standing on the balcony of his motel room in Memphis, Tennessee, when a sniper's bullet killed him, and the voice of freedom, non-violence and justice was stilled forever. Dr Martin Luther King Jr was 39 years old at the time of his death.

On 9 April 1968 a deeply moving funeral ceremony took place at the Ebenezer Baptist Church, where he had begun his life of service to the community.

'The pallbearers carried him out to a special hearse – a farm cart drawn by two mules, which symbolised his poor people's campaign, his own last and greatest dream. Then with bell shattering the humid day, the cart started forward to the clop, clop of the mules, carrying Martin Luther King on his last freedom march.' (Oates, 1982)

CHAPTER 4

MALCOLM X

'Ex-smoker. Ex-drinker. Ex-Christian. Ex slave....'

Malcolm X, a black American, was born on 19 May 1925 in Omaha, in the state of Nebraska. He was born Malcolm Little and changed his name during the course of transition and change in his life. Like Martin Luther King Jr, Malcolm X was the son of a Baptist minister, Reverend Earl Little. His father's death, when he was only six years old, had a profoundly negative effect on his life and that of his mother, who had to support nine children. Malcolm X's mother was later committed to an asylum.

His early life was not very stable. He left school in the eighth grade and after dropping out, he went to live with his older sister in Boston's Roxbury district. While in Roxbury, he took part in a number of criminal activities, including becoming a hustler and gang leader. During this period, he was known as 'Detroit Red' because of the redish colour of his hair. In 1946 and in 1952, he spent time in prison for burglary. He underwent a drastic change while still in prison when, through the influence of Elijah Muhammad, he joined an organisation known as the Nation of Islam.

The Nation of Islam was founded by Elijah Poole, the son of a Baptist minister. During his early life, Poole (now named Muhammad) was a share-cropper on a Southern plantation. In 1923 he migrated to Detroit, where conditions were so bad that he had to survive on charity, especially during the Great Depression (1929-1931). It was in 1931 that Elijah Poole met Wallace D Fard, sometimes known as Walli Farrad or the Prophet Fard. Elijah Poole became an ardent and devoted follower of 'Prophet Fard' and his loyalty was repaid when he was made chief assistant and lieutenant to Fard. He was subsequently made a 'Minister of Islam' by Fard and had to adopt a Muslim name, Muhammad. After Fard's mysterious disappearance in 1934, Elijah Muhammad established the Temple No 2 in Chicago, which became the headquarters of the Nation of Islam. One of the first things Elijah Muhammad initiated was the worship of 'Prophet Fard' as Allah. He gave himself the title 'Messenger of Allah'. Muhammad was henceforth addressed as 'the honourable'. He built his organisation, The Nation of Islam, on the philosophy of his predecessor, Fard. In addition, Muhammad combined aspects of Islam, Christianity and black nationalism, especially of the kind expressed by Marcus Garvey.

During World War II, Elijah Muhammad spent four years in jail for encouraging people to refuse to be drafted into the armed forces. With Malcolm X's assistance, the Nation of Islam grew to over half a million members and had a profound influence on millions of other people. In addition to its massive size, the Nation of Islam grew into an extremely healthy economic entity.

Malcolm, upon joining the Nation of Islam, changed his surname to X, which was symbolic of the fact that he had become an ex-smoker, ex-drinker, ex-Christian and ex-slave. Malcolm X was a first-rate speaker and one of the strong voices of the civil rights era in the United States from 1956 to 1965. He set to work extremely hard and organised black Muslim temples throughout the United States. He also established a newspaper called *Muhammad Speaks*. He was a prominent spokesman for the movement, which was against the integrationist movement and campaigned for racial separation. Malcolm X was appointed minister of Boston Temple No 11 of the Nation of Islam. His hard work and role as defender of the convictions of the movement gained him more favour with the hierarchy and soon he was made minister of Temple No 7 in Harlem. This post was one of the most important, after the headquarters of the movement in Chicago. Malcolm X was further honoured as the 'representative of the National of Islam' throughout the United States.

However, his meteoric rise to power within the movement was curtailed by Elijah Muhammad after Malcolm X made some callous remarks after the assassination of President John F Kennedy in 1963 (he had approved of the killing). Elijah Muhammad ordered Malcolm X to undergo a period of silence, but the ensuing tensions within the movement prompted Malcolm X to resign in March 1964, and soon afterwards he founded his own mosque, known as the Muslim Mosque, Incorporated.

Malcolm X then went on a pilgrimage to Mecca (1964) and while in Islam's Holy City, he became re-converted, this time into the orthodox brotherhood of Sunni Islam. He adopted the Islamic name of El-Hajj-Malik El-Shabazz. One of the consequences of this conversion was his renunciation of the beliefs of his former movement, The Nation of Islam. During 1965, he founded a political organisation known as the Organisation for Afro-American Unity. The purpose of the organisation was to bring to the attention of the world the plight of black Americans. Malcolm X wanted his new organisation to find common cause with Third World Nations and to move from being the champion of human rights to civil rights. However, his attempts were cruelly brought to an end on 21 February 1965, when he was assassinated by other black Muslims while delivering a lecture in Harlem. However, his ideas and other efforts laid the foundations upon which the Black Power Movement in the United States grew during the 1960s.

PART 5

MAJOR HUMAN RIGHTS ABUSERS

CHAPTER 1

JOSEPH STALIN (1879-1953)

INTRODUCTION

In 1953, one of the world's most powerful men, Soviet leader Joseph Stalin, died. He is reputed to have been one of the most ruthless men in history, who held the Soviet Union in his grip by police terror against his people. According to a number of his biographers, he industrialised the Soviet Union, enforced the collective system of agriculture and extended the sphere of Soviet influence and control to the Eastern Bloc countries. Stalin established a huge and ruthlessly totalitarian administrative structure in the Soviet Union. The result of the consolidation of his personal power was the destruction of such individual freedom as still existed prior to his coming to power in the Soviet Union. Apart from his very poor record with regard to freedom and human rights, Stalin built up a gigantic industrial machine, a very powerful army, and worked hard to make the Union of the Soviet Socialist Republics (now defunct) a nuclear power. Stalin was hailed as a great leader by his people in the early days of his rule. In fact, he promoted the creation of busts, statues, and icons of himself, thereby bringing into being a personality cult that carried on long after his death in 1953. In order to understand the nature and perhaps the personality of Stalin, it is important that some of his biographical features be examined.

Stalin ('Man of Steel') was from the Republic of Georgia in the former USSR. He was born on 21 December 1879, in the provincial town of Gori. His real name was Joseph Vissarionovich Dzhugashvili. His father was a poverty-stricken cobbler, who drank in excess and often administered severe beatings to his son. He spoke the local Georgian language and learnt Russian only when he went to a local school run by the Orthodox Church in Gori, between 1888 and 1894. His further education took place, strangely enough, at the Tiflis Theological Seminary. It was while he was at this seminary that the young Stalin first began reading Karl Marx's works, thereby gaining knowledge of international communism. He had to undertake this reading in secret as Marxist texts were forbidden by the Czarist regime in Russia.

Stalin's mother was a humble woman who washed clothes for a living. She made a number of attempts to get her son to become a priest, but both his psychological orientation and physical appearance made this unlikely. In 1899 Stalin went into exile as a result, it is said, of revolutionary activities.

Physically, Stalin was 'short, black-haired, had fierce eyes, one arm was longer than the other and his face was scarred by smallpox contracted as a child'. He was extremely shrewd and others who did him any harm were sure to receive some severe form of retribution at a later date. Stalin worked for a very short while in a clerical position in the Tiflis Observatory, this being the only period of work on record for which he was paid a salary. In 1900 Stalin became a member of the political underground and was very successful at organising workers, whom he duped into violent confrontations with the police, avoiding direct contact with the police himself. He was a member of the Social Democrats, who were in fact Marxist revolutionaries in disguise. However, the movement split into two distinct factions, one less militant, known as the Mensheviks, and their more militant and active counterparts, the Bolsheviks, whom Stalin joined in 1903. The leader of this movement was Lenin, and Stalin, still known by his birth name of Dzhugashvili at the time, became one of his most dedicated followers. For a 12-year period, from 1902 to 1913, Stalin was arrested a number of times for activities of a revolutionary nature. There was a period in those early days of political activity during which Stalin was said to have been in the pay of the Russian Imperial Police as an informer.

His rise to power was slow but steady. Between 1905 and 1907, he attended three conferences of the Russian Social Democrats in Finland, Sweden and London. During these three conferences, he made little progress in gaining a position in the party hierarchy. He is believed to have been party to the planning of an armed hold-up in Tbilisi (formerly known as Tiflis), to provide funds for the development of the party. He soon came under the eye of the leader, Lenin, and in January 1912, Stalin was asked, on a co-option basis, to serve on the Central Committee of the Bolshevik Party which had broken away from the Social Democratic Party. In 1913, Stalin was asked by Lenin to write an article based on Marxism and how it would help form the new society they were attempting to establish. It was at this time that he began to use the name 'Stalin', 'Stal', meaning steel in Russian. He became the editor, for a brief period, of the Bolshevik newspaper, *Pravda*, and was exiled in Siberia for five years (1913 to 1917). Stalin was later to use this type of banishment on his political enemies, real or imagined.

Earlier, in 1904, Stalin had married a humble Georgian woman named Ekaterina Svanidze, who died only three years later, leaving Stalin a son, named Jacob. Stalin, for some reason, despised his son and treated him with contempt. During World War II, the Germans took Stalin's son a prisoner of War. When the Germans offered Stalin the opportunity to exchange his son for other prisoners of war, Stalin coldly refused. After his return from Siberian exile, in 1917, Stalin once again became the editor of *Pravda*. During this second period of editorship, Stalin suggested that the Bolsheviks co-operate with the Duma, the provisional government that had taken power from the time the Czar had abdicated in February 1917. This government was led by Alexander Kerensky and made up of middle-class liberals. However, Lenin, for whom Stalin had boundless admiration, persuaded him to form the Bolshevik faction once more, a faction that advocated the violent seizure of political power. The opportunity to seize power came during the October Revolution of 1917, which put Stalin at the apex of the leadership group, only one rung lower than his rival Leon Trotsky.

His rise to power and prominence from this time on was meteoric. He took part in the civil war of 1918 to 1920 and was made a minister in the Bolshevik government. He held the post of Commissar for Nationalities and Commissar for State Control between 1917 and 1923. However, his ministerial posts were secondary compared with the all-important post of Secretary-General of the Central Committee of the Bolshevik Party from 1922 until he died in 1953, a total of 31 years. It was this post (Secretary-General) that provided Stalin with his base for amassing great personal power over all sectors of Soviet life. In addition to the post of Secretary-General, he was also a member of the Politburo and other committees. Before his death in January 1924, Lenin saw and understood the dangers lurking behind Stalin's ambitions and he issued a political testament in which he called for the removal of Stalin from the post of Secretary-General of the party. However, Stalin managed to evade the requests of Lenin on his deathbed, and survived his possible removal.

Stalin then began a calculated process of consolidating his position and eradicating his political rivals. He promoted the cult of Leninism and at the same time his own, by renaming the city of Volgograd (previously Tsaritsyn) Stalingrad. Power at this time resided in the persons of Zinoviev, Kamenen and Stalin himself. They practically cut off Trotsky from power. Stalin then moved against his co-government members in joining with two right-wingers, Nikolay Buhkarin and Alexsey Rykov. Stalin now was able to introduce his 'socialism in the country' policy and soon his new associates were also relieved of their leadership posts. Trotsky was exiled in 1920 and took up residence in Mexico, where authoritative sources say Stalin had him assassinated in 1940.

By 1928, Stalin began to discard the quasi-capitalist policies of Lenin and began an ambitious programme of state-organised industry. During this period, Russian peasants became the next target of Stalin's plan. He forced thousands upon thousands of small land-owning peasants (Kulaks) into co-operatives. That is, they were forced to amalgamate into bigger state-controlled collective farms. When the peasants resisted these measures, Stalin had them arrested and ordered units of the political police, OGPU, to attack them. Peasants who still resisted were arrested in their thousands, their leaders were shot dead, and thousands were exiled to Siberia. Thousands of others were forced into concentration camps and were worked to death under horrendous conditions. In the Ukraine, the 'breadbasket' of the Soviet Union at the time, a famine broke out as a result of the collectivisation of agriculture. During this time about ten million peasants are said to have been executed or died of famine.

Stalin then turned his attention to industrialising the Soviet Union. Here, too, his programmes were put into effect with a ruthless lack of concern for human lives. When targets were not reached, or some other failure had taken place, Stalin put on a number of farcical show trials in which several managers of industrial organisations were made to confess to 'crimes' they had not in fact committed. The industrial failures were largely the result of Stalin's own directives. However, despite many setbacks, Soviet industry did make a number of significant achievements. Stalin took the credit for these and was lauded by a number of other leaders, including Adolf Hitler, George Bernard Shaw and H G Wells.

Stalin had remarried his second wife, Nadezbda Alliluyeva, in 1919. She committed suicide 11 years later (1952). She bore him two children, a son named Vasily and a daughter, Svetlana. His son joined the Soviet Air Force and was raised to unmerited rank, but punished because of his severe alcoholism. He paid much attention to and lavished affection on his daughter, Svetlana. In later years, she left the Soviet Union and settled in the United States.

STALIN'S INFAMOUS PURGES

Towards the end of 1934, Stalin's grip on Soviet society was as such that he unleased a terror unheard of even in that violent country's history. He began a systematic purge of those very members of the Communist Party who had brought him to power. He started by having his arch-rival, Serge Kirov, murdered in Leningrad on 1 December 1934. He blamed his opponents for the murder and much blood was spilt with the eradication of his political opponents. This and other crimes against human life, dignity and civil rights were disclosed by his successor, Nikita Khrushchev, in an address in which he denounced Stalin at the 20th Congress of the Communist Party in 1956.

A number of other purges took place, one of the most notorious being in August 1936, when Zinoviev and Kamenev, in well-planned show trials, were forced to 'confess' fabricated charges against them. These sham Stalinist courts sentenced them to death almost immediately and had them shot. There were a number of other such sham trials, most notably one that took place in 1937. In June of that year, the Soviet Union's most distinguished military personality of the time, Marshal Mikhail Tukhachevsky, and a number of the USSR's leading generals, were court-martialled on charges of treason and executed.

After these executions, Stalin began a further series of purges that eliminated, among others, members of the Soviet Communist Party, veteran Bolsheviks, party hierarchy, managers in industry, high-ranking government officials, distinguished academics, legal and professional persons and even members of his own state police, the NKVD. The purges were of such a magnitude that experts say his political victims could number in the 'tens of millions' of people.

STALIN'S ROLE IN WORLD WAR II

Stalin was one of the most astute leaders of World War II. One of the first of several actions was an alliance he made with the German dictator, Adolf Hitler. Prior to this pact with Hitler, Stalin had attempted an alliance with the western powers. This was indicative of his Machiavellian nature in siding with any party in order to gain political advantage. When Hitler, encouraged by Stalin, attacked Poland, plunging the world into a major world war, Stalin acted swiftly and annexed the eastern section of Poland, Estonia, Latvia, Lithuania and parts of Romania. He also attacked Finland, but was unable to defeat this country. When Hitler invaded the Soviet Union, the conduct of the war against the Germans was placed in Stalin's hands when he appointed himself Chairman of People's Commissions, effectively making himself the absolute head of the government. He took part personally in the defence of Moscow and maintained close control over Chuikov's conduct of the battle of Stalingrad, which turned the tide against the Germans. At the end of the war, he was one of the three main representatives of the Allies at the Yalta Conference, where he outwitted his western allies.

When the war ended in 1945, Stalin took control of eastern Europe by imposing a form of 'colonial control' over a number of puppet communist governments subservient to himself personally. When Marshal Tito of Yugoslavia challenged Stalin's control in 1948 by breaking away into a form of 'independent' role, Stalin purged a number of Eastern Bloc leaders, many of them being either imprisoned or executed. In his final years, Stalin became almost completely paranoid. He turned against his wartime western allies and bolstered all things Soviet at the expense of all things western. Through his chief ideologist, Andrey Zhdanov, he declared war on Soviet intellectuals and artists, arresting and exiling many of them and executing others. On 5 March 1953, it was announced to the world that Stalin had died. His death, it is believed, may not have been completely natural.

CHAPTER 2

ADOLF HITLER (1889-1945)

Adolf Hitler, who rose to become Nazi Germany's dictator, was born on 20 April 1889, in the Austrian Village of Braunau Am Inn, the son of a minor civil servant in the service of the Habsburg customs ministry. Hitler's father, as he was illegitimate, had had his mother's name, Schicklgruber, and had adopted the name Hitler in 1876. Adolf went to school until the age of 16, but did not secure a school-leaving certificate. Hitler displayed some artistic talent, and dreamt of being a great painter, but this dream lasted only about two years, which he spent in the town of Linz. Despite the loss of his mother's support at her death in 1908, Hitler had his father's modest pension, which allowed him to maintain himself in Vienna.

Having failed two attempts to pass into the Vienna Academy, Hitler drifted from one lodging house to another. Even at this early stage, he showed signs of what his temperament would be like in the future. He could not maintain normal human relationships and was completely intolerant of the middle class and of any people who were not of German origin or who did not belong to the German social-political sphere of influence, and already showed signs of being very anti-semitic. He often gave way to violent outbursts of anger and had a tendency to live in a world of fantasy as a means of escaping the poverty and failure in his life. In 1913 he moved to Munich, but had to go back to Austria, where he was examined and found to be unfit for military service. He then returned to Germany and volunteered for war service. Hitler served quite well and was recommended for the Iron Cross after being wounded. Before the end of the war, Hitler was made a corporal and awarded the Iron Cross, First Class. During his war years, Hitler became reasonably self-confident, liked the discipline and companionship and approved of the authoritarian manner in which military organisations functioned.

After the war, Hitler felt strongly that Germany had been humiliated by the Treaty of Versailles. In 1920, he became a member of the German Worker's Party in the city of Munich, and soon his talent for political organisation earned him the post of Director of the Party's propaganda machine. This prompted him to leave the army and give his full attention to party politics. In the same year, the German Worker's Party was renamed the Nationalsozialistiche Deutsche Arbeiterspartei (NSDAP) – the term Nazi is an abbreviation of the name. The post-war resentment among most Germans, who regarded the Versailles Treaty as unfair, as well as widespread poverty and unemployment, made fertile ground for the growth of the Nazi party. An army coup d'état in 1920 had given Germany a strong right-wing government, and while in Munich, Hitler met Ernst Röhm, a district military commander who had joined the Nazi party even before Hitler. Röhm recruited the Nazi gangs which were used by Hitler to protect party meetings and for other, more sinister, reasons, such as attacking members of the Communist Party and other groups which opposed the Nazi party. Röhm later (1921) formed these gangs of Nazi thugs into a private Nazi army, known as the Sturmabteilung (SA), which became sufficiently powerful to help the Bavarian government stay in power.

Hitler was dissatisfied with the manner in which the Nazi party was being run and, after a confrontation with fellow members of the party executive, threatened to resign. The party hierarchy conceded, afraid that Hitler would make good his threat and the party would disintegrate. In this manner, Hitler was made President of the Party in July 1921, and was given unlimited power. He built up a mass movement through the use of every available means, including the use of the party news organ, the *Völkischer Beobachter* (The National Observer). It was during this period that Hitler began to gather a leadership group around him who would help him mould the party into the authoritarian instrument he wanted it to be. Among these men were Rudolf Hess, Alfred Rosenberg, Herman Göring and Julius Streicher.

Hitler's real movement into the German nation's political mainstream came when the Nazi party tried to seize power in what is referred to as the Munich Putsch of November 1923. In this incident, Hitler, in collaboration with General Erich Ludendorff, took advantage of the breakdown in law and order and tried to overthrow the Land government. They hoped that this action would have forced the regional Reichswehr commander to proclaim the commencement of a revolution against the Weimar Republic. The Putsch failed and consequently Hitler was arrested and tried, receiving a five-year prison sentence. Hitler did not serve the full five years of his sentence, spending only nine months in jail. It was during this period that he began writing the book *Mein Kampf* (My Struggle).

It was in *Mein Kampf* that Hitler's ideas on a number of issues crystallised. Most of his ideas though, were derived from other right-wing writers and an assortment of people who were on the fringes of right-wing intellectualism. To begin with, Hitler stated quite clearly that there was no equality between the races nor between human individuals. For him, racial inequality was accepted as part of the inherited natural order. Only one race, the Aryan race, he said, possessed any creative ability and the German people, he said, were the epitome of this Aryan creative spirit. The people, the Volk, were the natural unit of individuals clustered into a group, and the German Volk, he added, were the supreme example of a Volk. He derided democracy as a system of government, stating that the democratic process's assumption that all people are equal is false. The only equality, Hitler stated, existed in the person of the Volk leader, the Führer, who symbolised the unity of the Volk and was therefore endowed with absolute authority.

Hitler saw a number of prominent 'enemies' of Nazism. Among these he included social democracy and communism as expounded by Karl Marx and his adherents. For some reason, Hitler's hatred was concentrated on the Jewish people and his anti-semitism was openly proclaimed. He endowed Jews with every evil imaginable, even suggesting that it was the Jews who were responsible for the spread of international communism. He made some outlandish statements in moments of emotional frenzy. One or two such statements are reproduced hereunder to indicate the warped mentality of the man (Wepman 1985):

'The anti-semitism of reason, however, must lead to the systematic combating and elimination of Jewish privileges. Its ultimate good must implacably be the total removal of the Jews. Of both these purposes only a government of national strength is capable, never a government of national impotence.'

And:

'In his systematic efforts to ruin girls and women (the Jew) strives to break down the last barriers of discrimination between him and other people. The Jews were responsible for bringing Negroes into the Rhineland, with the ultimate idea of bastardising the white race which they hate and thus lowering its cultural and political level so that the Jew might dominate ... I believe ... that I am acting in the sense of the Almighty Creator. By warding off the Jews, I am fighting for the Lord's work.'

It was with such rash, ludicrous and inflammatory statements that Hitler whipped up the masses and created so-called German unity at the expense of not only German Jews, but Jews throughout Europe. Hitler was obsessed with Jews. In his youth in Vienna, Hitler had already made his attitude to Jews quite clear. He is reported to have confided to a friend at the time: 'If I am ever really in power, the destruction of the Jews will be my first and most important job. I will have gallows erected ... as many of them as the traffic allows (will be killed – own parenthesis). Then the Jews will be hanged, and they will stay hanging until they stink.' (Wepman, 1985) By 1935, the Nuremberg laws made it illegal for Germans to marry or conduct business with Jews and relegated people of Jewish origin or religious faith to second-class citizenship. Further legislation was passed making life for Jews almost impossible in Germany. What made the position even more difficult was that German Jews were the most assimilated into the society. Vast numbers of Jews were prominent businessmen, academicians, medical professionals, government functionaries and so on. In fact, during World War I, many German Jews fought for the country and distinguished themselves.

Very few German Jews read the signs correctly and even fewer emigrated. They were hopeful that Hitler's Nazism would be short-lived. But they were mistaken. The ninth of November 1938 was a day Jews in Germany and other parts of the world will not easily forget. An incident in Paris was the catalyst that prompted Hitler's Nazi apparatus to undertake the first substantial public display of anti-semitism. A German Jew living in Paris shot a German diplomat in protest at Nazi anti-semitism. In Germany, this resulted in what was called Kristallnacht (Crystal Night) because of the thousand of windows that were smashed. Led by Goebbels, Nazi thugs destroyed Jewish houses, looted their businesses and torched synagogues, with this type of action continuing into the next day. German police watched idly as gangs continued to wreak havoc upon the Jewish community. The toll on businesses and other Jewish assets was incredible. One source states that more than 800 Jewish shops were looted, 170 houses destroyed and nearly 200 synagogues were destroyed by fire or other forms of vandalism. In addition, nearly 100 Jews were murdered. Soon afterwards German police arrested nearly 20 thousand Jews and shipped them off to the notorious concentration camps.

When World War II started and the Nazi *Blitzkrieg* rolled through Europe, Hitler's wrath against the Jews continued in several other European countries. In Poland, Jews were rounded up and relocated into ghettos where they could be isolated from other residents of the urban areas. Once they were established in ghettos, the Germans began to ship them off to the concentration camps. On Hitler's orders, Heinrich Himmler and Reinhard Heydrich, who was head of Germany's security service, began preparing for a 'final solution to the Jewish question'. When German forces invaded the Soviet Union, orders were given that they should kill every single Jew they could find in the territory they occupied. More than 600 000 Soviet Jews were exterminated by special German forces known as the Einsatz-Gruppen. By 1942, the elimination of Jews began on a systematic basis. The Holocaust had begun, with genocide as the end result.

Jews were, however, not the only persons to be persecuted by Hitler's Germany. By 1942, Central and Eastern Europe were also earmarked for 'cleansing'. Roman Catholics, Communists and other political dissidents were also executed or put into concentration camps. Notorious concentration camps were built in several occupied countries. In Poland, the Bezzec Concentration Camp served as an eradication centre for vast numbers of Polish Jews, while those who could work were put into work camps where they were treated with utmost brutality. The murder of the Jews continued until, by the war's end, more than six million Jews and other minorities, especially gypsies, were executed in the cruellest ways. During the course of the war, most German citizens were aware that Jews were being brutally treated, but few knew that they were being killed on such a large scale. On 30 April 1945, a few days before Germany's unconditional surrender, Hitler committed suicide in his Berlin bunker, bringing to an end one of the world's most brutal periods of man's inhumanity to man.

CHAPTER 3

BENITO MUSSOLINI (1883-1945)

Benito Mussolini was born on 29 July 1893, in the village of Predappio, in the Romagna region of Italy. His father was the local blacksmith. His mother was a schoolteacher, but as a result of his father's profligate habits, such as spending money on his mistresses, the family was poor.

Mussolini's schooling was interrupted several times as a result of his temperament. As a child and a young man, he was described as quarrelsome, restless, unruly, disobedient and aggressive. His early teachers could not control or discipline the boy and his parents were forced to send him to a Roman Catholic Salesian school at Faenza. But here, too, he proved to be uncontrollable and, after assaulting a fellow pupil and one of the teacher-priests at the school, he was expelled. He was sent to another school, but there, too, he was expelled after attacking a fellow pupil with a pocket knife. However, Mussolini was extremely intelligent and passed his school certificate and obtained a teacher's diploma. After working as a teacher for a short period, he decided against this profession and left for Switzerland.

In Switzerland Mussolini took on odd jobs, slept wherever he could and lived the life of a Bohemian. He read widely and was conversant with the philosophers, particularly Kant, Spinoza, Nietzsche, Hegel and Sorel. At this point in his life, Mussolini did not yet have a concrete political philosophy of his own. However, he had a striking personality and generally displayed charismatic qualities which brought him to the notice of his peers, mostly a group of revolutionaries. His public-speaking abilities were excellent and he developed a special talent for political journalism. He got involved with a building trade union and after suggesting that they commence a general strike, he advocated the use of violence to achieve their aims.

He returned to Italy in 1904 and took up his original career as a teacher. He found a post near Udine, a town in the Venetian alps, but this life soon bored him, and he turned to a life of debauchery, drinking, womanising and getting involved in unbecoming conduct. He could not live this life for long and chose to return to journalism and involvement in trade union activities. His political extremism led to his arrest and imprisonment. In 1909, he fell in love with and married 16-year-old Rachele Guide. Soon afterwards, he was imprisoned once more by the Italian authorities for revolutionary activities on behalf of the Young Socialists, a group of which he was a prominent member.

As a socialist journalist Mussolini was very successful, first founding a newspaper of his own, called *The Class Struggle*. This was so successful that in 1912 he was appointed editor of the prominent socialist newspaper, *Avanti*. While its editor, he first wrote against Italy's involvement in World War I and later he did a complete about-turn and began supporting the war effort. This angered his socialist masters, who quickly disposed of this mercurial editor. Financed by a publisher, Mussolini assumed the editorship of another important Italian newspaper, the *Popolo d'Italia*. It was through the columns of this newspaper that Mussolini expressed his new political ideology and the philosophy that was to found Italy's Fascist Party. Mussolini fought in World War I, was wounded and returned from the war as a committed anti-socialist. Italy, he said, needed a strong man to lead them and he would be the man. He founded the Fascist Party with an initial membership of about 200. He organised numerous rallys to which he attracted thousands of people. The Fascist Party grew in strength and formed Fascist squads, known as Squadristi, who marched through towns and villages of Italy, shouting slogans, waving flags decorated with the Fascinae of the lictors, the symbol of the old Roman authority.

In the summer of 1922 the Fascists, led by Mussolini, found the ideal opportunity to bring down the Italian government: a general strike was called in Italy. Mussolini addressed a mass rally in Naples and threatened that, should the government fail to stop the strike, the Fascists would. He further threatened that Fascist militants would march on Rome and a coup d'état would begin. However, Mussolini hesitated to translate this last threat into action, but the anarchical situation continued to deteriorate in Italy and King Victor Emmanuel III of Italy summoned him to Rome and asked him to form a government. He became Italy's youngest prime minister. Among the powers he asked for, and received, was the power to rule with supreme authority for a period of one year. Mussolini proved popular with the Italian masses and through coercive force he managed to bring law and order to Italy and also began development projects that gave work to the unemployed. As one biographer put it (Brit p 751):

> 'He was undoubtedly more popular in Italy than anyone had ever been before…. He had transformed and reinvigorated his divided and demoralised country; he had carried out his social reforms and public works without losing the support of the industrialists and landowners; he had even succeeded in coming to terms with the papacy.'

Not happy to receive only the accolades of his native Italy, Mussolini began to develop territorial ambitions in Africa. He had his eyes and his heart set on Abyssinia (now Ethiopia). He made wild threats to the African country and in October 1935, his forces invaded. The League of Nations responded with horror and applied a number of superficial sanctions, but stopped short of imposing any really effective measures. On 9 May 1936 a jubilant Mussolini announced to a crowd of nearly half a million people in Rome that the invasion had succeeded and that Italy had an empire. He continued these military adventures by committing Italian troops to fight on the side of General Francisco Franco in the Spanish Civil War of 1936, and in 1939 he occupied Albania. These adventures placed a great strain on the Italian economy. To increase the burden, Italy had also acquired the territories of Tripolitania and Cyrenaica in North Africa and needed a period of peace in order to develop.

Mussolini was hesitant to enter the war in spite of having signed the so-called Pact of Steel with Hitler, because he knew that Italy was not ready, but as time went on he became convinced that Germany would win, so he entered the war in order to have a share in the spoils once it was concluded. His army chief of staff, Marshall Pietro Badoglio, made a last-minute attempt to convince Mussolini to delay Italy's entry into the war, but Mussolini, fired by a few quick German victories, replied:

> 'You, Marshall, are not calm enough to judge the situation. I can tell you that everything will be over by September and that I only need a few thousand dead so that I can sit at the peace conference as a man who has fought.' (ibid.)

Consequently, on 10 June 1940, Mussolini brought Italy into the war. From the outset, the war did not go well for Italy and her German allies treated her with distrust. Hitler never seriously consulted Mussolini about his plans and attacked Russia without revealing his strategy to his Italian allies. To avenge Hitler's treatment of him, Mussolini embarked on another costly adventure by attacking Greece without consulting the Germans. Mussolini's forces were defeated and the Germans had to extricate the Italians from this humiliating defeat. In North Africa, Italy's war effort did not fare much better and all but collapsed after British and Commonwealth troops defeated her armies in Abyssinia, Tripolitania and Cyrenaica. Here again Italy was bailed out by Germany.

A number of Italian leaders, unhappy with Mussolini's modus operandi, began to prepare for his downfall. On this occasion, both Fascists and non-Fascists attended a meeting of the Fascist Grand Council, the supreme body of the Italian state, on 24 July 1943. At this crucial meeting a resolution removing Mussolini from office was passed with an overwhelming majority. Mussolini disregarded the vote and continued to attend to his state duties until the next day, 25 July 1943, when he was arrested by command of the King. He was placed in custody on an island and later moved to the Gran Sasso d'Italia in the Abruzzi mountains. Despite being guarded, he was rescued by the Germans in a daring raid and taken to Germany.

Mussolini returned to northern Italy, where he established the short-lived Republica Sociale Italiana or Italian Social Republic. His government had little power to govern and even less of a military organisation. But he was able to order the arrest of a number of members of the Fascist Grand Council who had voted against him, including his son-in-law, Count Galleazo Ciano, and had them executed. As the Allied forces moved steadily northwards Mussolini attempted to flee to Switzerland or Germany disguised as a German soldier, but was recognised by partisans and was executed, together with his mistress, Claretta Petacci, near Azzano, on 28 April 1945. His body was taken to Milan where it hung upside down together with his mistress and 16 other followers who were also executed. Perhaps Mussolini might have had another destiny had he followed his own advice:

> 'No dictator can ever calculate with prudence, because all dictators in the end lose any sense of balance, as they pursue their obsessive ambitions into a world of unreality.' (Hartennian, 1988)

CHAPTER 4

IDI AMIN DADA (1925-)

INTRODUCTION

Africa too has had its share of dictators, but none fits the description better than Idi Amin, ousted President of the East African country of Uganda. Amin was born in the north-west of Uganda in 1925. His family were Muslims and, apart from some religious instruction at home, he had a very limited primary education. At the age of 21, Amin enlisted in the 4th Battalion of the King's African Rifles. He was a very keen sportsman and one of Africa's best boxers, becoming Uganda's heavyweight champion and keeping the title for nine years, from 1951 to 1960. He was also one of the country's best rugby players and was the only black person at the time to play for the Nile Rugby Club, traditionally an all-white institution.

Amin's rise in the military was meteoric. By 1959 he had been promoted, on merit, to the rank of Sergeant-Major and soon after to the rank of Effendi, equivalent to Warrant Officer. Just before Ugandan independence, he was made a full lieutenant, one of only two Ugandan officers to do so, and in November 1963 he was promoted to the rank of Major. Prior to this promotion, Amin had attended a course for commanding officers at Britain's School of Infantry in Wiltshire. Amin also did a paratrooper's course in Israel where he earned his wings. In 1964 there was a mutiny in the Ugandan Army and British officers left. Upon their departure, Major Amin was promoted to the rank of Colonel, which made him the Deputy Military Commander. The new deputy commander began to have financial problems and was soon the subject of a Parliamentary enquiry. During the enquiry he alleged that he had been paid large sums of money by Congolese (Zairean) revolutionaries for purchasing non-military equipment for them. He also stated that he had been to the Congo (now Zaire) under instructions from the Ugandan government. Trouble was also brewing between Colonel Amin and the Commander-in-Chief of the Ugandan Army, Brigadier Shabam Opolot.

In 1965 there was an unsuccessful attempt to overthrow the government of Uganda. Those involved in this plot were high-ranking military and political functionaries. One of the consequences of this attempt was the sudden promotion of Idi Amin to the post of Chief-of-Staff of the Ugandan Army and Air Force. He soon became commander of the Ugandan Army, one of the most powerful positions in the Ugandan body politic. The former commander of the Army, Brigadier Opolot, was given the post of Chief of Defence Staff within the Ministry of Defence. In October 1966, Opolot was dismissed from his post and from the army and was detained in terms of emergency regulations then in force in Uganda.

Earlier, in May 1966, Amin had ruthlessly suppressed a rebellion against the Obote government by the Buganda people. He was rewarded by being promoted to the rank of Major-General in 1968 and effectively became Commander-in-Chief of the Ugandan Armed Forces. President Milton Obote of Uganda did not trust General Amin and as a result formed a parallel military unit known as the General Service Unit (GSU). Dr Obote also made a number of appointments to the Ugandan Military hierarchy in order to counter Amin's influence. Most of the appointed officers were either from the Acholi or Langi Tribes.

AMIN TAKES OVER THE PRESIDENCY

In January 1971, Dr Milton Obote, President of Uganda, left for the Commonwealth Leaders Conference being held that year in Singapore. Prior to his departure he had ordered Idi Amin to prepare reports for him explaining the disappearance of certain arms and funds designated for the military. It was while Obote was away that GSU units moved to isolate Amin at his home in the hope of either capturing him or rendering him useless by placing him under house arrest. However, he had already been informed by a loyal soldier that the pro-Obote troops were on their way to him. Amin, always a popular figure with the army, secured a mechanised unit and the majority of the army and prepared to defend himself. He had the upper hand in the ensuing confrontation and defeated his opponents. On the morning of 25 January 1971 General Amin ousted Obote in his absence and took over as President of Uganda. His first move was to replace all high-ranking officers with members of tribes that were loyal to him. In addition to promotions based on tribalism, Amin also shared the spoils of victory with a number of fellow Muslims in Uganda. He had presented himself as a devout Muslim, tolerant of all religious persuasions, but there was soon evidence to the contrary: prominent Christians began to disappear without trace.

At the end of 1972 and early in 1973, a number of prominent Roman Catholics disappeared, including two who were leading members of the community – the Ugandan Chief Justice, Benedicto Kiwanuka, and Paul Kiggundu, the editor of the popular Catholic newspaper, *Munno*. At this stage, Idi Amin denied any involvement with the disappearances, suggesting instead that it was the work of pro-Obote activists.

He continued to make sporadic changes to the cabinet and other senior posts in order to ensure that no one could build a power base strong enough to threaten his hold on power. One of his biographers described his governmental style in the following manner (Van Rensburg 1975):

> 'Amin had developed his own formula for survival at the top: Keep ministers, senior civil servants, and commanding officers constantly on their toes and on the go. In a permanent game of musical chairs he sees to it that the people in top positions are changed around every two or three months, to make sure that none of them can build up a stronghold of power. For his frequent trips abroad, General Amin always appoints a different member of his Cabinet as acting President. And as additional insurance, Amin increasingly appoints senior officers from his own West Nile region.'

Amin's rule was marked by constant changes that were sometimes prompted by a mere whim of the dictator. In October 1973 he dismissed five cabinet ministers, including the influential Minister of Internal Affairs, Lieutenant-Colonel Obitre-Gama. Earlier in that year he had dismissed his entire cabinet, after some of them began questioning the wisdom of his mode of government. In January 1974, eight of his fellow West Nile tribesmen who were senior military officers were appointed to positions as Provincial Governors, which were posts created by Amin.

However, Amin did possess a number of charismatic qualities, which to some extent endeared him to his people. The rest of Africa and the first-world countries were not quite sure what to make of his system of government, which was based mainly on whatever affected him personally. At first, Amin promised that nationalisation of property and business enterprises would slow down. He toured the country promising a liberal internal policy as soon as the country was free of turbulence and law and order had been re-established. He managed to dupe many seasoned political observers, including the country's most famous political scientist, Professor Ali Mazrui, who suggested that Amin was the most charismatic leader Uganda had had. Amin was initially particularly careful not to upset Uganda's Asian population, who was very active in the Ugandan economy. He promised Asians resident in Uganda that they would be involved in the affairs of the nation and gave them assurances that their businesses and properties would be secure.

The Asians of Uganda held a virtual monopoly in the cultivation of sugar, cotton, tea and coffee. No sooner had Amin given his word, than on 17 September 1972, he suddenly changed his mind about the Asian population and gave them an ultimatum informing them that they had 90 days in which to leave Uganda. A great majority of Ugandan Asians had been born in the country, many of the prominent Asian families having been there for several generations. This action brought about a crisis in relations between Uganda and Britain, the former coloniser and the country to which most Ugandan Asians fled. Despite pressure from a number of countries, Amin proceeded with his forced expulsion of Asians and by the beginning of November 1972, approximately 50 000 had left. He vented his personal resentment against Britain by ordering a number of British companies in Uganda to sell their assets and leave the country. In January 1983, Amin announced that his government had taken over British firms in Uganda. In addition, he had serious differences with Uganda's East African Community partner, Tanzania, where the overthrown Ugandan President, Dr Milton Obote, was living in exile. He made a number of wild and unfounded accusations against Tanzania, including the allegation that Tanzania, together with Ruanda, Sudan, Burundi, Somalia and Zambia, were planning an invasion of Uganda.

AMIN'S COMPLICITY IN MASS KILLINGS AND ELIMINATION OF INDIVIDUALS

Amin turned his attention to the army, where individuals whom he did not trust or like were just never seen again by their relatives. In one mass killing, it is said that about 2 000 Obote supporters were executed in cold blood during 1971. Not trusting his fellow Ugandans, Amin hired a number of mercenaries to serve in his forces, many of them from southern Sudan and Zaire. Many other important Ugandans also disappeared without trace. Amin gave his loyal followers, including his hired mercenaries, properties that had formerly belonged to Asians who had been expelled from Uganda.

Amin several times gave the assurance that he would personally see to the problem of the mysterious disappearance of Ugandans, but nothing came of the dictator's promises and Ugandans from all walks of life continued to disappear, many of them being found brutally murdered. These included Wilson Oryema, a cabinet minister's son. Oryema had been trained as a fighter pilot in Germany. Soon after landing at Uganda's Entebbe Airport, he was abducted and killed. A prominent official in the Ugandan Foreign Ministry, Godfrey Kigalla, was seen at a meeting with Idi Amin and two of his bodyguards at Kampala's Fairview Hotel. Kigalla was seen leaving with one of the dictator's bodyguards and his badly mutilated body was found some time later. In February 1973, an East African medical conference was held in Uganda. As delegates filed in they were told that the conference director's assistant had disappeared without trace.

Amin had created an organisation known as the Public Safety Unit (PSU), a sinister security force made up of Amin's loyal followers and headed by Alli Towelli, who later became Deputy Commissioner of Police. Relatives of missing persons could contact the PSU and after payment of substantial bribes to officers of the unit were taken to the corpses of their loved ones.

THE ATTEMPTED COUP OF MARCH 1974

On 24 March 1974, army units dissatisfied with Idi Amin staged a coup attempt, but after heavy fighting over a six-hour period, the attempt was crushed. One of the most prominent military commanders, Brigadier Charles Arube, was alleged to have led the coup attempt. The state-controlled Uganda Radio said that Arube had shot himself, twice, and died a little later during an operation. The army at the time was made up partly of members of the Lugbara tribe. They apparently were upset because their leader, a Lieutenant-Colonel Michael Odega, had been killed under mysterious circumstances. Amin had announced that Odega had disappeared and had been found dead floating in the Nile. Amin had been informed of the discontent in the Lugbara section of the army and had taken action against them while the coup was still in the planning stages.

There were several other incidents which displayed Amin's excesses and his incredible cruelty and cunning. He brought Uganda, once described as the 'jewel of Africa', to its knees economically. His human rights record is one of the worst in Africa's turbulent history. He was finally ousted in 1978 by Tanzanian troops who, together with anti-Amin forces from Uganda, reinstated Dr Milton Obote. He was in turn ousted once more and today Uganda is in the process of reconstruction. Idi Amin is said to be living in exile in Saudi Arabia.

CHAPTER 5

JEAN-BEDEL BOKASSA (1921-)

Jean-Bedel Bokassa, one-time President and self-declared 'Emperor' of the Central African Republic, is another man whose human rights left much to be desired. He came to power, like most dictators, in a military coup which removed the former President, David Dacko, on 31 December 1965.

Bokassa was extremely well connected politically. He was born on 22 February 1921 at Bobangui, and his father was a village chief of the M'Baka tribe. The founder of the modern Central African Republic, Barthelomu Boganda, was his uncle, and the ousted President, David Dacko, was his cousin. The presidency of David Dacko was not a happy one as he brought his people much bitterness and disappointment as his policies unfolded. The coup that ousted him from power was thus welcomed by the general public and leaders in other sectors of the Central African Republic. Bokassa was the commander of the country's army at the time and held the rank of Colonel.

Bokassa was used to political intrigues – when he was six years old, his father was assassinated. His mother committed suicide soon afterwards, leaving behind a dozen children. Soon afterwards, the family was again struck by bad fortune when his uncle Boganda, founder of the nation, was killed in an aircraft accident.

Bokassa was educated at missionary schools at Mbaiki, Bangui, and in the Congo capital, Brazzaville. He was tempted to enter the priesthood in the Roman Catholic church, but instead opted to join the French army at the age of 18. As a soldier, Bokassa distinguished himself. In World War II, he fought with the Free French Forces and later in French Indochina. He was decorated 12 times for bravery and acts of gallantry in battle. His personal ambition won him favour with the French military authorities and in 1948 he was made a commissioned officer. Twelve years later he left the French army with the rank of Captain. When the Central African Republic became independent from France in 1960, Bokassa was requested by President Dacko to organise and set up the country's army. In 1963 he was promoted to Major and appointed Commander-in-Chief of the armed forces. Within a year he was moved to the post of Chief-of-Staff in the Ministry of Defence with the rank of Colonel.

The coup that brought Bokassa to power was executed in a manner that indicated the shrewd mind of a seasoned politician in a country used to political intrigue. He had an antagonist in the chief of the gendarmerie (police), a certain Izanio. Bokassa was displeased that the army had not received a fair share of the national budget allocation as a result of an excessive amount being given to the police department. The events of 31 December 1965 were of a nature that bordered on unreality. His opponent, Izanio, invited Bokassa to a New Year's cocktail party, but the shrewd Bokassa felt that something was amiss, as the two men had hardly been on speaking terms since the budget incident. Then a number of Bokassa's colleagues warned him that the invitation was a means of having him arrested. Bokassa therefore telephoned Izanio, asking him to come to a military camp to sign documents that had to be handed in prior to the year's end only a few hours away. Upon his arrival, Izanio was promptly arrested. A few hours later, while President Dacko was having dinner with friends, the army, under the command of Captain Alexander Banza, surrounded the Presidential palace and other key administrative buildings. On hearing of what was taking place, President Dacko made an attempt to return to his home district, but did not succeed. He was arrested by an army officer and brought back to the Presidential Palace, where, before the sun rose the next morning, he signed a statement handing over all power to Bokassa.

The houses of Dacko's ministers were attacked, some destroyed and their contents burnt in bonfires. The ministers were arrested and taken to military camps. On the morning of 1 January 1966, Bokassa addressed the nation on Radio Bangui, saying, among other things: 'As from 3.20 this morning, the government has been taken over by the armed forces. President Dacko and his ministers have resigned. The hour of justice has sounded. The bourgeoisie is no more, and a new era of equality between all citizens is beginning' (Van Rensburg 1975). Bokassa formed a Revolutionary Council and appointed a number of ministers. These included three men from the military, three former members of the Dacko Cabinet and three civil servants. The constitution was abolished and a new constitution was promised by Bokassa, now beginning to show dictatorial tendencies. He undertook to rule by decree with regular consultation with the Council of Ministers of the Revolutionary Council.

Gradually Bokassa's true dictatorial nature began to emerge. He made numerous promises to the public and tried to be all things to all people. Soon after the coup, several officers were given salary increases and promotions. Bokassa said that there had been a plot against the army and produced in evidence hundreds of weapons that supposedly were to be used by the Home Security Ministry against him. The scapegoat for the alleged move against the military was none other than his faithful bodyguard, Jean-Baptiste Mounoumbaye. Bokassa suggested that his one-time ally was the Chief of the dreaded 'Secret Police', and to make matters look serious and realistic, he put a price of 500 million francs on his head.

However, soon Bokassa became drunk with power and the ensuing excesses were of such a nature that the people of the Central African Republic were brutally shocked into realisation of his true nature. One of his biographers explains (Van Rensburg 1975):

'... He set out to inflict violence personally on 50 convicted thieves. In July 1972, Bokassa decreed that captured thieves would be mutilated. First offenders would have one ear cut off; second offenders, the other ear; and third offenders the right hand. A thief convicted for the fourth time would be executed publicly by firing squad ....'

The United Nations Secretary General protested against these excesses, but Bokassa dismissed Dr Kurt Waldheim's protests as those of a 'colonialist' and an 'imperialist'. In the following months, Bokassa did not display any enthusiasm for such trappings of democracy as elections, constitutions and the check on presidential powers, even announcing that he did not wish to hear such terms as 'democracy' or 'elections'. He said that he was the 'Guide' of the nation. 'I am everywhere and nowhere', he said. 'I see nothing yet I see all. I listen to nothing and hear everything. Such is the role of the Head of State' (Van Rensburg 1975).

From 1966 on, Bokassa endeavoured to develop a personality cult, with his portrait appearing in all public buildings, on school books and other prominent places. Development projects began to be named after him and he made certain that at any public ceremony or celebration, he would be revered to the same extent as his uncle Boganda, the first president of the Central African Republic. Among the things he did to secure adulation and respect was his self-promotion to the rank of full General. Upon returning from a trip to another African country, Bokassa had himself carried off the aircraft in a litter, thereby commencing a tradition that would one day lead him to proclaim himself 'Emperor' of the Central African 'Empire' in true Napoleonic style. During 1967, rumours circulated that his military officers were unhappy and about to take action against him. He summoned the help of his ally, France, and a famous French Parachute Division landed at Bangui to bolster his regime and protect him from possible threats from the enemies he was making. Two years later he felt secure enough again and the French troops left.

Bokassa continued to rule with an iron fist and in 1970 he issued a number of presidential decrees that affected more profoundly the lives of his fellow citizens. He decreed that articles to be published overseas would have to be censored. The press and radio in the Central African Republic could not put out statements without first having them approved by the minister responsible. Local authorities were given authority to call in troops to curb any strikes or other forms of protest, such as the assembly of people for the purpose of securing their rights. Strike leaders risked prison sentences of up to ten years. In another sinister development, no civilian in the Central African Republic was permitted to talk to or communicate in any way with members of the armed forces. Civilians were also not permitted on military property. With measures such as these, Bokassa became an absolutest dictator, involving himself in almost every aspect of his nation's life. He brooked no opposition and any form of action deemed to threaten his authority was met with strong and conclusive action. His one-time associate, Alexandre Banga, Minister of Health, was accused of plotting against him and after securing a quick conviction, Bokassa had him shot. Similarly, he imprisoned ministers or other officials who were popular and might therefore threaten his position.

Bokassa's economic policy was mercurial, even sometimes non-existent. He felt that as he was completely in control of the country, this meant that the natural resources of his country should be his to dispose of. He attempted, with success, to place the mining industry in his own hands. Here he came up against one of Africa's most honest and honourable officials, Blaise Onayo, head of the Department of Mines and Geology. Onayo did not comply with Bokassa's demands and was imprisoned for his trouble in 1968. The dictator then ordered the mining companies in his country to pay vast sums of money for mining permits, sometimes nearly 500 times more than the legal rate. When the mining houses refused to pay, Bokassa arrested all expatriate technicians at the mines and expelled them from the country. After protest from France, Bokassa relented and cancelled the expulsion orders. Misappropriation of funds, bad management and general dishonesty crippled the economy of the country and there were huge declines in agricultural production when he attempted to introduce the 'Bokassa Plan', a scientific socialism experiment. He often angered his French ally and relations between the two countries were often strained. However, economic necessity forced Bokassa to re-assess his relationship with France on a number of occasions. He tried to be all things to all people and in a special National Day Speech on 1 December 1971, he said (Van Rensburg 1975):

'A relentless search for friendship and co-operation among all peoples and nations, be they small or large, is one of the major aims of an external policy. In the past few years, we have expanded our diplomatic relations. We have, nevertheless, remained faithful to our traditional friendships – especially our friendships with France, with whom we maintain external ties of friendship and fraternity .... Our friends of the Soviet Union, Yugoslavia, Rumania, West Germany, the Republic of Korea and the Common Market have their place in our hearts.'

In due course, Bokassa became fascinated with the idea of absolute power and, harbouring a deep nostalgia for the old monarchical system of government, he declared his country an Empire, and crowned himself Emperor of the newly-established Central African Empire. This occasion came to the notice of the world, when this self-proclaimed 'emperor' used up 22 million dollars for the crowning ceremony alone. This represented one fourth of the country's annual budget. His excesses continued and he violated human rights and their conventions as he wished. In 1979, he once again came to the world's attention when he had several dozen school children murdered merely because they would not buy school uniforms supplied by one of his close supporters. This brutal action sealed his fate. France is alleged to have planned a coup and removed Bokassa from power, to the great relief of his tortured people.

THE LEGAL SYSTEM AND HUMAN RIGHTS – EARLY POLITICAL ACTIVISTS

PART 6

THE LEGAL SYSTEM AND HUMAN RIGHTS — EARLY POLITICAL ACTIVISTS

CHAPTER 1

HUMAN RIGHTS AND THE LEGAL
SYSTEM IN SOUTH AFRICA

The various governments in South Africa since 1910 have tended to ignore the issue of human rights, especially the Nationalist government, in power since 1948. During the post-1948 period, the Nationalist government concentrated its efforts on putting into practice a policy of racial separation and the maintenance of white domination in politics and, to a lesser extent, on economics.

Calls for the recognition of basic human rights accepted by many nations in the international community were largely ignored by the Nationalist government until quite recently, when it did a volte-face on the issue. Some commentators feel that the recent change of attitude towards the issue of human rights may be because of the fear that a majority government may not be positively inclined towards the minority. Although this may be partly true, the facts indicate that the white minority, and in particular the Afrikaners, are genuinely drawn towards a reappraisal of the human rights issue. The state as the supreme organ in society is fast losing ground and is being replaced by a genuine search for justice based on the traditions of equality for all citizens before the law and the maintenance, through the law, of human individual liberty.

An historical analysis of human rights generally and individual liberty in particular shows that South Africa has a poor record in this regard. The 1910 Constitution, an all-white document, made little if any mention of human rights or individual liberty or of equality between the races. The record speaks for itself. The adoption of the 1910 Constitution ignored the rights and liberties of black and Asian South Africans and dealt mainly with the conflicts inherent in white politics. White South Africa managed to hold its position in the pre-World War II era and little justification was necessary in explaining its racial policy to the world at large, especially to an almost disinterested League of Nations, forerunner to the more effective United Nations Organisation which came into being in 1945. Once Afrikaner nationalism triumphed in the 1948 election and the National Party came to power, the scene was set for a confrontation of values, legal and otherwise, over its policy of racial separation and its consequent violation of basic human rights.

The Nationalist government girded its political loins, ready for a policy of confrontation against its antagonists both within the country and in the international arena. The basic notion of the rule of law, a principle of law accepted throughout the world, with its emphasis on human rights, was unacceptable to the Nationalists. The post-1948 period was a time in which the Nationalist government enacted a maze of legislation, much of it repressive, to give legal force to its ideology of racial separation. When the Universal Declaration of Human Rights was adopted in 1948 by the General Assembly of the United Nations, South Africa persisted in its policy of racial separation. Attempts by the international community to have South Africa adhere to the human rights requirements contained in the Universal Declaration failed. The South African government had no interest in the pursuit of equality. In fact, prior to 1948, newspapers supporting the Nationalists actually published a draft constitution based on the ideology of separation and inequality. The draft was never adopted though it may well have provided guidelines for the party ideologues to follow.

There was an important period during the 1950s when the government began a process of constitutional changes to remove the 'coloured' population from the voters' roll in the Cape Province. It was quite clear from the process used that little consideration was given to the rights of people of colour. When first attempts were made to remove the coloured voters from the roll, the matter was referred to the Supreme Court as the ultimate protector of their rights. When the government saw that the courts, as they were constituted then, would and did support the view that the rights of coloured voters were protected by the constitution, they changed the law. That is, they introduced a Bill which created the High Court of Parliament. Consequently, the Appellate Division of the Supreme Court was packed with pro-separationists and the notorious Bill was accepted. This legal process in effect removed the right of judicial review from the courts, giving Parliament, and thereby the government, the ultimate right to pass or review legislation as it saw fit. Clearly this placed the government above the law with regard especially to human rights in particular.

According to one authority (Butler *et al* 1987) the government laid little emphasis on the accepted notion of the rule of law, particularly with regard to human rights. A sizeable number of writers, academics and judicial proponents of government policy published books and articles defending the policy of racial separation and the legislation introduced to implement this policy in every walk of life in South Africa. According to Professor John Dugard (Butler *et al* 1987), the Department of Foreign Affairs published a document entitled *South Africa and the Rule of Law* in 1968 outlining the government's views on the rule of law and, consequently, their views on human rights. There were a number of points raised in this document and for purposes of this study, they shall be reviewed below.

(a) The rule of law was viewed in the context of the writings of Dicey and other British constitutional lawyers. These suggest that the notion of the rule of law is a political and not a judicial notion. A number of judicial writers in South Africa at the time (*circa* 1956) argued that the notion or principle of the rule of law did not originate in the legal or judicial system, but was part and parcel of the political process and therefore was within the ambit of politicians rather than the judiciary. Among those holding these views were such persons as J P Verloren van Themaat, Professor of Law at the University of Pretoria, who, according to John Dugard (1987), produced the first constitutional text in Afrikaans. Verloren van Themaat argued that such ideas as 'personal freedom, equality before the law, trial by independent and impartial courts' were not traditionally part of the judicial process, but reflected a wish by the protagonists of the rule of law that Parliament should not infringe the rights and liberties of individuals. According to the same source (Dugard 1975 *in* Butler *et al* 1987) a similar view was advanced by Mr Justice J H Snyman, who held the view that the 'rule of law' as such was a political tool rather than a notion rooted within the legal process.

(b) The second point made in the document suggested that the principle of the rule of law originated in the humanistic approach to life, a view contrary to Calvinist philosophy. The point is clearly illustrated by F Venter of the Potchefstroom University for Christian Higher Education. He made the following comment (Butler *et al* 1987) that the rule of law was based on

'the broad fundamental humanistic assumption of human rights. (And) since the South African state is based on the Sovereignty of God, which stands in radical opposition to the humanistic point of departure, it follows that the rule of law and for that matter any doctrine of human rights, has no place in South Africa.'

During the period in which the 1983 Tricameral Parliament Bills passed through Parliament, the President's Council opposed the inclusion of a Bill of Rights on the basis that it was contrary to the Calvinist approach. The Council argued that the strong emphasis on human rights challenged the authority of the State which was one of the pillars upon which the Calvinist White South African rested.

(c) Thirdly, the document issued by the Department of Foreign Affairs argued that legal rules and the 'rule of law' were in effect the same practice. The argument proceeded by stating that the rule of law principle was monitored as long as any political organisation, such as the State, used the correct constitutional procedure to enact and put into effect any law, regardless of whether such law was contrary to human rights or was

generally repressive. The document went on to state:

'The rule of law may mean different things to different people, but there is general agreement that it requires that a person on trial be accused in open court; be given an opportunity of denying the charge and of defending himself and that he be given the choice of counsel. These rights are at all times assured by the South African courts.'

With this kind of judicial philosophy as a background, the government clearly indicated that it walked its own road with regard to the issue of human rights, choosing to ignore the internationally accepted conventions relating to human rights generally and personal freedom in particular.

The process of the erosion of the right of the courts to review legislation considered unconstitutional or contrary to natural justice began in earnest as early as 1910. The South Africa Act of 1910 made provision for the Cape Province to maintain a non-racial franchise on a qualified basis. The other provinces of South Africa did not favour this special dispensation for the Cape Province and in order to placate them, the 1910 Constitution made provision for changes to be effected by a two-thirds majority vote of both houses of Parliament sitting together. This constitutional provision was used success-fully against black voters (Africans) in 1936, who were removed from the common voters' roll. When the National Party came to power in 1948, they tried to remove the coloured voters from the roll in a similar fashion. However, on this occasion the government could not secure the necessary two-thirds majority in a joint sitting of Parliament. An attempt was made to remove the coloured voters by a separate sitting of the two houses of Parliament, namely the House of Assembly and the Senate.

In the classic case of *Harris v Minister of the Interior*, the Appellate Division of the Supreme Court ruled against the government, stating that the procedure was unconstitutional. Subsequently, the government attempted to remove the Supreme Court's power to test legislation by the introduction of the notion of the 'High Court of Parliament'. This tactic was also unsuccessful and the government was unable to get the required two-thirds majority of both houses sitting together by 1953. In 1954 Strijdom, the new Prime Minister, packed the Senate by increasing the number of pro-government senators and also increasing the number of Appellate Division judges from five to eleven. Many of the new appointees were favourable towards the government. This time, as a result of these new procedures, the government was able to remove the coloured people from the common votors' roll when the newly constituted Appellate Division ruled the process constitutional in 1957. A year earlier, the National Party had passed a law which excluded the courts from being able to test the legislation passed by Parliament. This process neutralised the courts' authority and vested the National Party with even greater arbitrary power over individuals and groups in South African society. Several prominent judges, among them Justice Albert van der Sandt Centlivres and Justice Olivier Deneys Schreiner, made their views regarding the undesirability of the process known and are on record as having protested strongly against the process used to remove the blacks and coloured persons from the voters' roll in the Cape Province.

As the erosion of personal and group liberty continued, the Progressive Party in 1962 set up a commission comprised of a group of experts to monitor human rights violations and to make recommendations concerning the protection of human rights. One of the main recommendations of the commission was that a Bill of Rights enforceable by the judiciary should be brought into being. This was accepted as party policy by the Progressive Party and the subsequent forms it took over the years. A number of prominent South African judges also supported the move to introduce a Bill of Rights.

Meanwhile, a wide range of people and organisations argued that the rule of law was being eroded and that repressive legislation being passed by the National Party majority in Parliament was in conflict with international standards of justice. Some of the repressive legislation included discretionary powers being vested in government officials, detention without trial and a whole host of legislation that infringed upon the rights of people of colour. The legal system was also criticised by human rights activists, who suggested that in many instances race and security laws were being interpreted in favour of the government, thereby violating one of the main tenets of Roman-Dutch law that ambiguous legislation be interpreted in favour of individual 'liberty and equality'.

Despite these negative developments, Afrikaner Nationalist viewpoints regarding human rights and liberties began to change. One of the proponents of a change of attitude was the Minister of Foreign Affairs, R F 'Pik' Botha, who in a 1970 speech called for the acceptance of the basic principle contained in the Universal Declaration of Human Rights. At the opening of Parliament in 1986, the former State President, Mr P W Botha, said (Butler *et al* 1987):

> 'We believe in the sovereignty of the law as a basis for the protection of the fundamental rights of individuals as well as groups. We believe in the sanctity and indivisibility of law and the just application thereof. There can be no peace, freedom and democracy without law. Any future system must conform with the requirements of a civilised legal order, and must ensure access to the courts and equality before the law. We believe that human dignity, life, liberty and property of all must be protected, regardless of race, colour, creed or religion.'

Having made the above declaration, however, the government continued to use laws that adversely affected individual liberty. However, the government did ask the Law Commission (1986) to investigate how the courts could become more active in protecting human rights. The government also asked the Law Commission to assess the desirability of introducing a Bill of Rights for South Africa. Changes were beginning to take place on several fronts within the ranks of Afrikanerdom generally, and the government in particular. A number of prominent Afrikaners (Butler *et al* 1978) began calling for changes both from within and outside the Government. Johan van der Vyver, a prominent Afrikaans academic, published the first text on human rights in Afrikaans in 1975, calling for the inclusion of a Bill of Rights for South Africa. Another prominent Afrikaner, D P de Villiers, the leader of the South African legal team that successfully argued South Africa's case in the International Court of Justice over the South West Africa issue, called for a review of legislation that threatened human rights, particularly security legislation. A number of Afrikaans academics called for a change in which the law would become the protector of human rights. Numerous other prominent Afrikaners in the legal profession and other leading members of the community have had a crucial role in prompting the government to accept the inclusion of a Bill of Rights in the Constitution for a new South Africa. Recently, a Draft Bill of Rights was published (see Appendix).

IMPORTANT CHARACTERISTICS
OF HUMAN RIGHTS

The issue of human rights is not a new one and has its roots in the early history of mankind. Most societies in the world are rooted in some form of philosophy, religious tradition or philosophical and juristic principle based upon human rights. However, different societies have different norms and values and may therefore have diverse opinions about what constitutes human rights. There are a number of societies that base their human rights criteria on the rights of the individual, while others lay emphasis upon the rights of the group, such as a tribe, religious group, clan, local community, a province or a state or any other group that may emerge in the human interaction process.

Since human societies differ from each other in many respects, it is possible that their interpretation of what constitutes human rights and how to apply these principles may differ. However, an attempt has been made to reconcile these differences, which led to the standardisation of a number of human rights through the Universal Declaration of Human Rights of 1948. The Declaration was brought into existence by the 14-member UN Commission on Human Rights and is dealt with in detail in an earlier chapter. Because of the incredible atrocities of World War II, especially the Holocaust (the killing of more than six million Jews by Hitler) the UN Declaration attempts to maintain strict adherence to the code included therein.

According to McQuoid-Mason *et al* (1991), there are a number of rights which citizens of a country should be aware of. These include legal rights, moral rights and human rights.

LEGAL RIGHTS

These are rights that are encoded either in some written or unwritten laws and can be defended in a country's law courts. There are a number of societies where legal rights are not written down or codified, but are traditionally accepted laws, norms and values relating to the protection of the rights of the individual or group. In a number of societies, legal rights are regarded as 'moral' simply because they are part of a codified system of laws. Many of these laws, as in the case of a number of apartheid laws, were not really moral and were in fact considered immoral by a vast majority of the population, especially as most of them discriminated against people on the basis of their colour, race or culture. Taking these factors into consideration, it seems reasonable to argue that human rights should be protected by a properly designed Bill of Rights which should, in turn, be codified or be part of the constitution of the country concerned. Individuals or groups would then have the protection of the law or be able to have legal recourse if their rights are violated by the state, or any other political-administrative organisation.

MORAL RIGHTS

Moral rights often differ from legal rights in that the latter are based on principles of a religious or philosophical nature. Moral rights are more often than not tied to belief systems other than the religious or philosophical. Often these are cultural and traditional beliefs which can be construed as being moral because they are based on long-accepted norms and values, especially in the tribal, clan or other traditional cultural groups. Moral 'truths' may often be the subject of divergent opinion and even disagreement among people, for example, concerning the use of certain drugs, such as alcohol. People of the Muslim faith hold firmly to the belief that alcohol is evil and may not be consumed by the adherents of this faith. Christian fundamentalist churches also have a negative attitude towards the consumption of alcohol by their members.

HUMAN RIGHTS

According to McQuoid-Mason (1991), human rights are 'universal moral rights'. That is, they are evolved from the natural rights of man generally and are accepted, in one form or another, by all human beings. 'They do not have to be earned, bought, or inherited!' These rights are ascribed and are the right of any individual by virtue of birth and apply equally to all of mankind without regard to race, colour, creed, language or any other such criterion. Human rights are accepted normally by all people, even though the society in which they are resident may not have a bill of rights or may, for some discriminatory reason, not subscribe to the principles of justice.

To many people, some human rights are more important that others. Sometimes it may happen that one group of people may consider a particular human right as no right at all. A good example is the issue of abortion. Roman Catholics and a number of other groups believe in the right to life; others believe that abortion should be performed on demand and that the woman concerned has the right to terminate her pregnancy if she so wishes.

There are a number of other rights which are important and form part of the greater spectrum of rights. These include the categories of civil and political rights, social and economic rights, and environmental, cultural and development rights (McQuoid-Mason et al 1991). Each of these will be dealt with separately below.

CIVIL AND POLITICAL RIGHTS

These rights are rooted in the traditions of liberty, fraternity and equality and are assumed to be basic rights of all individuals and groups. They include the right to political liberty, involving the right to freedom of speech, freedom of association, freedom to participate in legal political activity, freedom to vote and the right to vote freely for a candidate of one's choice. There are a number of other such rights, but the above-mentioned rights suffice as indicators of civil and political rights.

SOCIAL AND ECONOMIC RIGHTS

These rights are known as security-orientated rights, and include such important basic rights as the right to food, shelter and health care. Employment needed to provide such basic rights could also fall under this category of human rights.

ENVIRONMENTAL, CULTURAL AND DEVELOPMENT RIGHTS

According to McQuoid-Mason *et al* (1991), these rights include the right of people to live in areas that are free from industrial and other pollution. Under this category of human rights, people have the right to develop their cultural, political and economic potential generally. These rights, referred to as 'third generation rights' can also be seen as 'group rights'. That is, groups of people (as well as individuals) do have the need for their political, social and economic rights to be protected.

CHAPTER 3

TRADE UNION RIGHTS:
A SOUTH AFRICAN PERSPECTIVE

There are many South African trade unions, from a variety of political and economic opinions and steeped in a variety of ideologies. These include groups under the banners of the Congress of South African Trade Unions, (COSATU), The National Council of Trade Unions (NACTU), The South African Confederation of Labour (SACOL) and a number of other smaller movements. By far one of the biggest trade union organisations in the country is COSATU, comprising those trade unions under the umbrella of the Congress of South African Trade Unions. All trade unions function in terms of constitutions or charters which define their beliefs, ideologies and goals. Workers' rights are the prime concern of trade unions; it is therefore important to note the rights they stipulate for workers. A COSATU pamphlet lists these rights under seven basic categories, as follows:

1. *BASIC WORKER RIGHTS*
   (a) The right to join trade unions.
   (b) The right to a living wage.
   (c) The right to social security.
   (d) The right to education, training and skills upgrading.
   (e) The right to job security.
   (f) The right to work/full employment/job creation.
   (g) The right to healthy and safe working conditions.
   (i) Other rights.

2. *TRADE UNION RIGHTS*
(a) The right to bargain collectively.
(b) The right to determine the bargaining levels and bargaining issues.
(c) The right to strike (which includes the following sub-rights):
   (i)   The right to sympathy strikes.
   (ii) The right to picket.
   (iii) The right to job security while on strike.
   (iv) The right to protection against employers taking on scabs.
   (v)   The right to a strike fund.
(d) The right to appoint judges to the industrial court.

(e) The right to negotiate all laws affecting workers.

(f) The right to represent workers to state administrative bodies on labour issues.

3. PARENTAL AND RECREATIONAL RIGHTS

(a) Rights relating to workers enjoying family life.

(b) Social facilities for workers to enjoy their recreation.

4. WOMEN WORKERS' RIGHTS

(a) What women workers' rights should the workers' charter have in relation to:
    (i) Wages and upgrading.
    (ii) Education, training and skills upgrading.
    (iii) Job security.
    (iv) Taxation.
    (v) Sexual harassment.
    (vi) Contraception.
    (vii) Others.

(b) How must trade unions, worker political parties, all other mass organisations, employers and the state correct irregularities based on sex?

(c) How can we ensure all workers have equal rights and equal opportunities, regardless of race, sex and creed?

5. POLITICAL RIGHTS

(a) What political rights should workers have?

(b) Should trade unions be independent of the state and political parties?

(c) Should the state have any say in the running and control of trade unions?

(d) Should trade unions have the right to differ from the state?

(e) Should the state have powers to reverse/suspend worker rights, eg during a state of emergency?

(f) What access/control should trade unions have to all forms of media?

6. RIGHTS FOR ECONOMIC PLANNING

(a) What rights should workers have in a mixed economy, in managing private and state-owned companies?

(b) What rights and support should be given to co-operatives?

(c) What role should trade unions play in relation to economic planning at local, regional and national level?

7. RELATIONSHIP BETWEEN THE WORKER'S CHARTER AND THE CONSTITUTION

(a) Should the workers' charter be part of the constitution, or a separate

document?

(b) What should be the status of a workers' charter in a post-apartheid South Africa?

(NOTE: The above document was issued as a questionnaire by the Congress of South African Trade Unions, COSATU. The numerical presentation has been altered by the writer.)

When one studies this document a number of important issues come to the fore. The first is the extensive coverage given by COSATU to an array of rights, transcending mere work-related rights and dealing with almost all categories of rights that can affect the lives of workers. These include political rights, women's rights with regard to the workplace and the right of the worker to be part and parcel of socio-economic factors outside the normal scope of shop-floor activities. This is an indication of a broader vision for the rights of workers in the body-politic and hence involves the trade unions in quests for comprehensive rights, most of which originate in such documents as the Human Rights Charter. The document also seems to be linked to many of the rights that worldwide organisations such as the International Labour Organisation ILO attempts to secure for workers in all countries.

Another organisation that has stipulated workers' rights by way of a charter is the South African Communist Party (SACP). The draft Workers' Charter, which calls, *inter alia* for a number of rights for workers as a group and the worker as an individual. These include the following:

1.   THE RIGHT AND DUTY TO WORK FOR A LIVING WAGE

This really comprises several rights. Every adult worker has both the right and the duty to work and to be remunerated accordingly. It is strongly suggested that the state has the duty to create economic conditions conducive to full employment. It also stresses that the state must support unemployed workers and their families. There must be equal access to jobs, regardless of race, colour or creed. Another right claimed under this category is the state's duty to enforce a minimum wage in consultation with trade unions. Child labour and enforced or semi-forced labour is also forbidden.

2.   THE RIGHT TO ORGANISATION AND STRUGGLE

Under this heading, the SACP affirms the right of workers to organise themselves into political parties and/or trade unions. It states further that 'Trade union organisation shall be based on the principles of ''one industry, one union'' and ''one country, one federation'' (Bendix 1991). It also affirms that workers in all sectors of the economy shall have the right, through the mediation of the trade union, to engage in the collective bargaining process to achieve their aims, and the right to strike as a means of securing their goals.

3. THE RIGHT TO MEDIA ACCESS

Workers claim the right to be heard, either through the existing media or through newly worker-related sections of the media.

4. THE RIGHT TO FAMILY LIFE AND SOCIAL FACILITIES

With specific reference to South African society, no legislation may be passed that will interfere with the right of workers to enjoy a normal family life. The Charter also calls for the phasing out and eventual removal of the migratory labour system.

5. THE RIGHT TO HEALTH AND SAFETY

Work conditions must be as such that the 'health, safety and wellbeing' of workers shall not be threatened, nor should workers be subject to environmental risks that may impair their health. Workers must also be entitled to annual and sick leave and any worker injured while at work should be entitled to just compensation.

6. THE RIGHT TO SECURITY IN OLD AGE

Workers in general should be entitled to a sufficient pension upon retirement. An adequate pension should be paid to retired workers either by the state or the private company which employed the workers concerned.

7. THE RIGHTS OF WOMEN WORKERS

Women should be fully integrated into the economic system of the society. All forms of discrimination against women must be avoided and women's rights with regard to 'job allocation, wages, working conditions, training and other benefits in general' must be respected. Women should also have the right to education in order to be able to compete for and acquire all jobs for which they are qualified.

The Draft Workers' Charter of the South African Congress of Trade Unions also claims a number of rights for workers. It is important to look at the details of these rights both for general insight and for comparative purposes. This Charter claims the following rights for workers:

(a) All workers have the right to work.

(b) All workers have the right to freedom of movement, assembly and speech.

(c) All workers have the right to live with their families in decent housing near their place of work.

(d) All workers have equality of opportunity.

(e) Workers shall have the unconditional right to strike in support of their demands.

(f) Workers shall be paid a wage which enables them to satisfy the

minimum needs of their families.

(g) Workers have the right to free medical care, sick leave, annual leave and women workers shall be guaranteed the right to return to their jobs at the same rate of pay after maternity leave.

(h) There shall be a maximum eight-hour working day.

(i) Unemployed workers shall be the responsibility of the state.

(j) All workers shall be eligible for retirement with full pension.

(k) Health and safety shall be guaranteed.

(l) Women workers shall have the right to participate in all sectors of the economy without discrimination.

(m) All racist labour legislation shall be outlawed, including the racist Labour Relations Amendment Act.

(n) All workers shall have full political rights.

PART 7

MAJOR MOVEMENTS IN THE HUMAN RIGHTS STRUGGLE IN SOUTH AFRICA

CHAPTER 1

THE AFRICAN NATIONAL CONGRESS
OF SOUTH AFRICA

INTRODUCTION

The African National Congress of South Africa (ANC) was founded on 8 January 1912 in Bloemfontein, Orange Free State. At the time, the ANC was named the South African Native National Congress and changed to its present name in 1923.

The first President of the ANC was John Dube, the then leader of the National Native Congress, and the General Secretary was Sol Plaatjie, an activist from the African People's Organisation based mainly among the 'coloured' people. At its foundation, the ANC was primarily an organisation that promoted the interests of a professional African middle class, such as doctors, teachers, lawyers, businessmen and those of similar status. It was opposed to racial discrimination and attempted to gain rights and liberties for Africans generally. The ANC was always opposed to tribalism and subsequently developed into an organisation transcending race, colour, creed and gender. From the outset, it had a policy of peaceful protest, using mainly the process of lobbying for rights.

One of the first major protest campaigns undertaken by the ANC was against the 1913 Land Act, which effectively deprived blacks of the right to own land outside the reserves (homelands) created for them by whites. The ANC campaign was not successful, but protests continued during the course of World War I. After the war, the leadership of the ANC passed into the hands of a more radical element, based mainly in the Transvaal. The Transvaal leadership was more militant. By this time (1918 to 1920), the ANC still had a small membership, but was on the verge of becoming a mass-based organisation. The movement backed Witwatersrand mineworkers in pre-strike action during 1920.

Moves were afoot within the ANC to make it more militant, both in its philosophy and in its mode of protest. The President-General of the ANC in the period after 1920, J T Gumede, attempted to introduce radicalism into the movement. However, he was not successful, partly because of the ANC's association with the Communist Party of South Africa. The more 'nationalist' members of the ANC were still very powerful within the movement and consequently Gumede was ousted in 1930.

By the 1940s, the movement began to appeal to the masses, thus becoming a broadly based organisation. During World War II and its aftermatch, black political consciousness increased tremendously and with it the membership of the ANC. In 1943 it adopted a new constitution and a new programme of action aimed at securing full political rights for all. Another important development in 1943 was the formation of the Congress Youth League, which had a radical policy, demanding strikes, boycotts and other forms of protest such as civil disobedience. In 1949 the ANC adopted a radical line at a time when Parliament passed the Suppression of Communism Act, through which the state was able to silence the protest activity of several organisations at the time. Another development arising out of the promulgation of the Suppression of Communism Act was the decision by the SACP to disband, though Communist Party members continued working within the ANC.

A landmark decision was taken by the ANC to launch the 1952 Defiance Campaign whose aim was to protest against unjust laws. The Defiance Campaign was also a means of allowing the masses to participate in political action. The number of fully paid-up members of the movement stood at a little over 100 000 at the time. It was at this time, too, that the Congress Alliance was formed. This alliance consisted of the ANC, the South African Indian Congress, the Coloured People's Congress, the Congress of Democrats (a white organisation) and the trade union group, SACTU.

In 1953, the Alliance decided to call a Congress of the People, whose task would be to draw up a Freedom Charter for South Africa. The congress was the brainchild of Professor Z K Mathews, one of the members of the ANC hierarchy. It took place two years later, in June 1955, near the township of Kliptown, outside Johannesburg. It lasted only two days and was then broken up by police action. However, the Freedom Charter was adopted at this congress and has become the most important ideological and philosophical document of the ANC. In 1956, 156 delegates to the Congress of the People were charged with treason. The trial lasted five years and ended with the charges being dropped.

The essential elements of the Freedom Charter were:

(a) The reaffirmation of the multiracial nature of South African society.

(b) Equal status for all 'national groups'.

(c) Welfare provisions.

(d) Equal opportunities for all.

(e) The nationalisation of the mines, banks and monopoly industries.

It was at this time that a rift began to develop in the ANC, with an Africanist faction led by Robert Sobukwe, charging that the movement had betrayed the cause of black people. This faction contended that the ANC was in pursuit of a left-wing and communist-orientated class-struggle programme.

In November 1958 the Sobukwe-led faction broke away from the ANC to form the Pan Africanist Congress in 1959.

The year 1960 was a difficult year for the ANC. After the Sharpeville killings, when anti-pass-law protesters were shot by police, the government banned the organisation. The ANC felt that peaceful protest was not producing any result and consequently the organisation went underground. It was also in 1960 that the armed wing of the ANC, Umkhonto we Sizwe (Spear of the Nation), was formed in collaboration with the Communist Party of South Africa. The armed struggle policy was adopted and Nelson Mandela became Commander-in-Chief of Umkhonto we Sizwe.

A campaign of sabotage was started, but this did not last long. The police arrested a number of the leaders of Umkhonto we Sizwe at Lilies farm, Rivonia. Most of the leaders, including Nelson Mandela, Walter Sisulu, Govan Mbeki and others, were sentenced to life imprisonment. Once these leaders were jailed, the ANC increased its external activities and joined forces with other organisations with similar activities in their own countries. These included such organisations as SWAPO of Namibia and the Zimbabwe African People's Union (ZAPU).

The 1976 Soweto uprising prompted thousands of young people to flee South Africa and join up at a number of external missions of the ANC. Inside the country, dramatic changes began to take place, with demands being made on government by black people. In response, the government attempted to reform the apartheid system, but to no avail. The few changes it made were perceived to be cosmetic and were unacceptable to the masses. As anti-apartheid organisations' activities increased, so did the state's repression. It was in the aftermath of the 1976 Soweto uprising that black workers began to make demands for better conditions through the South African Council of Trade Unions (SACTU) and other channels. Externally, the ANC was being accepted and assisted by several sympathetic black countries as well as nations in Europe and elsewhere.

Within South Africa, the 1980s and early 1990s brought some dramatic changes. Organisations such as the United Democratic Front (UDF) were founded and began mass protests to demand the freeing of the ANC's leaders, as well as all political prisoners and activists. The 'Release Mandela' campaign gained momentum, until he was released in February 1990 upon the unbanning of all banned organisations. Since then, the ANC has become one of the main players on the South African political scene. Currently, it is one of several organisations that are attempting to resolve the constitutional crisis in the hope of establishing a new democratic system in South Africa.

The ideology and philosophy of the ANC is best summed up in the Freedom Charter, which was adopted by the Congress of the People on 26 June 1955. The Charter is reproduced below.

THE FREEDOM CHARTER

PREAMBLE

We, the people of South Africa, declare for all our country and the world to know:

That South Africa belongs to all who live in it, black and white, and that no government can justly claim authority unless it is based on the will of the people;

That our people have been robbed of their birthright to land, liberty and peace by a form of government founded on injustice and inequality;

That our country will never be prosperous or free until all our people live in brotherhood, enjoying equal rights and opportunities;

That only a democratic state, based on the will of the people, can secure to all their birthright without distinction of colour, race, sex or belief;

And therefore, we the people of South Africa, black and white, together as equals, countrymen and brothers adopt this FREEDOM CHARTER. And we pledge ourselves to strive together, sparing nothing or our strength and courage, until the democratic changes here set out have been won.

THE PEOPLE SHALL GOVERN!

Every man and woman shall have the right to vote for and stand as a candidate for all bodies which make laws;

All the people shall be entitled to take part in the administration of the country;

The rights of the people shall be the same regardless of race, colour or sex;

All bodies of minority rule, advisory boards, councils and authorities shall be replaced by democratic organs of self-government.

ALL NATIONAL GROUPS SHALL HAVE EQUAL RIGHTS!

There shall be equal status in the bodies of state, in the courts and in the schools for all national groups and races;

All national groups shall be protected by law against insults to their race and national pride;

All people shall have equal rights to use their own language and to develop their own folk culture and customs;

The preaching and practice of national, race or colour discrimination and contempt shall be a punishable crime;

All apartheid laws and practices shall be set aside.

THE PEOPLE SHALL SHARE IN THE COUNTRY'S WEALTH!

The national wealth of our country, the heritage of all South Africa, shall be restored to the people;

The mineral wealth beneath the soil, the banks and monopoly industry shall be transferred to the ownership of the people as a whole;

All other industries and trades shall be controlled to assist the well-being of the people;

All people shall have equal rights to trade where they choose, to manufacture and to enter all trades, crafts and professions.

THE LAND SHALL BE SHARED AMONG THOSE WHO WORK IT!

Restriction of land ownership on a racial basis shall be ended, and all the land re-divided amongst those who work it, to banish famine and land hunger;

The state shall help the peasants with implements, seed, tractors and dams to save the soil and assist the tillers;

Freedom of movement shall be guaranteed to all who work on the land;

All shall have the right to occupy land wherever they choose;

People shall not be robbed of their cattle, and forced labour and farm prisons shall be abolished.

ALL SHALL BE EQUAL BEFORE THE LAW!

No one shall be imprisoned, deported or restricted without fair trial;

No one shall be condemned by the order of any government official;

The courts shall be representative of all the people;

Imprisonment shall be only for serious crimes against the people, and shall aim at re-education, not vengeance;

The police force and army shall be open to all on an equal basis and shall be the helpers and protectors of the people;

All laws which discriminate on the grounds of race, colour or belief shall be repealed.

ALL SHALL ENJOY HUMAN RIGHTS!

The law shall guarantee to all their right to speak, to organise, to meet together, to publish, to preach, to worship and to educate their children;

The privacy of the house from police raids shall be protected by law;

All shall be free to travel without restriction from countryside to town, from province to province, and from South Africa abroad;

Pass laws, permits and all other laws restricting these freedoms shall be abolished.

THERE SHALL BE WORK AND SECURITY!

All who work shall be free to form trade unions, to elect their officers and to make wage agreements with their employers;

The state shall recognise the right and duty of all to work, and to draw full unemployment benefits;

Men and women of all races shall receive equal pay for equal work;

There shall be a forty-hour working week, a national minimum wage, paid annual leave, and sick leave for all workers, and maternity leave on full pay for all working mothers;

Miners, domestic workers, farm workers and civil servants shall have the same rights as all others who work;

Child labour, compound labour, the tot system and contract labour shall be abolished.

THE DOORS OF LEARNING AND CULTURE SHALL BE OPENED!

The government shall discover, develop and encourage national talent for the enhancement of our cultural life;

All the cultural treasures of mankind shall be open to all, by free exchange of books, ideas and contact with other lands;

The aim of education shall be to teach the youth to love their people and their culture, to honour human brotherhood, liberty and peace;

Education shall be free, compulsory, universal and equal for all children;

Higher education and technical training shall be opened to all by means of state allowances and scholarships awarded on the basis of merit;

Adult illiteracy shall be ended by a mass state education plan;

Teachers shall have all the rights of other citizens;

The colour bar in cultural life, in sport and in education shall be abolished.

THERE SHALL BE HOUSES, SECURITY AND COMFORT!

All people shall have the right to live where they choose, to be decently housed, and to bring up their families in comfort and security;

Unused housing space to be made available to the people;

Rent and prices shall be lowered, food plentiful and no one shall go hungry;

A preventative health scheme shall be run by the state;

Free medical care and hospitalisation shall be provided for all, with special care for mothers and young children;

Slums shall be demolished and new suburbs built where all shall have transport, roads, lighting, playing fields, crèches and social centres;

The aged, the orphans, the disabled and the sick shall be cared for by the state;

Rest, leisure and recreation shall be the right of all;

Fenced locations and ghettos shall be abolished and laws which break up families shall be repealed.

THERE SHALL BE PEACE AND FRIENDSHIP!
South Africa shall be a fully independent state, which respects the rights and sovereignty of all nations;

South Africa shall strive to maintain world peace and the settlement of all international disputes by negotiation not war;

Peace and friendship amongst all our people shall be secured by upholding the equal rights, opportunities and status of all;

The people of the protectorates Basutoland (now Lesotho), Bechuanaland (now Botswana) and Swaziland shall be free to decide for themselves their own future;

The right of all the peoples of Africa to independence and self-government shall be recognised, and shall be the basis of close co-operation.

Let all who love their people and their country now say, as we say here:

'These freedoms we will fight for, side by side, throughout our lives, until we have won our liberty'.

THE PAN AFRICANIST CONGRESS
OF AZANIA

The Pan Africanist Congress of South Africa (Azania) was formed when Robert Sobukwe broke away from the ANC. He took with him the more militant members of the ANC, whose political ideology was based on 'Africanism'. The breakaway took place in 1959.

The philosophy of Africanism provides for Africans working out their own destiny without assistance or interference from persons of other races, particularly whites. The doctrine of Africanism was first propounded within the ANC. The organisation's Youth League was formed soon afterwards. The Africanist element in the ANC, particularly the Youth League, became disenchanted with the broader Congress Alliance in which the ANC operated. The Congress Alliance comprised groups from right across the political spectrum.

The PAC referred to the ANC Alliance as the 'Charterists', namely those organisations that subscribed to the 1955 Freedom Charter as their common basis for the struggle. The breakaway PAC members were opposed to what they termed 'the multi-racial liberalism' of the ANC. The breakaway faction even founded their own mouthpiece, the newspaper called *The Africanist*.

The launching Conference of the Pan Africanist Congress took place at Orlando, Soweto, and its first president was Robert Sobukwe. The National Secretary of the PAC was Potalke Leballo. Sobukwe's first address in his capacity at President of the PAC laid down the main principle upon which the organisation was founded. The basic tenets of the PAC were given as follows:

❑ The PAC believed in government by Africans for Africans.
❑ Whites could not be part of a PAC government of the future because as a result of their current favoured status, they could not identify with the proper aspirations of the African people.
❑ The nature of the state in the PAC's view would be an 'Africanist Socialist Democratic Order'.
❑ The PAC based its ideology generally on the principles laid down by the All-African Peoples' Organisation Conference, held in the Ghanian Capital, Accra, in December 1958.

One of the first campaigns mounted by the PAC was the 'Status Campaign' of 1959. The thinking behind this campaign was to demand courteous treatment of blacks in shops and other commercial organisations by whites. The campaign was also intended to give blacks a sense of pride in themselves and also to remove the 'slave mentality' of many blacks. It also encouraged blacks to be more assertive in their daily activities. The campaign was also conducted by *The Africanist,* which argued, through its columns, that the battle for status was more relevant than the ANC's campaign in the economic sphere.

The PAC also became active in the trade union movements. It formed its own trade union organisation, known as the Federation of Free African Trade Unions (FOFATUSA), in the middle of 1959, with the help of labour organisations in other countries. One of its first moves was to attack its sister organisation within the Congress Alliance, the South African Congress of Trade Unions (SACTU). However, the PAC-backed FOFATUSA organisation did not succeed as a worker's movement and became redundant.

There is some confusion as to which organisation was responsible for organising the anti-pass-law campaign. The ANC announced its plans to step up anti-pass-law activities on 16 March 1960. The PAC announced similar intentions on 21 March 1960. One of the great tragedies of South African history, the Sharpeville killings, took place when about 5 000 people gathered outside the Sharpeville police station to protest against the pass laws. Sixty-seven people were killed when police opened fire on the crowd. On 30 March 1960, the PAC and the ANC were both banned by the government and a state of emergency was declared. From that time on, the PAC went into exile. For a brief period, the PAC joined forces with the ANC, the South African Indian Congress and the South West African National Union (SWANU) with the intention of opposing the South African government.

After the 1960 banning order, the PAC formed a military wing, POQO, meaning 'ourselves', within South Africa. This organisation worked underground and began attacking a number of targets within South Africa. However, by 1963, the PAC underground structures within South Africa were disrupted by a number of internal disputes that caused problems within the organisation. In 1981, John Pokela was elected Chairperson of the PAC and began to work for its cohesion. He died in Harare, Zimbabwe in 1985 and was replaced by Mr Johnson Mlambo. The PAC was unbanned in 1990, along with the ANC and a number of other organisations. Its present President is Robben Island political prisoner and activist leader, Clarence Makwetu. The PAC has a military wing, the Azanian People's Liberation Army (APLA), which has been active in a number of centres in South Africa.

CHAPTER 3

THE BLACK CONSCIOUSNESS
MOVEMENT

The Black Consciousness Movement developed during the late 1960s and 1970s. It had numerous followers, especially among the black youth of South Africa. During the 1976 Soweto riots and immediately after, the BCM was a vast grouping made up of approximately 18 different organisations. Its activities were curtailed when, in October 1977, the government banned it and detained Steve Biko, its leader and charismatic ideologue. Steve Biko died while in police custody in September 1977. His description of black consciousness in 1972 was as follows (Williams & Hackland 1988):

> 'In South Africa, political power has always rested with white society. Not only have whites been guilty of being on the offensive, but, by skilful manoeuvres, they have managed to control the responses of the blacks to the provocation. Not only have they kicked the blacks, but they have also told him how to react to the kick. With painful slowness he is now beginning to show that he realises it is his right and duty to respond to the kick the way he sees fit .... The philosophy of Black Consciousness, therefore, expresses group pride and the determination by the blacks to rise and attain the envisaged self.'

The BCM excluded whites from its ranks and was an exclusively black organisation. A black person, as far as the BCM was concerned, was anyone who was not white. Thus Africans, Indians, Asians and coloured persons were considered black. This view is similar to that of the Pan Africanist Movement.

The philosophy behind the movement was based on blacks liberating themselves psychologically from the 'obedience syndrome' perpetuated by the white government and white society. The Africanist (PAC) philosophy of Africans freeing themselves is particularly pertinent to the Black Consciousness Movement. Another source of ideological infusion into the BCM was the black theology movement in the United States. This same theology was represented in South Africa by the University Christian Movement. Moreover, the BCM also believed that race, rather than class, was the major factor in determining the nature of the struggle against oppression.

One of the first movements to emerge from the BCM was the South African Students' Organisation (SASO) in 1969. SASO was predominantly a University Students' Organisation. Other BCM-affiliated organisations were formed, representing a wider spectrum of black society than merely the intelligentsia. One of these was the Black People's Convention (BPC), which had a philosophy of 'black commercialism'. A trade union, the Black Allied Worker's Union (BAWU) was also formed. However, neither the BPC nor the BAWU ever gained much grassroots support.

It has been suggested that the Black Consciousness Movement was not very effective. One authority (Nolutshangu 1983) argues to the contrary. He suggests that the Black Consciousness Movement played a key role in political events during a critical period of black protest against the apartheid system. He states:

'The evidence was provided by the events which began in Soweto on 16 June 1976 … in the relative ease with which the key organisations with which we associate the movement, SASO (the South African Student's Organisation), BPC (Black People's Convention) and BCP (Black Community Programmes), among others, were able to attract adherents in spite of severe measures taken against them …. The emergence of the Black Consciousness Movement was perhaps the single most important development in the internal politics of South Africa in the period 1967 to 1976.'

One of the affiliates of the BCM, the South African Student's Organisation (SASO) has in fact been very active for some time, particularly on university campuses. However, SASO as an activist movement has never attempted to replace such structures as the ANC, the PAC or any other movement as a political party. SASO defines itself as a supplementary movement to the main political actors, namely the ANC and PAC. It has never presented itself as an alternative political movement to the traditional ones, which at that time were headquartered in exile.

Another BCM offspring, the Black People's Convention, was founded in 1972. Its main aim was to spread the notion of black consciousness to the black community at large. Through the medium of 'Black Communalism' the BPC undertook several community projects, including literacy campaigns, health-related projects, cultural and other activities in order to create a 'self-help' consciousness among black people. One of the other activities of the BPC was the establishment of the Black Allied Worker's Union (BAWU). However, despite having about 40 branches, it did not flourish and was banned in 1977, along with other black consciousness movements.

CHAPTER 4

THE UNITED DEMOCRATIC FRONT

The United Democratic Front (UDF) was founded in Johannesburg in August 1983. The movement comprised about 30 anti-apartheid organisations, among them the Natal and Transvaal Indian Congresses. About 100 delegates came from all over South Africa for the founding meeting.

The UDF was the brainchild of Dr Allan Boesak, then President of the World Alliance of Reformed Churches. At its height, the UDF had more than 2 million members and about 700 organisations affiliated to it. The main tenet upon which the UDF was founded was its opposition to the tricameral system of Parliament instituted in 1983, which excluded blacks from participation. Boycotts of coloured and Indian elections were organised, resulting in a low percentage poll of between 20 % and 30 %. The UDF also undertook campaigns against the Black Local Authorities system sponsored and implemented by the government.

Although the UDF is now defunct, its campaigns at the time gave notice to the government that opposition to it could not be suppressed and that political rights would have to be given to all in South Africa unconditionally. The UDF as a mass movement was ideologically part of the tradition of the Congress Alliance and its philosophy was based on the pronouncements of the Freedom Charter. The UDF seemed at the time to be a sort of 'shadow ANC', even sporting the colours of the then banned movement.

Several leaders of the organisation were detained by police and security forces, but the organisation was not banned outright. In 1986, the UDF became an 'affected organisation' and could not receive money from overseas sources such as governments, private or public organisations or sympathetic individuals. At grassroots level, the UDF operated through street committees, established for the express purpose of reaching the masses and allowing them to participate in anti-apartheid activities.

The very structure of the UDF made it very difficult for the state apparatus to deal with it, the large number of organisations of which it was made up being a form of insurance against prohibitive government action. In addition, the leadership of the UDF was composed of several distinguished activists. These included such persons as Archie Gumede, Mrs Albertina Sisulu, Oscar Mpetha, Dr Allan Boesak, Mrs Winnie Mandela, Popo Molefe and Patrick 'Terror' Lekota. The UDF was disbanded after the release of Nelson Mandela and the unbanning of the ANC and other political movements in 1990.

CHAPTER 5

INKATHA YENKULULEKO YESIZWE

The Inkatha Movement was defined by its founders as a national cultural liberation movement. The movement's main founder, Dr Mangosuthu Gatsha Buthelezi, said at its inception in 1975 that its philosophy was basically cultural.

According to Maré & Hamilton (1987), Inkatha's constitution closely resembles that of the Zambian United National Independence Party (UNIP). In addition, the movement also adopted part of the structure of a previous Inkatha Movement of 1928, the Inkatha Ka Zulu, founded by Dr Buthelezi's uncle, King Solomon ka Dinzulu.

To gain some insight into the founding principles of Inkatha, it may be useful to examine a statement made by one of the movement's hierarchy. The then (1987) Secretary-General of Inkatha, Dr Oscar Dhlomo, said that Inkatha's constitution was derived from the Lusaka Manifesto of 1969, which was drawn up by 14 African states and subsequently adopted by the UN General Assembly. The Lusaka Manifesto was drawn up for, *inter alia*, the purpose of abolishing racial discrimination. It also called for all Southern African people to have the right to elect and take part in their own government.

The structure of Inkatha is as follows:

At the apex is the National Council, the policy-making body, consisting of about 300 members. Below that is the General Council and the Central Committee. The Central Committee is composed of members of the KwaZulu Legislative Assembly, who are also members of Inkatha. There are also representatives from the regions and from the Inkatha Brigades' Executive. Each affiliated organisation has a representative member on the Central Committee. The General Conference is composed of all members of the National Council, including a number of representatives of each branch of Inkatha throughout the country.

However, the Central Committee and the National Council are the highest policy-making bodies and delegate functions to a number of subcommittees (Maré & Hamilton 1987). These subcommittees include:

- ❏ the Defence and Security Committee;
- ❏ the Political, Constitutional, Legal and Foreign Affairs Committee;
- ❏ the Economic and Finance Committee;
- ❏ the Social and Cultural Committee;
- ❏ the Election, Publicity and Strategy Committee; and

❑ the Appointments and Disciplinary Committee.

In addition, there are a number of structures within Inkatha. Among these are the Inkatha Brigades. The Women's Brigade is particularly powerful and functions at the various branches of Inkatha throughout the country. The Women's Brigade's main function is to mobilise women in the struggle for both freedom and the objectives of Inkatha as an organisation.

The Youth Brigade of Inkatha functions along with the other national Inkatha branches and is charged with the task of upholding the 'gains made by the movement' (Maré & Hamilton 1987).

For a period prior to the unbanning of the other liberation movements in 1991, Inkatha did play a role in keeping the internal campaign for liberation going. However, its policy was one of non-violence and pressure on government to review its apartheid policy, in which respect it differed from the 'armed struggle' policies of the ANC and PAC. On numerous occasions, Inkatha made its general policy clear (Maré & Hamilton 1987).

> 'Inkatha's opposition to economic pressure against South Africa is based on a few simple arguments: first, that such measures are (or will be) ineffective, a view directly contradicted by the simultaneously held position that sanctions will ruin South Africa and leave a destroyed economy for a future black government to take over; second, that they will hurt black South Africans much more than they will whites or the state; third, that such measures have never been supported by Inkatha members or African people in general.'

Inkatha has undergone a number of changes over the years, but in principle has not deviated radically. Its current political thinking is along the lines of a federal system of government as an option for consideration by the constitution-makers of the country. Inkatha has also come under strong attack from other liberation movements for working within the system. Recently, it has embarked on a 'Natal option' policy and is therefore seen (right or wrongly) as a regionally based movement restricted mainly to predominantly Zulu-speaking Natal. Sadly, violent clashes have taken place and are still taking place in Natal and the Transvaal between Inkatha supporters and those who oppose its policy. Death, destruction of property and the maiming and injuring of people is still part of everyday life in Natal-KwaZulu. However, despite its detractors, Inkatha as both a cultural and political movement will play a role in the future dispensation in South Africa, even if that role is restricted to the Natal-KwaZulu region.

CHAPTER 6

LAWYERS FOR HUMAN RIGHTS

According to the publication *Rights* vol 3, November 1992, Lawyers for Human Rights was established in South Africa to serve the public. Its services are, however, available to individuals and groups who are the subject of alleged human rights violations. The Mission Statement of the movement explains its structure and the function in detail.

MISSION STATEMENT (LHR)

> Lawyers for Human Rights, established in 1979, has consistently worked to uphold and strengthen human rights associated with the Rule of Law and Administration of Justice and the protection of Fundamental Liberties in accordance with the Universal Declaration of Human Rights.
>
> In 1987, a full-time Directorate was instituted and a number of projects initiated in the areas of research; human rights education and promotion; the monitoring of infringements and campaigns lobbying for the protection and enforcement of fundamental human rights; and legal and quasi-legal assistance through litigation to victims of human rights abuses.'

LHR identifies with the International Human Rights Movement and has ongoing contact with international human rights groups by attending conferences and delivering papers worldwide.

LHR's objective is to represent the rights and interests of the individual and to ensure that its services are accessible to the oppressed. Currently, LHR has 13 regional offices operating effectively throughout the country. They are staffed by competent para-legals who work in conjunction with Regional Directors as well as the local regional committees of lawyers.

Officers operating in rural areas are located in Klerksdorp, western Transvaal, in Colesberg, Cape, in Umtata, Transkei and in Pietersburg, northern Transvaal. Recently, offices were established in Kimberley, the Boland, and Bophuthatswana.

The Lawyers for Human Rights is centralised, its structure having a National Council, with executive members, a National Directorate and offices in several regions of South Africa. Most of the appointees to the hierarchy of the organisation are from the legal profession. Regional Directors are appointed and are normally qualified attorneys or advocates of the Supreme Court. Below the Regional Directors are Regional Organisers, who are normally legally qualified, but need not necessarily be attorneys or advocates. At grassroots level are field workers who have some paralegal qualifications. They are normally assigned to the rural areas of South Africa. The regions provide such services as legal advice to individuals or groups who may feel that their rights have been infringed, for example, a person who may feel that he or she has been unfairly dismissed from employment. The regions also undertake human rights education courses, paralegal training workshops and other such projects. The structure of the organisation is set out in an appendix at the end of the book.

Lawyers for Human Rights also deal with other aspects of justice, including capital punishment, women's rights, environmental rights, socio-economic rights, prisoner abuse, equality in the administration of criminal justice, rural justice and access to justice for all. The movement also monitors judicial reform and the constitutional transition process. Indeed, the number of facets relating to human rights is too large to elaborate upon in this study.

CHAPTER 7

THE HUMAN RIGHTS COMMISSION
OF SOUTH AFRICA

INTRODUCTION

The Human Rights Commission (HRC) came into existence in 1988, follow-ing the banning of a number of anti-apartheid organisations in February of that year. One such organisation was the Detainees' Parents Support Com-mittee (DPSC), with an established reputation for monitoring and publicising human rights violations in South Africa. In response to the information vacuum created by the neutralisation of the DPSC, a group of organisations concerned with human rights decided to create the HRC, which was launched on 20 September 1988.

THE STRUCTURE OF THE HUMAN RIGHTS COMMISSION

The HRC is an independent organisation, not affiliated in any way to any political party or grouping. However, it makes its research findings available to any body, political or otherwise, which asks for them, including govern-ment agencies, and will co-operate with such bodies in any projects which the HRC believes will lead to the alleviation of human rights abuses.

The membership of the HRC has four components. At the core of its structure are the working groups, located in each regional centre, consisting of skilled full-time researchers assisted by part-time volunteers. Guiding the activities of the working groups are the management committees, drawn from members of the community of the area in which the working group is located. A great deal of importance is attached to this linkage with grassroots com-munities which bear the brunt of repression. The third component comprises the commissioners of the HRC, whose duty it is to act as spokespersons. They are elected at the AGM for a one-year term of office and are drawn from all regions. Finally, there are the subscribing organisations, national organisa-tions not affiliated to any political party, which are directly concerned with human rights issues and which subscribe to the objectives of the HRC.

THE OBJECTIVES OF THE HUMAN RIGHTS COMMISSION

At the outset, the stated objectives of the HRC were to monitor, and dissemi-nate information about, the observance or violation of human rights by the South African government. The yardstick for assessment is the Universal

Declaration of Human Rights adopted by the United Nations General Assembly in 1948. Special emphasis is laid on repression, defined by the HRC as actions perpetrated by the proponents and supporters of apartheid against its opponents and victims for the purpose of maintaining or defending the system of apartheid. The ultimate objective of the HRC is, of course, to make a contribution towards the total eradication of apartheid, a system which the international community has declared a crime against humanity.

THE ACTIVITIES OF THE ORGANISATION

The HRC gathers information from various sources, including community structures, lawyers, the media and the government itself. National coverage is assured by a network of collection points located in Johannesburg, Cape Town, Port Elizabeth and Durban.

The information is collated into a systematised format and disseminated in the form of publications of three general categories:

- Instant response (special alerts, special briefings, press statements);
- Regular reports (weekly, monthly, annually); and
- In-depth single-issue Reports (fact sheeets, special reports, articles).

Distribution of these publications is aimed, both nationally and internationally, at a wide audience of organisations and individuals concerned with human rights issues in South Africa. Means of dissemination include normal mail, electronic mail, fax and direct contact through conference briefings.

In addition to the distribution of publications, the HRC also appears before and submits evidence to bodies enquiring into human rights violations by the government and its agents and supporters. The HRC has not only participated in such enquiries within South Africa, but has also responded to requests from such international bodies as the United Nations, the Commonwealth, the Organisation of African Unity, Amnesty International, the Association of Western European Parliamentarians Against Apartheid and many others.

SERVICES PERFORMED BY THE HRC

The HRC offers up-to-date reports, information and in-depth analysis on all aspects of repression aimed at maintaining the dominance of apartheid-supporting forces in South Africa. This information is in constant demand by the media, the diplomatic corps, governments, political organisations, community organisations, church groups, trade unions and business groups, human rights organisations, solidarity groups and academic institutions.

The HRC also conducts briefings on specific issues for the media, diplomats and special interest groups. In addition, it is also available for making submissions to commissions and conferences on areas within its field of competence.

Finally, the HRC encourages communities affected by apartheid repression to use HRC services to draw attention to their plight.

PUBLICATIONS ISSUED

HRC publications are available on request to organisations and individuals who are able to indicate their interest in the issues of human rights violations and repression in South Africa. Such requests should be made in writing to the head office in Johannesburg. A charge may be made for distribution costs.

REGULAR PUBLICATIONS:
- ❑ *Weekly Repression Report* (fax only);
- ❑ *Human Rights Update* (monthly);
- ❑ *Area Repression Report* (monthly);
- ❑ *Monthly Summary Report* (fax only); and
- ❑ *Human Rights Review* (annually).

OCCASIONAL PUBLICATIONS:
- ❑ Press statements (fax only);
- ❑ Fact sheets;
- ❑ Special briefings; and
- ❑ Special reports.

NATIONAL OFFICES OF THE HRC
The offices of the HRC are located in the following centres:
Head Office/Transvaal TEL: (011) 403 4450/1
FAX: (011) 339 1422
P O Box 32723
BRAAMFONTEIN
2017

Natal TEL: (031) 305 9460
FAX: (031) 305 7380
Room 66 Ecumenical centre
20 St Andrews Street
DURBAN
4001

Eastern Province TEL: (041) 546 284
FAX: (041) 547 394
Room 502
Alfin House
Main Street
North End
PORT ELIZABETH
6001

Western Province TEL: (021) 474 767
FAX: (021) 474 744
Industria House
350 Victoria Road
SALT RIVER
7925
South Africa

(PROFILE, HRC 1992)

CHAPTER 8

THE HUMAN RIGHTS TRUST

The Human Rights Trust (HRT) was established in Port Elizabeth in 1986. At the time it was known as the Operation Real South Africa. The HRT is currently operating in the Eastern Cape Region only, although it does interact with other human rights groups throughout South Africa. Its two founders were the late Andrew Savage, then PFP Member of Parliament for Walmer, and Rory Riodan, who became its Director. According to an Annual Report (31 March 1990), its objectives are defined as follows:

'The Trust has the following objectives:

The Trust will concern itself with the identification of areas of deprivation or suffering as a result of discrimination by law, regulation, custom or practice and will verify such circumstances by thorough investigation and deal with them by publication and public education and the marshalling of whatever assistance individual cases or situations may require with a view to carrying out the principle objects of the Trust which are, in the public interest:

1. To provide assistance, comfort and relief without charge and in such manner as the Trustees may determine in their discretion, to any persons in South Africa irrespective of race, religion, gender, language or political affiliation:

1.1 who are deprived of human rights, dignity or worth in any manner whatsoever and arising from whatsoever cause;

2. To educate the public of South Africa in regard to human rights and to foster an awareness of and an interest in matters of and relating to human rights, in a systematic or formal way as the Trustees may determine in their discretion.'

The Human Rights Trust also runs a number of activities related to the pursuance of human rights, civil liberties and assistance programmes. According to a document released by the HRT (*Projects of the HRT* 1993), some of the functions and services of the organisation are given. They include the following projects:

1. The Port Elizabeth Human Rights Festival
The Human Rights Trust is seven years old in 1993, and will run its sixth annual Festival of Human Rights to celebrate this event.

The Festival is an ambitious undertaking, and each year it involves:

(i) a **Conference** on Human Rights issues;

(ii) human rights **Theatre** – the Festival has traditionally brought human rights theatre to Port Elizabeth's Opera House. Such performances receive massive attendance, and encourage many people, who would not otherwise be exposed to such ideas, to begin to wrestle with human rights topics;

(iii) a human rights **Film Festival** – 1992 brought to the public a festival of the finest South African human rights films. Previous festivals have brought to Port Elizabeth such films as *A World Apart*, *Mapansula*, etc, which would not have made the commercial circuit in Port Elizabeth;

(iv) a **Photographic Exhibition** – the Conference and film festivals have traditionally been accompanied by suitable photographic exhibitions;

(v) a **Child Art Competition** – in 1990, the Trust's festival was accompanied by an art competition, as well as a human rights essay competition. The Universal Declaration of Human Rights was circulated to thousands of South African schools, and entries inspired by it were encouraged; thousands were received, and suitable prizes awarded;

(vi) the **Andrew Savage Memorial Lecture**, begun in 1990, commemorates the founder of the Human Rights Trust and is an integral part of the Festival.

2. Education programme on rights issues

The HRT in conjunction with Lawyers for Human Rights, co-ordinates the Lawyers for Human Rights 'Human Rights for All' education programmes in the Eastern Cape.

3. Bursary fund

The HRT runs a bursary fund for black students at tertiary education level, and at present has about 25 such students at tertiary education institutions. The administration of this programme is enormously time-consuming, as all book accounts, etc are paid by the Trust.

4. National Peace Initiative, Human Rights Commission,
*   Alternative Monitoring Board*

Trust staffers are involved in the Eastern Cape branches of all of these projects.

5. Platforms for rights speakers

The HRT invites a range of speakers to address rights issues at universities, schools, etc, as well as providing staffers to do this all over South Africa and in other countries.

6. Marginalised youth

The Trust is involved in three projects in this regard. The Director is on the steering committee of both the JEP and the HSRC investigations in this regard, and is a Trustee of the Idayasa/Read Eastern Cape project for the rehabilitation and upliftment of Eastern Cape marginalised youth.

7. Socio-economic rights

The Trust co-ordinated a workshop in 1993 as part of the National Lobby Group programme on socio-economic rights, in an attempt to get consensus from human rights NGOs on how, or if, such measures should be constitutionalised before lobbying accordingly.

8. Development

Trust staffers are playing an important part as negotiators in and supporters of the Port Elizabeth One City Process. It is the Trust's belief that Port Elizabeth's black townships being taken over by a domocratically elected municipality with a properly functioning City Council is the quickest route to improvements in the lifestyle of the residents of black areas.

Further to this commitment, the Trust in 1992 organised a trip of 30 Eastern Cape municipal personalities to the USA, Germany, Russia and Switzerland, to learn about municipal government and to study transition and other relevant issues. The group included the Town Clerk, Director of Administration, City Treasurer and City Engineer of Port Elizabeth, as well as three DP Councillors and 22 people from ANC structures working in One City issue, headed by Thozamile Botha, Head of the ANC Local Government Department, and one-time Rivonia trialist, Raymond Mhlaba. The tour was a resounding success, and helped to give further impetus to the Eastern Cape's One City process.

The Trust is involved in a wide range of publications, including:

❑ *Monitor* magazine, a very widely circulated publication, covering political, economic, rights, constitutional and other issues pertinent to South Africa's transition. *Monitor* has been used as a teaching aid at most universities in South Africa and overseas.

❑ *Research* – Both coupled to *Monitor*, and independent of it, the Trust undertakes a variety of research programmes. These include the Eastern Cape's only door-to-door market-research programme in all communities on political and rights issues.

❑ *Occasional publications* – Many occasional publications are written by Trust staffers, ranging from chapters in books to journalistic articles.

National Human Rights Lobby

In 1990, the Human Rights Trust pioneered the conception of a South African

Human Rights Movement, open to all NGOs that:

(i) accept the Universal Declaration of Human Rights, and whose programmes are nowhere in conflict with the Universal Declaration; and

(ii) whose work is aimed at strengthening adherence to the clauses of the
Universal Declaration in South Africa.

There are well over 50 such organisations, and the HRT invited them to
begin the formation of a lobby group on human rights issues, to impact on the
writing of the new South African Constitution and Bill of Rights.

The first meeting of the group requested a set of principles on which to
base the lobby group's detailed proposals and a meeting of an invited
committee came up with the following guidelines:

1. The future South African Constitution and Bill of Rights should in all ways
be consistent with the Universal Declaration of Human Rights.

2. The issues on which controversy and disagreement can be expected
include the following:

(i) Second and Third Generation Rights – whether they should be
constitutionalised and, if so, how?

(ii) Affirmative Action – whether it should be constitutionalised and, if
so, how?

(iii) Quotas as mechanisms for constitutionalising affirmative action;

(iv) Capital Punishment – should it be prohibited?

(v) Abortion – should abortion on request be allowed?

(vi) Property rights and land rights – should they be constitutionalised,
and, if so, how?

(vii) Minority and group rights – what is meant by them, what is
legitimately to be constitutionalised and, if so, how?

(viii) Should rights issues be heard by ordinary courts, a special
division of the Appeal Court, a constitutional court, or other
mechanisms and if so, what and how?

(ix) Gay rights and rights to privacy – are they separate from other
personal rights?

(x) Freedom to dissociate – is it separate from the right to privacy?

(xi) Anti-discrimination measures, including hate speech.

The initiative moved to a full conference of the South African Human
Rights Movement, which was held in Port Elizabeth on 1 and 3 June 1992.
The conference was a resounding success. It was attended by 99 delegates
from 69 different human rights NGOs.

The above issues were extensively debated, a substantial report drafted
and returned to delegates for comment, beginning the process of obtaining
consensus on these important human rights issues. Equally importantly, two
committees were formed to carry the process further.

In 1993 this process continued, with workshops to aid the move towards consensus on the substantive rights issues and with the formation of a lobby group to present the groups proposal to the National Constitutional Forum.

Amnesty International

The HRT has received approval to begin founding Amnesty groups in South Africa, leading to the establishment of a full Amnesty International Region in South Africa. The Trust has hosted an Amnesty official on his visit to South Africa. This project is felt to be of inestimable value in getting ordinary South Africans involved in campaigns around rights issues, and should be a valuable tool for creating a rights climate.

Amnesty groups are up and running and the Trust is allowed to call this process an 'Amnesty Initiative'. All groups are non-racial, and the trust projects 20 groups nationwide by the end of 1993.

(HRT Document 1993)

CHAPTER 9

OTHER HUMAN RIGHTS MOVEMENTS
IN SOUTH AFRICA

THE BLACK SASH

This is a white women's organisation founded in 1955 with the express purpose of fighting apartheid in all its forms. It was originally founded as the Women's Defence of the Constitution League. It came to be called the 'Black Sash' because protesting women wore black sashes during the silent protest vigils. The black sash came to symbolise mourning for the lack of appropriate constitutional rights for people other than whites in South Africa.

One of the first protests it undertook was against the removal of 'coloured' people from the common voters' roll. The Black Sash became involved with the daily problems experienced by blacks in South Africa, establishing a network of advice offices throughout the country to help people experiencing problems related to the unjust racial laws in the country.

The Black Sash has ideologically supported the views expressed in the 1955 Freedom Charter. One of its other major activities was helping to establish the End Conscription Campaign (ECC) which protested against compulsory military service for white males in South Africa.

THE SOUTH AFRICAN INDIAN CONGRESS

The South African Indian Congress was formed in 1920 by the unification of the Natal Indian Congress, founded in 1894 by Mahatma Gandhi, and the Transvaal Indian Congress.

One of the most significant developments in the history of the SAIC was the pact signed with the ANC in 1947. As a member of this Congress Alliance, the South African Indian Council was involved in the 1952 Defiance Campaign, which led to a number of SAIC activists being imprisoned by the authorities. The SAIC participated as a full member of the Congress Alliance in the 1955 Congress of the People at Kliptown. Despite the fact that the organisation was banned by the state, some SAIC members were imprisoned and often harassed by the state apparatus.

One of the most eminent persons in the Congress movement, Mewa Ramgobin, re-established the then defunct Natal Indian Congress in 1971. One of its main aims was to oppose the establishment of the South African Indian Council by the government. As a consequence of the NIC campaign, only about 10 % of voters turned out in the 1981 elections for the pro-government Council. In 1983, the Transvaal Indian Congress was revived and took part in the UDF-led campaign against the apartheid system.

THE AZANIAN PEOPLE'S ORGANISATION (AZAPO)

The Azanian People's Organisation came into existence in May 1978. The previous year (1977) had seen the banning of the Black Consciousness Movements, thus leaving a political vacuum, which Azapo hoped to fill.

AZAPO's ideology is reflected in its motto: 'One People, One Azania.' The organisation was found attractive by the black intelligentsia, particularly in the main urban areas. The movement has moved beyond black consciousness, and until the unbanning of the major liberation movements, it subscribed to the notion of 'class struggle' as part of its strategy and philosophy.

The Azapo movement favoured trade union activity as a major element of its strategy of fighting for the rights of workers as a class. Azapo's role in the arena of the struggle for human rights has been strong, but is has met with strong opposition from the state.

THE PORT ELIZABETH BLACK CIVIC ORGANISATION (PEBCO)

The Port Elizabeth Black Civic Organisation (PEBCO) is one of the most active mass community structures in the country. It was founded in 1979 as a union of a number of civic organisations in the greater Port Elizabeth region of the Eastern Cape.

The main aim of the organisation was vigorously to oppose apartheid and its structures, particularly in the townships. PEBCO has also been in the forefront of the struggle for equal civic rights for black people in the region where it operates. One of the prime targets of PEBCO was the Urban Community Councils set up by the government.

PEBCO has been involved in several strikes and one in particular is significant. This took place at the Ford Motor Company in Port Elizabeth and was prompted by an attempt to dismiss a prominent civic leader working at the plant, Thozamile Botha. One of the results of the strike action was the formation of the trade union, the Motor Assembly and Component Workers' Union of South Africa (MACWUSA).

THE NATIONAL UNION OF SOUTH AFRICAN
STUDENTS (NUSAS)

The National Union of South African Students (NUSAS) was founded in 1924. Its original purpose was to create unity between English and Afrikaans students at white universities in South Africa.

However, in 1933 the Afrikaans universities left NUSAS because the organisation supported the admission of the black Fort Hare University to its ranks. Fort Hare University was not admitted until 1945, when it became an affiliate member. Soon other black universities followed suit.

NUSAS began early on to oppose segregation in tertiary educational institutions. During the 1980s, it broadened its scope to include opposition to apartheid in general. However, when the Black Consciousness Movement was established, it criticised the white liberal elements of NUSAS and black campuses terminated their membership of the organisation. A crisis developed within NUSAS as a result, but this was soon overcome. The organisation became more radical and participated in the creation of non-racial trade unions in South Africa and also became involved with other organisations working for a democratic South Africa. As a result of this radicalisation, a number of conservative white universities, including Rhodes University and the Pietermaritzburg campus of Natal University, withdrew from NUSAS.

NUSAS continued its involvement in working for change in South Africa, co-operating with such organisations as the Azanian Student's Organisation, (AZAPO) and the Congress of South African Students (COSAS). The movement went through difficult times between 1960 and the 1970s. It was subjected to close scrutiny by the authorities and funding from overseas was stopped. During the height of its anti-apartheid activities, NUSAS playing a significant role in involving university students in the struggle for rights and liberties.

CONCLUSION

There are numerous other organisations that have been, and still are, involved in the process of fighting for human rights in South Africa. It is not possible, within the scope of this study, to deal with all of them, except to say that they have all made their contributions to the struggle for justice, freedom and the dignity of all South Africans.

PART 8

HUMAN RIGHTS ACTIVISTS: SOUTH AFRICA

CHAPTER 1

JOHN TENGO JABAVU (1859-1921)

One of the most famous founding fathers of African political activism was John Tengo Jabavu. He was born in the village of Healdtown in the Eastern Cape in 1859 and attended school there. At the early age of 17, he became a teacher in the town of Somerset East. He was very energetic and besides his teaching job, he learned the printing trade during his spare time by apprenticing himself to a newspaper in the town. He also continued his studies under Professor Kyd, a member of staff of Gill College.

From an early age, Jabavu became an activist, beginning with numerous letters he wrote to newspapers locally and elsewhere in the Cape. His missionary teachers attempted to curb his enthusiasm for political activity, but the young activist persisted, becoming more and more involved in the political struggle.

In 1881, Jabavu became the editor of the black publication, *Isigidimi Sama Xhosa*, and was soon elected Vice-President of the Native Educational Association. He used his positions as editor and vice-president of the NEA to protest strongly against discrimination. The year 1884 was an important one for Jabavu because he entered active politics by backing a liberal independent white candidate, James Rose Innes, for election to the Cape Parliament. Through the offices of the Native Electoral Association, Jabavu called on Africans to support this candidate. The African vote, which still existed in the Cape at that time, swung the election in favour of Rose Innes, who was elected to Parliament as the Member for Victoria East. Soon after this, Rose Innes's brother and James Weir, another sympathetic investor, financed Jabavu in setting up his own newspaper, *Imvo Zabantsundu*. This was a very important development as several other black newspapers and publications were started as a result.

Jabavu's newspaper was instrumental in bringing about unity between divergent black opinions and also brought about an interaction with whites through its airing of a number of black grievances. Among the most serious were maladministration in the courts and discriminatory legislation such as the pass laws applicable only to blacks, regulations relating to locations, the liquor laws and other legislation prejudicial to blacks. The role of *Imvo* as an instrument of protest was very significant. It became the leading medium through which African opinion on a range of issues was aired and a number of protest actions were launched by and through it. In 1887, Jabavu mobilised mass political opinion against the Parliamentary Voters' Registration Act, promulgated when the Transkeian territories became part of the Cape Colony through incorporation. The Act ostensibly extended the African vote to the recently incorporated Transkeian Territories, but did not regard tribal land tenure as legally valid. Since becoming a voter required a property ownership qualification, this Act effectively curtained the black vote.

Jabavu organised political meetings throughout the Eastern Cape, protesting strongly against the Act. In addition, he sought the intervention of such organisations as the Aborigines Protection Society and the Friends of Natives in Britain, as well as members of the British Parliament. Through the Native Educational Association, Jabavu made representation to the Cape government and formed a committee whose purpose was to keep the British Colonial office informed of developments and, if need be, to send a delegation to Britain to vent the grievances directly to London. Consequently, black representatives, mainly from 13 regions of the Eastern Cape, met at King William's Town in 1887 to discuss what was to be done about the recent legislation.

However, other important issues were also discussed, including the general rights of Africans in the Cape Colony's body politic. An organisation known as the Union of Native Vigilance Association was established, with the hope that it would eventually become an all-embracing political organisation to protect black rights. Part of the UNVA's organisation consisted of decentralised village-level branches, which would function all year and meet on an annual basis under the Native Vigilance Association's auspices. The organisation set itself the task of monitoring the black voter registration process and if necessary, taking test-cases to the Supreme Court when prospective voters were disqualified on one ground or another. Blacks at the time had a strong influence on voting patterns in the Cape Colony and in fact controlled the balance of power in many constituencies. The following excerpt will give a clear indication of the black voter situation at the time in the Cape Colony (Odendal 1984):

'As a result of the Parliamentary Voters' Registration Act, the names of 20 000 people were struck from the 1886 Voters' Roll. The overwhelming majority were blacks. Despite this, the black vote still affected the results in a number of constituencies. By 1891, blacks comprised 30 % of the electorate in 12 constituencies and in a further ten constituencies, they accounted for between 20 % and 29 % of the vote.'

It was this strong black position in the voting pattern that prompted a number of individuals and groups to call on Parliament to do something to curtail the number of black votes. Consequently, the Franchise and Ballot Act of 1892 was enacted and promulgated, raising the property qualifications for blacks and at the same time introducing a literacy test. Jabavu's reaction this time was a little more cautious. He had become more aligned with party-political processes and his connections with Rose Innes and his other two important liberal colleagues, J W Sauer and John X Merriman, were quite strong. These three men were members of the 'Afrikaner Bond-backed' Cabinet of Cecil John Rhodes. As a result of a political scandal, the three resigned in 1893. Sauer and Merrimen soon broke with the Afrikaner Bond-Rhodes alliance as a result of the negative political effects of the failed Jameson Raid in 1896. The Bond took an anti-Rhodes and anti-British stance in the aftermath of the Raid. This could have caused a clash of loyalties for Jabavu, but this problem was short-lived, for both Merrimen and Sauer canvassed the black vote in the 1898 elections when they needed it to win in their constituencies. In addition, J H Hofmeyer, leader of the Afrikaner Bond, made an impassioned speech in March 1898, in which he supported the African franchise rights. Jabavu was elated at this and gave Hofmeyer his support, having to go against his liberal associates and friends in the ensuing elections.

One of the major consequences of Jabavu's support for Hofmeyer and the Afrikaner Bond was that he was estranged from a large portion of important black political opinion. Strong political cleavages ensued, with Jabavu and his predominantly Mfengu supporters siding with Hofmeyer's Afrikaner Bond on the one hand and a group of mainly Xhosas who were opposed to Afrikaner political aspirations on the other. The Xhosa group mainly supported the 'English Parties' and unfortunately the split in the political support process took on an ethnic character. In the 1890s these cleavages increased and were complicated by the fact that the Xhosas established a newspaper of their own, called *Izwi Labantu*, and founded the South African Native Congress. This SANC was opposed to Jabavu's political stance. Jabavu did not wish to see a broad political group develop for a number of reasons. It has been argued (Odendaal 1984) that he wanted to protect his own powerful political position in black politics. However, another reason was that he favoured a non-racial political process, involving both blacks and whites in a future political dispensation. The promotion of non-racialism was paramount in his philosophy. Despite these political differences, John Tengo Jabavu's name has gone down in South African history as one of the fathers of non-racialism, a prerequisite for the resolution of most of South Africa's political, social and economic problems.

CHAPTER 2

DR ABDULLAH ABDURAHMAN
(1872-1940)

Abdullah Abdurahman was born in Cape Town's famous District Six in 1872. His father was a teacher, who sent him to elementary school at the Marist Brothers College in Cape Town and later to the South African College (SACS). This institution, started in 1829 and later to become the University of Cape Town, was the first secondary school in the country.

It was soon after Abdurahman graduated from SACS that the government of the day passed regulations prohibiting non-whites from enrolling at the College. Soon afterwards, however, Abdurahman's parents moved to Britain, where he enrolled at the University of Glasgow in Scotland and read for a medical degree. He qualified as a medical doctor in 1893. While in Scotland, he married a Scotswoman. On his return to his native South Africa, he became a private medical practitioner, opening a surgery in Cape Town. His practice was very successful and Dr Abdurahman's popularity increased.

Soon after he started his career as a medical practitioner, he became very interested in the social, political and economic conditions of black as well as coloured people. In 1902, he entered the political arena, becoming a founder member of the African People's Organisation (APO), which was based in Cape Town. Three years later, in 1905, he was elected President of the APO as a result of his popularity and his keen insight and organisational ability. In 1904 he was elected to the Cape Town City Council, being the first 'coloured' person to be a councillor. In 1914 he was elected to the Cape Provincial Council, an institution that was abolished with the introduction of the tricameral parliamentary system.

Dr Abdurahman served on the City and Provincial Councils until his death in 1940. One of his main political objectives was to cut across racial and ethnic differences. He argued with relentless vigour in favour of a unitary form of constitution in order to safeguard the Cape's non-racial policy. He also pressed for political unity between the African, Indian and Coloured people. To this end he organised, together with D D T Javabu and other community leaders, a series of conferences between 1927 and 1934. These resulted in the formation of the Non-European Unity Movement, which eventually affiliated with the African National Congress in 1943.

Earlier in his political life, Dr Abdurahman had gone, together with fellow African leaders, to London in 1906 and again in 1909, to protest against the draft constitution creating the Union of South Africa. However, the South Africa Act of 1910 effectively ignored direct non-white representation in the country's highest legislative body. In addition, this Act brought in segregation, a practice Dr Abdurahman abhorred and fought against throughout his active political life. After Union, he continued to advocate the political unity of all people of colour, stating that this was the only means of ending the all-white monopoly of political power.

On a personal level, Dr Abdurahman was an admirer of General Jan Smuts and the party he led, the now defunct United Party, but opposed its many political measures that entrenched segregation and even campaigned against South Africa's rule of South West Africa, now Namibia.

Near the end of his life, Dr Abdurahman was challenged by more radical political militants, among them his own daughter, Zainunissa, who teamed up with James La Guma and John Gomas. They formed the National Liberation League in opposition to the APO. However, Dr Abdurahman continued as President of the APO until his death in 1940.

CHAPTER 3

JOHN LANGALIBALELE DUBE (1871-1946)

The Reverend John Langalibalele Dube was born on 12 February 1871, in Inanda, Natal. He was a clergyman, writer and politician who had the distinction of becoming the first President of the African National Congress.

Like a number of his peers, Dube was educated at missionary schools in the region where he lived. One of these was the Amanzimtoti College, later known as Adams College. After finishing secondary school, Dube enrolled at the famous Oberlin College in Ohio, USA, in 1889. He graduated from the College in 1893, with the degree of Bachelor of Arts. During his stay in the United States he published his first book, entitled: *A Talk upon my Native Land*. In 1897, John Dube was ordained as a minister of religion. While in the United States, he met a number of influential black thinkers and intellectuals, among them Booker T Washington, John Hope and W E B du Bois.

On his return to South Africa in 1901, the Rev Dube founded the Zulu Christian Industrial School, which later became known as the Ohlange Institute, in Natal. This industrial school was run along the lines of the world-famous Tuskeegee Institute in the USA, founded by Booker T Washington. Dube's school was one of the first such schools in Africa providing industrial arts training for African men and women.

One of the highlights of the Rev Dube's career was the founding of the first Zulu language newspaper, *Ilanga Lase Natal* (The Natal Sun), which he founded together with a distinguished black journalist, Nganzana Luthuli. Dube became the first editor of the newspaper, using its columns to champion the cause of his fellow blacks, whose rights were being hampered by the white authorities.

Through his articles in *Ilanga*, Dube built up a big following among blacks, but he also incurred the wrath of the white authorities in Natal. In 1909 he wrote a major treaties entitled 'Zulus' Appeal for Rights and England's Duty'. In this treaties Dube called upon the British government to face up to the challenge in South Africa, specifically with regard to repression and black people's rights in the then Natal Colony.

Dube attended the inaugural meeting of the South African Native National Congress (SANNC), which later became the African National Congress. The meeting was held in Bloemfontein, where, on 8 January 1912, he was elected first President-General of the Congress. Almost immediately, he had the task of opposing the all-white government's introduction of more unacceptable legislative measures, among them the Land Act of 1913. This Act brought about a number of discriminatory land practices, in that it denied blacks the right to own land or to buy land in so-called white areas. The Act was vigorously opposed by the SANNC. Dube and a delegation went to London in 1914 to attempt to prompt the British government to act, but the delegation was not favourably received in Britain, particularly by the colonial office. Dube was unhappy with the results of his visit to London and returned to South Africa. Further efforts to fight the Land Act were interrupted by the outbreak of World War I.

In 1943, during World War II, Dube was elected to the government-created Native Representative Council, as a representative for Natal. This post was later filled by Chief Albert Luthuli in 1946, the year of Dube's death.

Dube was a very versatile man, having an interest in politics, religion, literature and scholarship in general. His writings include:
- ❑ Zulu folk and dance songs;
- ❑ a political work, *The Greatest Enemy of the Black is the Black Himself* (1922);
- ❑ a novel, in English, entitled *Clash of Colour* (1926);
- ❑ a historical novel *Vieque Isila Ka Tshaka*, on the court and life of the Zulu king. In 1957, this work was translated into English as *Jeqe, the Body Servant of King Tshaka*;
- ❑ a biography of the Zulu prophet Isaiah Sembe, *U-Shembe*; and
- ❑ a book, *Good Manners* or *Ukuziphatha Kahle*.

In 1926 Dube attended the International Conference of Christian missions in Belgium. Ten years later, he was the first African to be awarded the degree of Doctor of Philosophy (PhD) by the University of South Africa. John Langalibalele Dube, clergyman, newsman, politician-activist, scholar and writer, died on 11 February 1946 in Umhlanga. He was 75 years old.

CHAPTER 4

ALFRED BITINI ZUMA (1893-1962)

Alfred Bitini Zuma was one of South Africa's most distinguished scholars, medical men and political activists. He was born in the Transkei in 1893, a member of an aristocratic Xhosa family. He was a man of remarkable talents who rose to become President-General of the African National Congress between 1940 and 1949.

He first became a teacher, but went on to enrol at the Tuskeegee Institute, Alabama, USA, where he studied agriculture. He then enrolled for a medical degree course at the University of Minnesota and completed the degree of Doctor of Medicine (MD) at the North-Western University in Evanston, Illinois. From there he went to Europe to specialise in gynaecology. He also undertook further studies at the two Scottish Universities of Glasgow and Edinburgh.

On his return to South Africa, Dr Zuma settled in Sophiatown, Johannesburg, where he opened a surgery in 1927. He used most of his energies to improve his medical practice, but soon found himself more and more involved in political opposition to discriminatory practices directed against blacks by the government of General J B M Hertzog. Dr Zuma joined the Johannesburg Joint Council, but as the political situation deteriorated, he involved himself in the politics of protest and was elected to the position of Vice-President of the All-Africa Convention, with D D T Javabu as President.

His continued efforts in the struggle for justice earned him the respect of the black community in general and consequently he was elected to the post of President-General of the African National Congress in 1940. It was the efforts of Dr Zuma which led to the transformation of the ANC into a mass-based political movement. He paid particular attention to the young element in the ANC and it was during his presidency that many young people were brought into leadership positions.

In 1944, a Youth League subcommittee of the ANC was established. Significantly, the Youth League was then led by three outstanding young men who later became leaders in the struggle for human rights. They were Nelson Mandela, Walter Sisulu and Oliver Tambo, two of whom are still active in the struggle for human rights in South Africa. They were in favour of a more militant form of human rights programme, but Dr Zuma differed with them on this issue.

It was also during Dr Zuma's presidency that the ANC developed links with other political movements in the hope of broadening the struggle for human rights, particularly for blacks. To this end, it developed a closer relationship with the SA Indian Congress, which was also in the forefront of the fight for justice for all in South Africa.

On the international front, Dr Zuma opposed the inclusion of the Mandated Territory of South West Africa (now Namibia) into South Africa. However, he was a moderate man in all things and this attitude cost him the presidency of the ANC in 1949, with J S Moroka taking over the post. The opposition to Dr Zuma's moderate stance was led by the ANC Youth League.

Dr Zuma died on 28 February 1962.

CHAPTER 5

JAMES SEBE MOROKA (1891-1985)

James Sebe Moroka was born in 1891 in Thaba Nchu, the great-grandson of the Tswana chief, Moroka. He received his education at the Lovedale Training College near Alice in the Cape Province, where a number of other political activists were also educated. In 1911, he registered for a medical degree at the University of Edinburgh in Scotland, graduating as a qualified medical doctor in 1918.

After continuing his studies in Vienna, Austria, he returned to his home in Thaba Nchu, where he established a medical practice. His medical abilities soon gained him the respect of his community, including many Afrikaners who were among his patients. Dr Moroka once confided to someone that he was indebted to an Afrikaner by the name of Piet Steytler, who had assisted him financially during his studies. His non-racial attitude towards all people was proved beyond doubt, for he assisted four white students and several African students in the completion of their studies. In addition to his medical practice, Dr Moroka was a reasonably prosperous farmer.

Dr Moroka had a distinguished and interesting political career. This began in earnest in 1930, when he opposed the notorious pass laws, the liquor laws as they applied to blacks, and racial discrimination generally. In the Cape Province, he campaigned vigorously against attempts by the government to remove blacks from the Common Voters' Roll. During the mid-thirties, Dr Moroka joined the All-Africa Convention and was made its leader. He led a delegation to see the Prime Minister, Dr Hertzog, confronting him on the issue of the 1936 Land Act which effectively confined blacks to only 13 % of the land.

His activism against discrimination continued and by 1942 he was elected to the Native Representative Council. This government-created body had little real power and he believed that the NRC could best be destroyed by activity from within.

The year 1946 was a critical year in Dr Moroka's political activism. It was a year in which a civil disobedience campaign was instituted in South Africa. Black miners went on strike and government reacted with harsh countermeasures, resulting in the death of eight miners and injuries to more than a thousand people. The response by the members of the NRC was to call for an indefinite adjournment of its proceedings. In 1948, many of the NRC members resigned, but Dr Moroka did not join them, delaying his resignation until 1950. Paradoxically, he had by then been President of the ANC for a year.

The manner in which Dr Moroka gained the presidency of the African National Congress is interesting, as he was not a member of the organisation at the time. During 1949, the militant ANC Youth League was disenchanted with the moderate stand of the then President of the ANC, Dr A B Zuma. Those who opposed Dr Zuma included Nelson Mandela, Oliver Tambo, Walter Sisulu, Lambede and others. The Youth League leaders wanted a more vigorous effort in opposing the government. They demanded a programme calling for non-cooperation with the government, nationwide strikes and stay-aways.

As a result, Dr Moroka was favoured to head the ANC and institute a more militant programme. He accepted the presidency and was a popular leader, both with the other members of the ANC hierarchy and the general masses. He was very active from the outset, addressing meetings throughout South Africa. When Nelson Mandela led the Defiance Campaign in 1952, he was readily supported by Moroka. However, Dr Moroka insisted that the campaign should be non-violent in nature and that the method of passive resistance should be used.

The Defiance Campaign was the culmination of a number of appeals and approaches to the government of the day, requesting at least an understanding of the desires and needs of black South Africans. In fact, Walter Sisulu wrote to the Prime Minister at the time, Dr Malan, asking for a sympathetic hearing on the issue of black political, social and economic rights. These requests were met by more laws, curbing further the human rights of blacks. According to one source, Malan suggested, by way of a reply, that the ANC did not represent a majority of the people.

Not afraid to take part in the struggle for human rights, Dr Moroka addressed a mass gathering of blacks on 6 April 1952, in Johannesburg. He said (*inter alia*) (UNECHUE 1991):

> 'Africans must master all their forces of mind, body and soul to see that this state of affairs, these crushing conditions under which they live shall not continue any longer.'

In the speech, Dr Moroka also called for 10 000 volunteers to defy the laws of apartheid. The government reacted by arresting him, along with Mandela, Sisulu and a number of other ANC leaders, in November 1952. They were charged under the Suppression of Communism Act for organising the Defiance Campaign. For some reason, Dr Moroka decided to engage separate legal representation from the other accused. All the trialists were found guilty of furthering the cause of communism (ie statutory communism).

In mitigation of sentence, Dr Moroka stressed a number of factors, among them his friendship with Afrikaners and the fact that he had on occasion assisted a number of them. He received a sentence of nine months' imprisonment, suspended for two years. His attitude at the trial had a negative influence on his political career. In December 1952, at the Annual Conference of the ANC, he was not re-elected to the presidency. His successor was Chief Albert Luthuli.

Dr Moroka returned to his home in Thaba Nchu, continued to practice medicine and lived on his farm. He always insisted that blacks and whites in South Africa needed and complemented each other. In fact, he supported the Homelands policy of the Nationalist government, justifying this support on the basis that it gave at least partial control of the country to blacks. Dr Moroka remained self-confident and carried himself with his usual dignity until his death at the age of 94 in November 1985.

CHAPTER 6

ALBERT JOHN MVUMBI LUTHULI
(1898-1967)

'The Road to Freedom is via the Cross'

Albert Luthuli, Nobel Prize Winner, tribal chief and teacher, was born in Zimbabwe in 1898. He was the son of Buynan Luthuli, a missionary, who had gone up to the then Rhodesia to follow his Christian calling. Between 1952 and 1960 he was the leader of the African National Congress. It was in recognition of Luthuli's non-violent struggle against racial and other forms of discrimination that he was awarded the prestigious Nobel Prize for Peace in 1960.

He was ten years old when his missionary father died, making it necessary for the young Luthuli to return to South Africa. From that age he was brought up by his uncle, who was chief of Groutville, a community which was part of the American Congregational Mission in Natal. In his uncle's household he learned the traditions of the Zulus, a culture he valued deeply.

Luthuli's formal education culminated in his graduation from the American Board Mission's Teacher Training College at Adams, near Durban. His educational training was a struggle, as his mother, a washerwoman, used her hard-earned money to assist him. He also earned a scholarship which enabled him to complete his studies and became one of the first three black instructors. It was during this period (1927) that he married Nokukhanya Bhengu, also a teacher, who was the daughter of a clan chief.

He taught until 1936, when he withdrew from the profession and was elected to the post of chief of the Groutville community, several thousand strong at the time. It was during this period that Chief Luthuli became more aware of the great degree of poverty, the need for adequate land and the lack of a political voice for blacks in his community and in South Africa generally. In 1936 he had yet to become involved in mainstream politics, but he was involved in a number of organisations:
- Secretary of the Natal African Teachers' Association;
- Secretary of the South African Football Association;
- He founded the Zulu Language and Cultural Society;
- Member of the Christian Council Executive of the Joint Council of Europeans and Africans; and

❑ Member of the Institute of Race Relations in Durban.

Albert Luthuli joined the African National Congress in 1945. In 1946, he was appointed by the government to the Native Representative Council, an organisation consisting of traditional chiefs and intellectuals. The NRC advised the government on a number of issues relating to black needs. It was at this very time that the government ordered troops and police to deal with a black miners' strike. The result was that eight people died and nearly 1 000 others were injured. Luthuli began to doubt the value of the Native Representative Council and protested against its powerlessness.

In 1948 he undertook a tour of the United States as a guest of the Congregational Board of Missions. In public speeches and private conversations, he warned that Christianity was facing a crisis of confidence in Africa as a result of race discrimination, both in South Africa and the African colonies of Britain and other European countries.

When Luthuli returned to South Africa, he found that the National party, a predominantly Afrikaner organisation, had come to power. Following closely on this event, Luthuli was elected to the Natal presidency of the African National Congress. The ANC's strategies at the time attempted to secure human rights for its oppressed people through sending deputations to the government, petitions and mass protests, which had been used since 1912 by the ANC, but all its appeals had fallen on deaf ears.

The year 1952 was an important one in Luthuli's life. Young black intellectuals were agitating for action against unjust laws and to further this aim, the ANC joined forces with the South African Indian Congress. A nationwide campaign of defiance against unjust laws was organised. Using some Gandhian tactics, more than 8 000 people went to prison on a voluntary basis. The government for its part did little to accommodate the demands and in fact gave Luthuli a choice: he had to resign his leadership of the ANC in Natal or resign his position as a chief. In keeping with the dictates of his conscience, Luthuli refused to do either, whereupon the government deposed him as chief.

Despite the fact that he was deposed, his people continued to regard him as their *de facto* chief. In 1952, the year that he was deposed as chief, Luthuli was elected President-General of the African National Congress of South Africa. Henceforth, the government repeatedly banned him in terms of the Suppression of Communism Act. During periods when he was not restricted under banning orders, Luthuli toured the country addressing meetings, attending gatherings and generally encouraging people to continue the struggle for human rights. He undertook these functions despite being seriously ill at the time.

In 1956 Luthuli and 155 others were detained and charged with high treason. It was a long and laborious trial, but the State failed to prove the charge of treason, or that of a suggested communist conspiracy, or one of using violence to achieve political ends. In 1957, Luthuli was released from custody. His quiet style of leadership and his reserved personality were respected by many, including many foreigners. As a result of his dignified style of leadership, Luthuli was nominated for the Nobel Prize for Peace.

In 1957, Luthuli's call for a stay-at-home strike was heeded by thousands of black people. His quiet confidence also moved a number of whites who began to attend his meetings. As a consequence, he was confined to his rural region by the government in 1959 and effectively banned from gatherings for a period of five years. The government of the day justified its actions by stating that Luthuli was 'promoting feelings of hostility between the races'.

The year 1960 was a critical one, both for Luthuli and the country as a whole. It was the year of the Sharpeville shootings in which 69 demonstrators against the pass laws were shot dead by police. Luthuli immediately called for a period of national mourning and burnt his own pass book. He was charged and found guilty, but illness prevented him from serving his prison sentence in Gandhian style. He paid a fine instead. The same year saw the banning of the ANC and its rival movement the Pan-Africanist Congress (PAC).

In December of 1961, Luthuli was given permission by the government to go to Oslo, accompanied by his wife, to receive the Nobel Peace Prize. In his speech accepting the prize, Luthuli told of the great non-violent struggle by black South Africans for basic human rights. He also noted that despite the struggle, blacks were no closer to achieving these rights.

Hardly a week later a group calling itself Umkhonto we Sizwe (the Spear of the Nation) attacked installations throughout South Africa, thereby signalling the abandonment of the policy of non-violence. Albert Luthuli returned to an enforced isolation in his rural region. He spent his time on his small farm near Stanger, Natal, dictating his autobiography and sometimes receiving visitors when the police approved.

On 21 July 1967 he was crossing a railway line near his smallholding when he was struck by a train and killed. The voice of Albert Luthuli was stilled, but as one of his biographers put it: 'His vision remains intact for posterity'.

CHAPTER 7

ALAN STEWART PATON (1903-1988)

World-famous author and activist Alan Paton was born on 11 January 1903 in Pietermaritzburg, Natal. After completing his primary and secondary education, he went to the University of Natal, from which he graduated with degrees in Mathematics and Physics. He also obtained a Teacher's Diploma and then worked as a teacher for 20 years.

His teaching career took him to the Natal town of Ixopo and the Pieter-maritzburg College, where he taught from 1925 to 1935. In 1935, the government moved the administration of African reformatories from the Prisons to the Department of Education. This was to change Paton's life. He was appointed to the post of principal of the Diepkloof Reformatory near Johannesburg by the then Minister of Education, Jan Hofmeyr, a liberal in the Cabinet of Prime Minister Jan Smuts.

Paton brought in a number of positive changes in the administration of the reform school at Diepkloof. At that time Alan Paton was still an ardent admirer of the Afrikaners and their way of life. He learnt Afrikaans, becoming fluent in the language, and attended the 1938 Voortrekker Monument cere-monies. While there he took note of what he considered to be the intolerance and bigotry of the Nationalist Afrikaner political movement. It was at this stage, too, that he began to understand the maze of oppressive legislation under which the black population suffered. During 1946, Paton toured a number of countries, including Britain, the United States and Scandinavia, where he studied penal and reform processes. With his mind full of new impressions, Paton wrote his first novel, *Cry, the Beloved Country*, which brought him into the international limelight. That year (1948), also saw the coming to power of the National Party. The novel depicted the lives of blacks and whites under a segregationist and discriminatory socio-political system. 1948 was also the year in which his friend Jan Hofmeyr died, leaving a large gap in his life. He later published a biography of Hofmeyr.

The post-1948 period was difficult for Paton, who increasingly disagreed with the harsher laws brought in by the apartheid system. This made him resign from the civil service and, with other persons of like mind, he formed the Liberal Party in 1953. One of its pivotal principles was the recognition of the need for universal suffrage. In 1955, Paton was elected leader of the party, which had black as well as white members. His second novel, *Too Late the*

Phalarope, a book about love between people of different races, was banned in 1953. He also published *South Africa: The Land – Its People* (1955) and, together with Don Weiner, *South Africa in Transition* (1956).

His political activities in the 1950s made Alan Paton a household name both in South Africa and internationally. He co-operated with the anti-apartheid protest movements such as the Congress Alliance and the African National Congress, which had then not yet been banned. In 1960 he went to the United States where he was awarded the prestigious Freedom Award in recognition of his efforts to win human rights for all in South Africa.

In South Africa, the situation continued to deteriorate and upon his return from the USA, his passport was withdrawn by the government. It was only returned ten years later, in 1970. He also received other awards in the form of honorary degrees, including an LLB from Yale University. Other universities to confer honorary degrees on Paton were the University of Natal in 1968 and the University of Durban-Westville in 1986.

1968 was a sad year for both Alan Paton and the Liberal Party. In that year, the passing of the Prohibition of Improper Interference Act made it impossible for racially mixed political parties to function and it became evident that the Liberal Party had to cease to exist or face a banning order. With the demise of the Liberal Party, Alan Paton's political career came to an end.

He continued to write, however, and his other published works were:
- ❏ *Debbie Go Home* (short stories) (1961);
- ❏ *Instrument of Thy Peace* (1968);
- ❏ *The Long View* (1969);
- ❏ *Kontakion for You Departed* (1969);
- ❏ *Apartheid and the Archbishop* (1973);
- ❏ *Knocking on the Door* (1975);
- ❏ *Ah, But Your Land is Beautiful* (1980); and
- ❏ *Towards the Mountain* (an autobiography) (1980).

Paton's political views brought him much sorrow. He was despised by most Afrikaner nationalists and their supporters. Blacks also did not accept him fully, leaving him in a political vacuum. He suffered the loss of his wife, Doris, in 1967, but married a second time, to Anne Hopkins. In the years preceding his death, he called for the creation of a non-racial federation in South Africa.

Although he did not fully accept the Tricameral Parliamentary system, Paton felt that it at least broadened the representative basis to South Africans of Indian and Coloured descent. He opposed sanctions as a weapon against apartheid, believing that they would cause unemployment and impact particularly on the poor. He was fearless in his fight for human rights and was especially opposed to the laws that deprived the majority of South Africans of the right to be represented directly in Parliament. Alan Paton died at his home in his beloved Natal on 12 April 1988.

CHAPTER 8

ROBERT MANGALISO SOBUKWE
(1924-1978)

Robert Mangaliso Sobukwe, the first President of the Pan-Africanist Congress (PAC), was born in the Karoo Town of Graaff-Reinet in the Eastern Cape on 5 December 1924. His family was poverty-stricken, but the young Sobukwe had an impressive intellectual aptitude. He won a number of scholarships enabling him to study at Lovedale College. He left the College in 1945 and registered at Fort Hare University College, from which he graduated in 1949 with an Honours Degree in History, Literature and Education and a Teacher's Diploma.

Sobukwe soon became politically active and joined the Youth League of the ANC. He became the Chairman of the League's Victoria East branch in 1949. From the outset, he clashed with the authorities. He became a teacher in Standerton in 1950, but two years later, in 1952, he was dismissed from his post for taking part in the Defiance Campaign. In 1953 he joined the staff of the Department of Bantu Studies at the University of the Witwatersrand, where he was a language assistant. He remained in the academic world until 1960.

Sobukwe was politically active during his years at the University and by 1957 he had become the editor of the influential journal *The Africanist,* the official mouthpiece of the ANC at the time. It was also during this crucial period that he and a number of his close associates began to feel uncomfortable with ANC policy. These were younger leaders who felt that the role of the Communist Party in the ANC was undesirable as it increased its own power at the expense of the ANC. The Sobukwe faction also felt that the multiracial character of the ANC would adversely affect the development of black consciousness. By 1958, the rift between the Sobukwe faction and the rest of the ANC had reached a point where a split became inevitable. On 6 April 1959, Sobukwe and his followers founded the Pan-Africanist Congress (PAC). Sobukwe was elected its first leader on a policy of strict African Nationalism.

One of the principles upon which the PAC was based was the notion that in order to overcome racial inequalities in the country, blacks had to regain their dignity and self-respect in order to receive reciprocal respect from whites. Sobukwe felt that only black people could gain their own inde-

pendence and freedom. This exclusivism led to Sobukwe and his PAC
colleagues being accused of racism, but he insisted that the PAC wanted to
establish a non-racist South Africa, once the apartheid system had been
removed or had collapsed. Black awareness was one of his main themes, later
serving as an inspiration to the establishment of the Black Consciousness
Movement by Steve Biko.

Despite his critics, Sobukwe's leadership of the PAC resulted in a mass
following. He organised a campaign against the hated pass laws as a major
more towards eventual total liberation. Mass demonstrations were held in a
number of places, including one at Orlando, Soweto on 21 March 1960.
Sobukwe was arrested during this demonstration and charged with incitement. He was given a three-year hard labour sentence, part of which he served
in the Stofberg Prison in the Orange Free State. In April 1961 he was
transferred to the Pretoria Central Prison. After completing his sentence he
was detained, this time in the notorious Robben Island Prison. While on
Robben Island, he studied through London University, choosing economics
as his major subject.

Sobukwe was released in 1969, but was immediately banned for a
five-year period. This banning order placed Sobukwe under house arrest in
Kimberley in the Northern Cape. In 1974 the government renewed the
banning order. Sobukwe continued his studies through the medium of correspondence and in 1975 he was awarded a law degree. This was a difficult
period of his life, especially as he had a lung ailment. He was taken to Cape
Town where he underwent chest surgery at Groote Schuur Hospital in 1977.
Despite the operation and post-operative care, his health did not improve and
on 27 February 1978 he died in the Kimberley Hospital.

Robert Mangaliso Sobukwe died at a relatively young age, but his ideals
are still enshrined in the PAC's present ideology and principles. He was an
ardent believer in Pan-Africanism. He was an excellent organiser and had a
refined oratorical ability, coupled with a deep love for his native land and the
continent of Africa as a whole.

CHAPTER 9

STEPHEN BIKO (1946-1977)

Steve Biko, the founder of the Black Consciousness Movement in South Africa, was born in King William's Town on 18 December 1946. He did his pre-university education at the Brownlee Primary School and the Charles Morgan Institute, but had to complete his matriculation at the Marianhill Catholic Institute in Natal in 1965.

Biko attended the University of Natal's Medical School between 1966 and 1972, but as his interest in politics grew, his studies began to suffer and he did not complete his medical degree. He became the principal exponent of the Black Consciousness Movement, which began taking root in the latter years of the 1960s. Black identity was the assertive call of the movement and all its efforts were aimed at countering the society that denied it.

Biko's main philosophical precept was that blacks had to liberate themselves through self-reliance. Blacks, he asserted, must speak for themselves and not depend on white liberal elements to be their spokesmen. He also felt that it was not possible for white people to put themselves into the place which blacks found themselves, just as blacks would have difficulty in placing themselves in the white person's position. Biko did not oppose white liberals as such, but stated that persons opposing the apartheid system were not necessarily allies in the black struggle for human rights and political improvement.

In Biko's political ideology it was not acceptable to have 'benign' white liberals lead the struggle as they would not be forceful enough in the process. However, he did not regard himself or his ideology as racist in nature simply because of his emphasis on black self-upliftment. South Africa, he stated, was a society in which the myth was propagated that whites were superior, blacks inferior. This attitude had no foundation and had to be countered by the ideology of Black Consciousness. Blacks, he suggested, should have their own organisations that would work for the development of pride in themselves as a group. They should also develop a feeling of humanity in order to help overcome the psychological and physical suffering caused by the system of apartheid. This philosophy brought Biko and the Black Consciousness Movement into direct conflict with the Nationalist government.

One of the BCM's most important actions was the establishment of the South African Students' Organisation (SASO). This was an all-black organisation and was formally established in July 1969 at the University of the North. Biko was elected its first President. SASO's main aim was to create unity among black students at universities throughout the country. SASO was at the time affiliated to the National Union of South African Students (NUSAS). It cancelled its affiliation in 1970, but still recognised NUSAS as the national student representative organisation.

The Black Consciousness Movement began to flourish and persons other than students began taking an interest in its activities. Biko's personal initiative was vital in the ensuing years. He helped to establish Black Community Programmes, sports organisations, financial trust funds and several other all-black bodies aimed at the upliftment and empowerment of black people. In 1972, an over-arching organisation, the Black People's Convention, was formed, bringing together over 70 black organisations. Steve Biko was elected the first Honorary President of the organisation.

Also in 1972, Biko made a literary contribution to a book entitled *Student Perspectives in South Africa*, published in association with the Abe Bailey Institute of Inter-racial Studies. The book was banned by the authorities. He also wrote an essay entitled 'Black Theology: The South African Voice', which was published in London. He was also expelled from the University of Natal in 1972, thereby ending his medical studies. He then joined the Black Community Programmes in Durban, serving as an organiser. However, in March 1973, the government served a banning order on him, which stipulated that his movements were restricted to the King Williams Town magisterial district. Other conditions were that he was not permitted to communicate with more than one person at a time and he could not write articles that would be quoted or otherwise reproduced in public. He came under close Security Police scrutiny.

Biko's life under restriction in King Williams Town was difficult, but he registered with the University of South Africa, doing a degree course in law by of correspondence. In addition to his studies, he established Black Community Programmes in the region and acted as its executive director responsible for the Eastern Cape region. These activities were, however, curtailed once more when, in December 1975, his banning order was altered to include restrictions on his doing this work.

Biko underwent serious personal difficulties in the years between 1974 and 1977, the year of his tragic and premature death. He was detained four times, including a period exceeding one hundred days. He was prosecuted for a number of alleged offences including minor traffic violations, violating his banning order and interfering with witnesses. None of the allegations was proved in court and Biko was found not guilty each time. The legal costs were high and he often had to request financial assistance from the Black People's Convention.

On 19 August 1977 the Security Police set up a roadblock outside Grahamstown and Biko was stopped and arrested. He was detained without trial in terms of the security legislation in force at the time. The reasons for his detention were that he was allegedly involved in riots in Port Elizabeth and that he had drafted pamphlets calling for violence. These allegations were never tested before a court of law. The events that followed, leading to his death, sent shock waves throughout the country and in several countries in the world. It was alleged that he was held in chains and was not allowed to exercise in the fresh air. On or about 7 September 1977, he went into a coma after about 22 hours of constant interrogation. Strong-arm tactics are said to have been used against him during this period. Doctors were called in to examine him and they concluded that there was nothing seriously wrong with him. The police noticed that for a five-day period, Biko could neither eat nor drink and they decided to move him to Pretoria for treatment.

Biko was put into the back of a Land Rover vehicle, still manacled and allegedly naked. On 12 September 1977 he died in Pretoria. A post-mortem report, signed by four pathologists, including one representing Biko's family, found that he had died of a brain haemorrhage probably sustained during his detention. There were also injuries to his left ribs and a number of bruises and abrasions.

Steve Biko's life ended at the age of 30, but despite his young age, he had accomplished much. He was a leader of outstanding ability and was very charismatic. He worked tirelessly and fearlessly for the cause he believed in. He had no ambition to increase his personal popularity, preferring to remain in the background. His hope was that South Africa would move non-violently through a transition to a more egalitarian society, violence becoming an option if all else failed.

Steve Biko became a household name both in South Africa and abroad.

CHAPTER 10

NELSON ROLIHLAHLA MANDELA (1918-)

Nelson Rolihlahla Mandela was born on 18 July 1918, in Umtata, Transkei. His father was a chief, who had four wives. According to Mandela's own autobiographical record (Mandela 1990), neither of his parents had attended school. In 1930, when he was 12 years old, his father died and he was left in the care of acting Paramount Chief David Dalindyebo.

In his biographical account (op cit), he says that he is related to both Sabata Dalindyebo, Paramount Chief of Tembuland (1964) and Kaizer Matanzima, former Prime Minister of Transkei. Both are his nephews according to Tembu custom.

Mandela became politically aware very early in life. He described this early experience thus (Mandela 1990):

'My political interest was first aroused when I listened to elders of our tribe in my village as a youth. They spoke of the good old days before the arrival of the white man. Our people lived peacefully under the democratic rule of their kings and councillors and moved freely all over the country. Then the country was ours. We occupied the land, the forests and the rivers. We set up and operated our own government; we controlled our own armies and commerce. The elders would tell us about the liberation and how it was fought by our ancestors in defence of our country, as well as the acts of valour performed by generals and soldiers during those epic days. I hoped, and vowed then, that among the pleasures that life offered me, would be the opportunity to serve my people and make my own humble contribution to their struggle for freedom.'

Nelson Mandela grew up in the tradition of his people and at the age of 16 he went to a circumcision school on the banks of the Bashee River, where his ancestors had undergone the same process. After these ceremonies were completed, he was accepted into manhood, with all the rights and duties afforded by the customs of his people. At the age of 23, he left his home region and moved to Johannesburg, in the company of his nephew, Justice Mtirara, in search of a job. They applied for work at the Crown Mines and both were employed, Mtirara as a learner clerk and Mandela as a mine policeman. After a while, he (Mandela) left the mines and became an estate agent at a salary of £2 (R4,00) a month. He did not particularly enjoy this work and in 1942 he left the job and articled himself to the legal firm of Witkin, Sidelsky and Eidelman.

Mandela's political career began in earnest in 1944 when he joined the African National Congress. He worked hard, both at his job and in his political activities. In 1952 he was elected Chairman of the Transvaal branch of the ANC and later in the year he became Deputy National President of the organisation. Hardly had he taken up his political post, however, than he was forced by the government to resign in 1953. In the same year, he was sentenced to nine months' imprisonment for his part in arranging and organising the ANC Defiance Campaign against unjust laws. In 1956 he faced another major test; he was arrested and charged with high treason. The case was a lengthy one, lasting five years, at the end of which, in March 1961, he was discharged. One month later he went underground, spending much time organising the May 1961 strike.

In 1962 Mandela visited several African countries, including Tanganyika (now Tanzania), Ethiopia, Sudan, Egypt, Libya, Tunisia, Algeria, Morocco, Mali, Senegal, Guinea, Sierra Leone, Liberia, Ghana and Nigeria. He also paid a visit to Great Britain, where he met Hugh Gaitskell, the Labour Party leader, and the leader of the Liberal Party, Jo Grimond. In the African countries he met the heads of state and other prominent government and community leaders.

THE RIVONIA TRIAL OF 1963-1964

Soon after his visit to the African countries, Mandela returned to South Africa by being smuggled across the border. However, on 6 August 1962, he was arrested near Howick, Natal. He was put on trial in Pretoria's Old Synagogue in November of the same year, charged with incitement and leaving the country illegally, and found guilty on both counts. He was sentenced to a period of five years' imprisonment and sent to the Pretoria Central prison to serve the sentence.

It was during this period of imprisonment that the police raided the underground headquarters of the ANC at Lilieslief Farm, Rivonia, outside Johannesburg, and arrested a number of leading activists. They included Walter Sisulu, Govan Mbeki, Raymond Mhlaba, Ahmed Kathrada, Dennis Goldberg, Lionel Bernstein and others. The police also found documents relating to the manufacture of explosives, the diary detailing Mandela's African tour and most important of all, a draft of the proposed guerilla struggle entitled 'Operation Mayibuye'.

In October 1963, the famous Rivonia Trial began. Mandela was brought from prison and arraigned with the other eight accused on charges of conspiracy to overthrow the government by revolutionary methods and of assisting an armed invasion of South Africa by foreign troops. The accused were charged in terms of the Suppression of Communism Act and the General Laws Amendment Act. The marathon trial, lasting 11 months, dealt with 193 allegations against the accused and persons recruited by the accused and drew international attention.

Nelson Mandela's statement, made to the court on 20 April 1964, is now an historical document and deserves particular attention. It was a dramatic statement which traced the history of black South Africans' struggle for human rights and justice.

Mandela admitted that he was one of the persons involved in founding the armed wing of the ANC, Umkhonto we Sizwe (the Spear of the Nation). He told the court that two factors contributed to his decision to do so. One was that the government left no other means of legal protest, including peaceful demonstrations. Having no recourse to other means of protest, the ANC had no option but armed struggle. The other was the fact that blacks had no other way of overcoming white supremacy, which was constitutionally entrenched. Blacks, Mandela said, would not accept a permanent state of inferiority in the land of their birth.

He also openly admitted being one of the main individuals responsible for the Defiance Campaign. This campaign, he stated, was organised on the basis of passive resistance, in which 8 000 people volunteered to take part and also to bear the punishment in the Gandhian sense. Mandela told the court that these volunteers were referred to as 'Amadelakufa' ('those who are prepared to die'). In other words, they knew full well what they were undertaking and were prepared to accept the consequences. They distributed pamphlets and conducted other activities which, although illegal, were nevertheless moral as an instrument of the struggle for justice. Up to that period, the ANC did not have a policy of violence, Mandela stated. This was borne out by the fact that all the 156 in the previous trial were found not guilty by the court and discharged.

The Sharpeville tragedy and the banning of the ANC in 1960 were also important milestones in the history of the struggle, he said. These were followed closely by the Referendum of 1960, in which only whites were asked to decide whether South Africa should become a Republic outside the British Commonwealth. As a consequence, the ANC had no option but to call the All-in Africa Conference and Stay-at-Home in 1961. It was critical stage in the development of the ANC, a period in which the government used force to govern, while not allowing any form of political protest.

The decision to use violence, Mandela said, had been taken only after the most serious consideration. The ANC, he said, feared that its followers were becoming impatient with the restraint called for by their leaders. He was afraid that when violence flared up it would result in confrontation with whites and that black-on-black violence would also erupt. He said (Mandela 1990):

'At the beginning of June 1961, after a long and anxious assessment of the South African situation, I, and some colleagues, came to the conclusion that as violence in this country was inevitable, it would be unrealistic and wrong for African leaders to continue preaching peace and non-violence at a time when the government met our peaceful demands with violence.'

Mandela told the court that the decision to form Umkhonto we Sizwe was taken for three basic and important reasons. The ANC was a mass-based organisation and as such could not be used to further the cause through violence, as members had joined the organisation on a policy of non-violence. Using the whole ANC structure for violence would change the nature of the organisation, possibly turning it into a small cohesive body as a 'military' requirement. The ANC was prepared to change its policy, but only to the extent that it would condone and conduct controlled violence. He said (op cit):

'I say ''properly controlled violence'' because I made it clear that if I formed the organisation I would at all times subject it to the political guidance of the ANC and would not undertake any different form of activity from that contemplated without the consent of the ANC. As a result of this decision, Umkhonto was formed in November 1960.'

Mandela further stated that the ANC felt that the prospects for a civil war in South Africa seemed strong and that it viewed such a situation with alarm, but wanted to be ready if it came. Although not wanting to commit itself to civil war, the ANC, through Umkhonto, considered four possible forms of violence against the state: sabotage, guerilla warfare, terrorism and open revolution. He then described the way in which Umkhonto we Sizwe would and did undertake actions against its chosen objectives. These included economic targets, government buildings and other targets that would not harm persons. He outlined the policy thus (op cit):

'Attacks on the economic life-lines of the country were to be linked with sabotage on government buildings and other symbols of apartheid. These attacks would serve as a source of inspiration to our people. In addition, they would provide an outlet for those people who were urging the adoption of violent methods and would enable us to give concrete proof to our followers that we had adopted a stronger line and were fighting back against government violence.'

Mandela then outlined the structural and functional characteristics of Umkhonto we Sizwe, which, he added, were based on the command structure of the Jewish nationalist underground organisation, Irgun Zvai Leumi, which operated in Palestine between 1944 and 1948. Umkhonto's structure consisted of a High Command under which fell a number of Regional Commands. The High Command was responsible for the 'determination of tactics, targets, training and finance'. The Regional Commands were in charge of local sabotage groups.

Mandela then traced the history of atrocities committed by the state against blacks over a long period of time in South Africa. These included such actions from the state's violent response to the 'Masabala' protest in Port Elizabeth in 1920, in which 24 people were killed, to such recent tragedies as Sharpeville.

He then dealt with the allegations of the State in the trial. He denied that the Lilieslief Farm at Rivonia was the headquarters of either the ANC or its armed wing, Umkhonto. He also discounted the allegations by the State that the ANC and the Communist Party are one and the same. Mandela said, *inter alia*, (op cit):

> 'The ANC has never at any period of its history advocated a revolutionary change in the economic structure of the country, nor has it, to the best of my recollection, ever condemned capitalist society.'

He went on to say that he had gained much from both East and West with regard to democracy, justice and the rights of man. The fight was, among other things, against two crucial enemies in South Africa, namely 'poverty and lack of human dignity'. He then gave a detailed analysis of the conditions under which blacks had to live. The lack of sufficient health facilities, the lack of appropriate educational facilities and the poor quality of education. He also described industrial and commercial discrimination against blacks, indicating the lack of opportunities, job-reservation and general lack of economic opportunities. The breakdown of family life suffered by blacks as a result of the pass laws and other legal restrictions was another critical factor prompting the ANC into action.

Mandela and seven of his colleagues were found guilty. He was convicted on four charges of sabotage. They were all sentenced to life imprisonment. The other accused were Walter Sisulu, Govan Mbeki, Raymond Mhlaba, Elias Matsoaledi, Andrew Mlangeni, Ahmed Kathrada and Dennis Goldberg. The date was 11 June 1964. Mandela was to spend about 27 years in prison, beginning with incarceration on the notorious Robben Island Prison in Table Bay, where he spent many years. Later he was moved to Pollsmoor Prison on the mainland. In December 1988, Mr Mandela was moved to a clinic for treatment of an ailment and then to a house in the grounds of Victor Verster Prison, near Paarl. He was freed from prison on 11 February 1990.

Despite many trials and tribulations, Mandela never wavered in his dedication to his life's work. He has been the recipient of honours from universities and organisations throughout the world. These include:

- ❑ Hon LLD – University of Strathclyde, Scotland, 1985
- ❑ Le Prix Ludovic-Tranieux, Bordeaux, France, 1985
- ❑ Hon PhD – University of Zimbabwe, 1986
- ❑ Hon LLD – Bayero University, Kano, Nigeria, 1988
- ❑ Hon LLD – Lagos, 1990
- ❑ Commander, Order of Nigeria, 1990

These are but a few of the international honours bestowed upon Dr Nelson Mandela, current President of the African National Congress. He is one of the main leaders in the current movement towards a new democratic South Africa. It is not possible in a study of this nature to do justice to the biography of a man of his stature. In 1993, Nelson Mandela was awarded the Nobel Peace Prize together with the State President, F.W. De Klerk. Now in his seventies, Dr Mandela's tireless effort for justice and freedom for all continues with vigour and a humble wisdom.

On his release from the Victor Verster Prison, on 11 February 1990, he addressed his first public gathering for 27 years on Cape Town's famous Parade. Thousands upon thousands of people thronged the square and, in full view of his people and the national and international media, he said, *inter alia*:

'I am not a prophet ....'

This was a measure of the man, one of South Africa's greatest sons.

CHAPTER 11

OLIVER REGINALD TAMBO (1917-1993)

The name of Oliver Tambo has been associated with the struggle for human rights for decades. Oliver Reginald Tambo was born on 27 October 1917 at Bizana, in the Eastern Cape. He attended the Methodist Mission School and the Holy Cross Mission School (Anglican) at Flagstaff. He later enrolled as a boarder at St Peter's Secondary School in Johannesburg, where he graduated with distinction in 1938.

He returned to the Eastern Cape and enrolled at the University of Fort Hare, where he obtained a Bachelor of Science degree in 1941. While studying for a diploma in education, Tambo was expelled (1942) from the university for his refusal to attend church services, which were compulsory at the time. He returned to St Peter's Secondary School in Johannesburg, this time as a science and mathematics teacher. A number of his pupils later made a contribution to the struggle for human rights, men such as Duma Nokwe, Joe Molefi and Joe Mathews. Tambo's political career began at this time, when he helped to establish the Youth League of the African National Congress in 1944.

Despite being a keen science and mathematics teacher, Tambo felt an urge to study law. In 1948, he articled himself to a Johannesburg law firm and in 1952, together with Nelson Mandela, he opened a legal practice. This was the first black legal practice in South Africa.

He now became more active politically, holding key portfolios in the ANC and related organisations. He was National Secretary of the ANC Youth League. He was also Transvaal President and National Vice-President of the League between 1948 and 1949. He was elected to the National Executive of the ANC in December 1949 and served as its Secretary-General between 1955 and 1958. His next position was that of Deputy President-General of the ANC, a post that was warranted by the fact that the then President (Albert Luthuli) was restricted to his home region in Natal by the government.

During the 1950s Tambo had the task of reassessing the constitution of the ANC. This resulted in a new constitution being accepted in 1957. Prior to that date, Tambo was served with a banning order in 1954. In terms of the order, issued under the Suppression of Communism Act, he was forbidden to attend public gatherings and restricted to the magisterial districts of Benoni and Johannesburg. The ban was effective for a two-year period. However, he remained active in the ANC and was instrumental in campaigning against the introduction of the notorious Bantu Education System.

In 1956, Oliver Tambo, a man of deep Christian conviction, was accepted as a candidate for ordination into the priesthood by Bishop Ambrose Reeves. However, his ordination process was cut short by his arrest in December of that year on charges of high treason. In the following year, the charges against him and others were dropped. Two years later, in 1959, he was again banned and was prohibited from attending public gatherings for five years.

At this time, the National Executive of the ANC became convinced that the authorities would ban the whole organisation in the country. With this in mind, the Executive asked Tambo to leave the country and establish an ANC mission overseas. Before he could leave, the Sharpeville tragedy took place and the banning of both the ANC and the PAC was discussed openly by the authorities. Tambo, together with Ronald Segal, left for Botswana, then Bechuanaland, and became the head of the ANC's external mission.

During these difficult days, Tambo travelled much on behalf of the ANC. He visited the United States, several European countries, the Soviet Union, Cuba, India, North Korea, the People's Republic of China and a number of African countries. He visited the United Nations on several occasions and attended meetings of the Organisation of African Unity on a regular basis. During the 1960s he worked tirelessly to create a united front of the external anti-apartheid organisations, including the ANC, PAC and South African Indian Congress. However, the unity of the movements collapsed.

In 1965, through Oliver Tambo's efforts, a guerilla training camp was established at the Tanzanian town of Morogoro, a few kilometres from Dar-es-Salaam. This camp later became the military headquarters of the ANC. When Albert Luthuli died in 1967, Tambo was elected acting President of the ANC, a position he held until recently, when Nelson Mandela was elected President, whereupon Tambo was elected Chairman. One of the more difficult moments of Tambo's political career was in 1984, when he was refused a transit visa through the People's Republic of Mozambique because of the Nkomati Accord signed between that country and South Africa. During his years in exile, he lived in Tanzania, Zambia and Britain. During the difficult years of exile, Tambo was the symbol of unity, strength and direction of the African National Congress. His fugitive lifestyle took its toll and he suffered from ill-health. He returned to South Africa after the release of his lifelong colleague, friend and partner, Nelson Mandela, and settled in Johannesburg. He was a quiet, unassuming man who shunned the limelight, preferring to live quietly and remain in the background. He was a dedicated family man; he and his wife Adelaide Tambo, a nurse and also a political activist, had three children, now all adults. His death in April 1993 was the end of an era in the ANC's history. His funeral service was attended by thousands of his fellow South Africans and numerous dignitaries from around the world.

CHAPTER 12

WALTER MAX ULYATE SISULU (1912-)

Walter Sisulu was born in 1912 in the Engcobo region of the Transkei. He was brought up by his mother and his uncle, who was a headman in the area. One of his biographers (Gastron 1987) said that Sisulu was of 'mixed ancestry and his light appearance set him apart from his peers. He was conscious of this and resented his family's deferential attitude towards whites'.

Sisulu attended a missionary school (The Anglican Missionary Institute), but when he was 15, his uncle died and he had to leave school. He left the Eastern Cape and found employment in Johannesburg, where he obtained employment in a dairy, but soon moved back to the Eastern Cape, where he was a domestic worker in East London. During this period, he was influenced by Clements Kadalie and the Industrial and Commercial Worker's Union.

In the early 1930s Sisulu moved back to Johannesburg, taking his mother and his sister with him. He worked at several jobs, most of them in factories. One work-related incident left its mark on the young man. During 1940 he was employed in a bakery, but felt that the wages they paid were inadequate and organised a strike, which led to his dismissal. Sisulu continued to campaign for better working conditions while with other employers, always confronting them on such issues as better wages. He became disenchanted with working for others and constantly clashing with his employers, however, and decided to open an estate agency. This venture lasted for only two years before he gave it up.

While he was in the Transvaal, Sisulu undertook private study and was very active in cultural activities. He was a member of the Orlando Brotherly Society, a group steeped in Xhosa history and culture. The group also attempted to make blacks economically independent of whites.

Sisulu's political life began in 1940 when he became a member of the ANC. He was soon elected treasurer of the ANC Youth League, taking a strong and militant attitude towards whites. During the war, Sisulu actively campaigned against black people joining the army.

Sisulu's activism landed him in prison when he was involved in a scuffle on a Johannesburg surburban train. A white ticket-collector had confiscated a season ticket from a black child and Sisulu came to her defence rather vigorously.

His activities in the ANC Youth League soon earned him the respect of his peers. He was involved in numerous activities and in 1946, during the African Mineworker's Strike, Sisulu tried to call for a general strike in their support. He became a member of the ANC's Transvaal Provincial Executive and in December 1949 was elected Secretary-General of the ANC due to his role in the Youth League, whose programme of action was accepted by the Conference of that year.

In June 1950 Sisulu was involved in the call for a work stoppage in conjunction with the Indian Congress and the South African Communist Party. A co-ordinating committee was formed and elected Sisulu and Yusuf Cachalia as joint secretaries of the united movement for action against the race laws. The then President of the ANC, Dr James Moroka, lived in the Orange Free State and was unable to attend to the day-to-day functions required of him, so Sisulu took over many of these functions, particularly those pertaining to the Transvaal. The result was that he was propelled into the Joint Planning Council in preparation for the Defiance Campaign. With passive resistance as their mode of operation, the Congress Alliance led by Walter Sisulu protested against the country's racial laws. He was arrested and imprisoned for a short period, after which he was banned under the Suppression of Communism Act.

In 1952 Sisulu, among others, was sentenced to nine months' imprisonment for his part in the Defiance Campaign, though the sentence was suspended for two years. He was re-elected to the post of Secretary-General in December 1952. At this time he also undertook a trip through China, the Soviet Union, Romania, Israel and Great Britain. While in the Soviet Union, he was made aware of Stalin's authoritarianism and he reacted against it. The overseas trip as a whole also had a profound influence on Sisulu, who changed his views on exclusive racial nationalism, choosing instead a multiracial approach to achieving a just society in South Africa.

Sisulu's banning order was a great hindrance to his political activities because he could not attend gatherings and other necessary meetings and functions. In 1954 he was forced to resign from the ANC as a result. One of the historical gatherings he was unable to attend was the 1955 Congress of the People that he had worked so hard to prepare for. He continued his work underground and became more and more multiracial in his approach to the struggle for human rights in South Africa. This did not make him popular with the exclusively Africanist faction of the ANC.

In 1956, Sisulu was one of the 156 people charged with high treason. It was a long case which was concluded only in March 1961. All the accused were found not guilty and discharged. While the trial was still proceeding, Sisulu and a number of the treason trialists were detained without trial for several months during the 1960 state of emergency.

Subsequent events were difficult for him. When the ANC and PAC were banned, he was placed under house arrest, making it even more difficult for him to function within the ANC structure. In 1962 he was arrested six times and charged on only one of those occasions. During 1963, he was convicted on charges of organising the 1961 stay-away protest and generally 'furthering the aims of the ANC'. The court released him on bail pending an appeal against his sentence, but once more his temporary freedom was curtailed. He was placed under 24-hour house arrest. In April 1963 he went underground, joining the armed wing of the ANC, Umkhonto we Sizwe. On 26 June 1963, it was Sisulu who made a clandestine broadcast from a secret ANC radio station.

On 11 July 1963, in the company of other high-ranking ANC members, Sisulu was arrested at Lilieslief Farm, Rivonia, and held for 88 days in solitary confinement. In June 1964, he was sentenced to life imprisonment for his part in planning acts of sabotage and revolution, and imprisoned, together with Nelson Mandela and others, in the notorious Robben Island Prison. In April 1982 he was admitted to Cape Town's Groote Schuur Hospital for a routine check-up and, together with Mandela, was transferred to Pollsmoor Prison at Tokai, near Cape Town.

Walter Sisulu was released unconditionally from prison in 1989 and in 1990, he was elected President of the ANC Committee to establish the movement's structures within South Africa. He is still an active member of the ANC National Executive Committee.

CHAPTER 13

JOE SLOVO (1926-)

Joe Slovo was born on 23 May 1926, in Lithuania. At the age of nine, he came to South Africa with his parents. He came from humble beginnings: his father worked as a van driver in Johannesburg. After he left school he worked as a clerk while he studied law at the University of the Witwatersrand, where he earned the degrees of BA LLB. He fought in World War II and after the war took an active part in the Springbok Legion, an ex-servicemen's organisation with radical tendencies. Between 1946 and 1951 he studied at the London School of Economics.

Slovo was a founder member of the Communist Party of South Africa and was active in the party during the 1940s. Once qualified, he was called to the Bar and as an advocate he defended many activists in political trials. In 1949 he married Ruth First, the daughter of Julius First, who was then the treasurer of the SA Communist Party. In 1950 Slovo and his wife, together with hundreds of others, were 'listed' in terms of the Suppression of Communism Act. The listing imposed a number of restrictions on them, one of which was that they could not be quoted in the press.

In 1953 Slovo was among the founder members of the Congress of Democrats, which he represented on the consultative committee of the Congress Alliance. It was through the Congress Alliance that the Congress of the People was called. In 1954 he was banned in terms of the Suppression of Communism Act, which meant that he could not attend gatherings in South Africa and Namibia (then South West Africa). However, he continued his political activities covertly, even helping to draft the Freedom Charter. He could not attend the Congress of the People held in Kliptown because of his banning order, but overcame this impediment by watching the proceedings from a rooftop, using binoculars.

In the 1956 Treason Trial, Slovo was charged with other members of the Congress. He was also a member of the defence team. In 1958 the treason charges against him were dropped. Two years later, during the 1960 state of emergency, he was held in detention for a period of four months.

Slovo was one of the first persons in the Congress Movement to join the ANC's armed wing, Umkhonto we Sizwe. He was a keen member of the organisation, attending regular meetings at the Liliesleif Farm, Rivonia. He left South Africa in 1963 and so missed being detained with the others later in the year. However, his wife Ruth was detained a few months after the arrest of the Rivonia trialists. Soon after her release, she left South Africa with their three daughters. She was killed by a parcel bomb in Maputo, Mozambique, in 1984.

Joe Slovo continued his political activities for both the ANC and the SA Communist Party while overseas. In 1977, he established a base for the ANC in the Mozambican capital, Maputo. In 1984 he was asked to leave Mozambique as a consequence of the Nkomati Accord signed between South Africa and the People's Republic of Mozambique during the presidency of Samora Machel. He returned to Britain and while there, a court awarded him damages of £25 000 against a South African newspaper that had alleged in an article that he had been party to his wife's murder.

Slovo was for a time Chief of Staff of Umkhonto we Sizwe and was Secretary-General of the South African Communist Party from 1986 until he stepped down on account of ill-health in 1992. He is still very active in protest politics and the negotiation process in South Africa.

CHAPTER 14

CHRIS MARTIN THEMBISILE HANI
(1942-1993)

Chris Hani, politician, activist and Latin scholar, was born at Cofimvaba, Transkei, on 28 June 1942. He attended a number of schools, including the Matanzima Secondary School, Cala, then enrolled at the Lovedale Institute, from where he matriculated in 1958. During his years at a Roman Catholic primary school, he came into contact with Latin, a language he learnt to love. The Catholic influence motivated him and already at the age of 12 he wanted to become a priest. His father, who played a vital role in his political education, did not like the idea and moved him to a public secular school.

When he entered Fort Hare University in 1959, Hani studied Latin classics and through these studies came to the realisation that politics involved a struggle between the opposing forces in society. His readings on the roles of patricians and plebeians in Roman society, coupled with a strong Dickensian description of England during the Industrial Revolution, helped him formulate his political attitudes. He moved to Rhodes University, where he graduated with a BA degree in Latin and English. Between 1962 and 1963 he was an articled clerk in the legal firm of Schaeffer and Schaeffer, but he did not complete his articles.

As stated earlier, Hani's father Gilbert had a profound influence on his son's political thinking. Gilbert Hani was a migrant worker who had moved to Cape Town, where he worked in the construction industry, before becoming self-employed as a pedlar. He was politically active and a member of the ANC. While in Cape Town he had been chairman of the Langa Vigilante Association, but in 1962 he was banished from Cape Town to the Transkei. He did not accept this condition and left the country, moving to Lesotho where he sought political asylum.

Chris Hani was also strongly influenced politically by his uncle, Milton Hani, who was a resident of the Kayamandi Location outside Stellenbosch and a member of the SA Communist Party. Another person who had a strong influence on Hani's political thinking was Govan Mbeki, the father of Thabo Mbeki, who had been Hani's schoolmate. These two men, together with a number of his teachers, helped him comprehend the intricacies of Marxism-Leninism.

Chris Hani became a member of the ANC Youth League in 1957, while he was at the Lovedale Institute. He took an active part in the protests against the University of Fort Hare being taken over by the then Department of Bantu Administration in 1959. In 1961 he took part in the protest campaign against the establishment of a Republic based on an all-white referendum and was suspended from Fort Hare University as a result.

While he was in Cape Town, Chris Hani's perceptions of wealth and the need for its redistribution took root. During the period in which he was articled to the firm of attorneys he came into close contact with the South African Congress of Trade Unions (SACTU). Through this contact he was able to see at first hard the workers' struggle to achieve a better life. He also saw the very poor conditions under which his father had had to live in 'bachelor's quarters' and the generally poor conditions to which migrant workers were subjected. The Freedom Charter of the ANC became a guiding principle for his struggle for economic and social justice.

Hani now embarked on a course of action which brought him to prominence within the ANC and SACP structures. When the ANC was banned, he joined Umkhonto we Sizwe and became a member of a group known as the 'Committee of Seven', which was in reality the leadership structure of Umkhonto we Sizwe in the Western Cape. From then on he was forced to live a clandestine life. In 1962 he was arrested at a roadblock for having in his possession pamphlets objecting to the 90-day detention law. He was held at the Phillipi police station and later at the Roeland Street gaol, before being charged in terms of the Suppression of Communism Act. He was released on R500 bail, but went to Lobatsi in Botswana to attend an ANC conference. He was re-arrested at the Lobatsi border gate when he returned to South Africa. At his trial he was found guilty and sentenced to 18 months' imprisonment, but was released on bail pending his appeal against the sentence. When he lost his appeal, the ANC instructed him to go underground in Cape Town. Some months later, he moved to Johannesburg and was told to leave South Africa in order to undergo military training.

Hani surfaced again in 1967 as Commissar of the Luthuli detachment of Umkhonto we Sizwe. He fought in Rhodesia alongside the forces of the Zimbabwe African People's Union (ZAPU) and was involved in a number of battles in the Tjolotjo region near Wankie. However, consistent pressure from the Rhodesian security forces forced him to move to Botswana towards the end of 1967. In Botswana he was arrested and tried for being in possession of arms, found guilty and given a six-year sentence. After serving two years, he was released and moved to Zambia.

In 1974 Hani was back in South Africa, where he was instructed to establish a political infrastructure for the ANC in the Cape Province. After a number of operations in the Cape, he moved to Lesotho and remained there for seven years. In 1981 explosives were planted in the vehicle he was using, but the assassination attempt failed. In 1982 he was recalled to Zambia and made Political Commissar and Deputy Commander of Umkhonto we Sizwe. In 1973, at the age of only 32, he was elected to the ANC's National Executive. In 1987 he was appointed Chief of Staff of Umkhonto we Sizwe. He served as a member of the Politburo of the South African Communist Party and on Joe Slovo's retirement he became Secretary-General of the SACP, a post which he held until his untimely death in April 1993.

CHAPTER 15

CHRISTIAAN FREDERICK BEYERS NAUDÉ (1915-)

Christiaan Frederick Beyers Naudé, known throughout South Africa as Beyers Naudé, is one of South Africa's most respected activists and human rights advocates. He was born in the Transvaal town of Roodepoort on 10 May 1915. He was one of eight children, the son of Jozua Franchoise Naudé, one of the founders of the Afrikaans language and a Dutch Reformed Church minister. Beyers Naudé's struggle for human rights and justice is all the more remarkable in view of his conservative origins.

He was reared in the Afrikaans tradition, both in the Transvaal and the Eastern Cape town of Graaff-Reinet, to which the family moved in 1921. He attended the Afrikaans Hoër Volkskool, from which he matriculated in 1931. He went on to Stellenbosch University and obtained a Master's degree in languages. In 1939, he graduated from the School of Theology of Stellenbosch University and in 1940 was appointed assistant-minister at Wellington's Dutch Reformed Church. It was during this period that Beyers Naudé was inducted into the secret organisation, the Afrikaner Broederbond.

For two decades Beyers Naudé served congregations in various parts of South Africa and remained very much within the parameters of National Party ideology. These began to change, however, when, in 1960, he attended the Cottlesloe Constitution. The Sharpeville tragedy in the same year also left a profound mark on his mind and spirit.

During this time he had risen in the church hierarchy to become acting moderator of the Southern Transvaal Synod. In April 1961 he was appointed moderator within the same jurisdiction. However, he had also helped to found the Christian Institute, an ecumenical organisation whose aim was the unity of all christians regardless of their ethnic origin. He edited the Christian Institute's controversial publication, *Pro Veritate*, and from this time on, he underwent what can best be described as a Damascus experience regarding the issue of social justice. He paid a high price for his new beliefs.

The year 1963 was a watershed year for Beyers Naudé. He resigned as moderator and as pastor to his congregation. He became the Director of the Christian Institute and also resigned from the Afrikaner Broederbond, giving his reasons for doing so in the press. He had been a member of the secret society for 22 years and his step did not endear him to the other members, most of whom held positions of power in the government and other institutions in South African society. An incident in March 1965 was indicative of the resentment he had to face because of his beliefs. His appointment as an elder of the Dutch Reformed Church in Parkhurst, Johannesburg, caused very bitter controversy and he had to suffer the humiliation of being removed by force from a meeting at which he was to address a group of young people in Belgravia, Johannesburg.

A Pretoria professor, A P Pont, suggested that Beyers Naudé and Professor A S Geyer were 'communist fellow-travellers'. Naudé and Geyser sued for libel and were awarded R10 000 each by the court. His biographer says (Gastrow 1987):

> 'As Director of the Christian Institute, Naudé was invited to address many meetings where he repeatedly warned about growing militant black power consciousness, increasing uncontrolled racial flashpoints and the temporary rejection of white liberal organisations by blacks. He repeatedly opposed the use of violence as a means of change.'

Beyers Naudé undertook a series of tasks including travelling to Europe. On 8 May 1972, he became the first Afrikaner to preach at Westminster Abbey, London. In September 1972 the Free University of Amsterdam awarded him an honorary doctorate in Theology. During this period, the Christian Institute was subject to pressure from the state in the form of harassment of members of the CI's staff. Some were banned and others deported. The offices of the CI were raided several times and staff and members were questioned by the security police.

In 1973 Parliament appointed the Schlebusch Commission to investigate The Christian Institute, The University Christian Movement, The National Union of South African Students (NUSAS), and The Institute of Race Relations.

Beyers Naudé was called to give evidence to the Commission, but he refused and was harassed even further. In November 1973 he was forced to surrender his passport.

The following year he received two further distinctions – an honorary doctorate in law from the University of the Witwatersrand and the prestigious Reinhold Niebuhr Award for working for peace and justice in South Africa. He shared this prize with the distinguished Russian dissident, Andrei Sakharov. The authorities returned his passport, thus enabling him to travel to the United States to receive the award.

The Schlebusch Commission's findings were released in 1974, and included the recommendation that the Christian Institute's external financial assistance be stopped, which had a serious and negative effect on its functioning. In 1975 Beyers Naudé was invited to address the Royal Institute of

International Affairs in London. However, his passport had been withdrawn again and his speech had to be read for him.

In 1976 Beyers Naudé found himself in further difficulties. He had appealed against the sentence handed down to him for refusing to testify before the Schlebusch Commission, but the appeal failed and he was fined R50 or one month's imprisonment, with an additional three months conditionally suspended for three years. He refused to pay the fine and on 28 October 1976, he went to prison. However, his fine was paid by Dr Jan van Rooyen, a DRC minister, and he was released after spending the night in goal.

The year 1977 was not much better for him. In October of that year, he was banned for another five years, along with the Rev Theo Kotze, a one-time Director of the CI's Cape regional office, and an Anglican priest, the Rev David Russel. Two more international awards were bestowed on him while he was banned, one from the Swedish Free Church and the other from the Austrian Bruno Kreisky Foundation.

In 1980, along with three fellow ministers and theologians, Beyers Naudé broke away from the main Dutch Reformed Church (the all-white church) and was admitted to the NGK in Africa, the black wing of the DRC. The year 1982 came, and with it an extended banning order for another three years. He was asked to appeal against the extended ban, but he refused. In December of that year his banning order was eased a little, but it made little difference, since he was still restricted to the Johannesburg magisterial district and could not address meetings of a political nature. He was further forbidden to address students, to teach or communicate with other banned persons. He could also not be quoted.

A number of representations were made to the authorities, including one by the Potchefstroom Calvinist journal *Woord en Daad*, asking them to rescind the banning order. In addition, thousands of signatures were collected throughout South Africa and presented to the Minister of Justice asking for the banning order to be lifted. In September 1984, the Government conceded and lifted the banning order.

Naudé's next important post was that of Secretary-General of the South African Council of Churches (SACC). The post had fallen vacant when Desmond Tutu became Anglican Bishop of Johannesburg in January 1985. On 27 March 1985, Beyers Naudé was arrested when he and the Rev Allan Boesak led two hundred others in a demonstration march in Cape Town. However, the charges against them were dropped.

Beyers Naudé was awarded further honours in recognition of his selfless service to the fight for justice and human rights. The University of Cape Town awarded him the honorary degree of Doctor of Literature (DLit) in 1983. Two American honours were also conferred on him in 1984 and 1985 respectively

– the Freedom of Worship Medal, awarded by the Franklin D Roosevelt Foundation, and the Robert F Kennedy Memorial Human Rights award.

CHAPTER 16

GOVAN ARCHIBALD MVUYELWA MBEKI
(1910-)

Govan Mbeki, one-time National Chairman of the African National Congress, was born in 1910 in the Nqamakwe district of the Transkei. His father was a chief who had been deposed by the government. He attended several schools, among them the one at Healdtown, and went on to the University of Fort Hare, from which he graduated with a BA in 1937. In addition to his degree he completed a teacher's diploma in education.

He became a member of the African National Congress in 1935, while he was still studying. He was influenced politically by Edward Roux, a leader of the Communist Party of South Africa. For a while, he was also influenced by a black American Communist, Max Yergan, who had been sent to South Africa on secondment to the YMCA. However, Yergan's enthusiasm for communism diminished and he became a supporter of the National Party.

Mbeki taught at various schools, including Adams College and the Clarkebury Institute. In common with other activist teachers, he was dismissed because of his political activities. He then became a businessman, running a co-operative store near Idutywa in the Transkei. He also edited the *Territorial Magazine* for seven years, between 1938 and 1944. Mbeki was an ardent student and continued his studies through the University of South Africa, being awarded the degree of BCom in 1940.

Mbeki's political career began in earnest with his appointment as Secretary of the Transkei African Voter's Association. He entered mainstream politics when, in 1943, he was elected to the Transkei bunga for a four-year period. He was active in the ANC and in 1943 was involved in discussions relating to the Atlantic Charter, the document that was eventually adopted as the UN Charter. He also had a hand in drawing-up the Freedom Charter. In 1950 his co-op store was destroyed by a tornado and he had to begin teaching again in order to make a living. He found a post in Ladysmith, Natal, but he could not resist political activity and was once more dismissed from his post.

He moved to Port Elizabeth in 1955, where he became the regional editor of *New Age*, a left-wing newspaper. He was not yet a member of the South African Communist Party, but he made no secret of his support of the left wing. As editor of *New Age*, he reported on issues throughout the Eastern Cape, including Transkei. At the same time he kept close touch with affairs at his alma mater, the University of Fort Hare, serving as the convocation's representative on the Council of the University.

Mbeki's hard work in the Eastern Cape, and Port Elizabeth in particular, helped make the ANC's regional branch one of the most successful. He put into effect a system of cell groups, called the M plan, which had been initiated by Nelson Mandela, and made the Eastern Cape one of the strongholds of the ANC in South Africa at the time. He opposed the government's Bantu Administration system, especially its Bantu Education policy. He took part in planning the Congress of the People in 1955 and was made leader of the ANC in the Eastern Cape. In 1956 he was elected National Chairman of the ANC.

Govan Mbeki and Kaizer Matanzima had been close friends for a number of years, but this relationship broke up in 1957 over the issue of bantustans. The quarrel between the two men continued when Matanzima tried to stop a dock-workers' strike in Port Elizabeth by importing truckloads of workers to the area. The strike continued and succeeded. In retaliation, Matanzima issued orders to his headman and councillors that if any members of the Mbeki family were seen in the Qamata region of Transkei, they should be brought to him. Govan Mbeki never returned to the area.

During the 1960 state of emergency Mbeki was detained for five months. After his release, he worked hard at organising the All-in-Africa Conference at Pietermaritzburg. In 1961 he joined the SA Communist Party and in December of that year, he was arrested and charged under the Explosives Act. He spent several months in solitary confinement before being brought to trial, at which he was found not guilty. In 1963, while under house arrest, he joined Umkhonto we Sizwe, serving as the Secretary of its High Command. In July 1963, together with his fellow leaders of the ANC, Mbeki was arrested at Lilieslief Farm, Rivonia. Found guilty of sabotage, he was sentenced to life imprisonment on Robben Island.

He was released in 1987, but restricted in the same year. The restrictions were lifted in 1990 and he is now a member of the National Executive Committee of the ANC and a member of the Central Committee of the SA Communist Party. One of the many honours he has received is the honorary degree of Doctor of Philosophy in Social Sciences from the University of Amsterdam.

CHAPTER 17

NOMZAMO WINNIE MANDELA (1934-)

Winnie Mandela was born in Bizana, Pondoland, in 1934. Her father was a prominent Transkei politician who left teaching for a post in the Cabinet, that of Minister of Agriculture and Forestry. Her mother was a trained Domestic Science expert. She attended school at Bizana and later at Shawbury. At 16 she enrolled at the Jan Hofmeyr School of Social Work and was the first black person to become a medical social worker. She worked at the Baragwanath Hospital in Soweto.

She met Nelson Mandela and married him during 1958. She was active in politics at the time, serving on both the National and Provincial Executive of the ANC Women's League and the Federation of South African Women. She was also chairperson of the Orlando branch of the ANC until the organisation was banned in 1960. She was an ardent activist and was in almost constant difficulty with the authorities. Those confrontations included:

❑ 1959: charged in terms of the Terrorism Act, but found not guilty on appeal.

❑ 1962: banned in terms of the Suppression of Communism Act and restricted to Orlando West Township. She was forced to give up her job.

❑ 1965: more stringent banning orders were served on her.

❑ 1967: charged twice with allegedly violating her banning order. She was sentenced to a year's imprisonment, but the sentence was suspended, with the exception of four days.

❑ 1969: detained in terms of Section 6 of the Terrorism Act, resulting in her being held in solitary confinement for 17 months. She was acquitted on these charges twice.

❑ 1970: served with another banning order and also placed under house arrest.

❑ 1971: received a suspended sentence for allegedly communicating with another banned person.

❑ 1974: had to serve a six-month prison sentence for another contravention of her banning order.

Despite constant pressure on her from the authorities and her periodic imprisonment for her activities, Winnie Mandela continued to work for what she believed in. Her banning order expired in 1975 and almost immediately she assisted in the founding of the Black Women's Federation and the Black Parents' Association. The latter organisation's function was to assist the victims of the 1976 Soweto riots. In 1977 both these organisations were banned by the government. She was detained again in 1976 and served with another banning order on 28 December.

In the following year (1977), Winnie Mandela's banning order was amended in order to remove her from her Soweto home. She was moved, against her will, to Phatakhale, outside the Orange Free State town of Brandfort. This still did not quench her spirit and she faced a number of charges for violating her banning order. In 1982 she was once more banned, with the order being renewed after one year.

In August 1985 her Brandfort home was fire-bombed and she defied her banning order and returned to her home in Soweto. The authorities relented a little, allowing her to live anywhere in the country, except in the magisterial districts of Johannesburg and Roodepoort. On 21 December 1985, Mrs Mandela was removed from her Soweto home by police, but returned once more. She was arrested again and held in custody overnight.

She visited her husband in prison in Cape Town over Christmas. When she returned to Johannesburg, she was once again arrested and charged with violating her banning orders. The charges were withdrawn in February 1986.

After the release of her husband, Nelson, and other members of the ANC hierarchy in 1990, Mrs Mandela became head of the Social Welfare Department of the ANC. She was later replaced as head of Social Welfare. Among the many honours bestowed upon her was an honorary LLD degree conferred by the University of Utrecht, Holland. She and her husband have now separated.

CHAPTER 18

MATAMELA CYRIL RAMAPHOSA (1952-)

Cyril Ramaphosa has had a distinguished career, both as a trade unionist, and as a politician. He was born in Johannesburg, where his father was a policeman, on 17 November 1952. He attended the Sekano-Ntoane High School in Soweto and later the Mphaphuli High School in Sibasa, Northern Transvaal. He matriculated in 1971. The following year he registered at the University of the North (Turfloop) for a BProc degree. He immediately joined the South African Students' Organisation (SASO) and in 1974 was elected chairman of the Student Christian Movement (SCM), an organisation that went beyond dealing with spiritual matters, also encompassing political and social issues. In 1974, a rally supporting the Mozambican Frelimo Movement was held at the University. As a consequence, Ramaphosa was detained under Section 6 of the Terrorism Act at the Pretoria Central Prison.

Upon his release, Ramaphosa became active in the Black People's Convention as a member of its committees. He also articled himself to a firm of attorneys in Johannesburg. However, when the June 1976 riots broke out in Soweto, he was once more detained under the Terrorism Act and held for six months. On his release he resumed his legal articles and continued to study by correspondence at the University of South Africa. He was awarded the degree of BProc in 1981. He also completed his articles, but chose not to practice as an attorney. His calling was working for the underprivileged and he felt that legal practice was not the best way of assisting those in need, particularly the workers.

Ramaphosa joined the Council of Trade Unions of South Africa (CUSA) as its legal advisor. Through the labour movement, he continued to work for freedom and justice. In this respect, 1982 was an important year both for him and for CUSA. The labour organisation chose to form the National Union of Mineworkers (NUM) and Ramaphosa was chosen as its first Secretary-General. The NUM's membership rose from a mere 6 000 workers to nearly 400 000 by 1987. It was also the first unregistered trade union to be recognised by the Chamber of Mines.

Cyril Ramaphosa, with his legal training, was the ideal person to begin the struggle for better conditions for the workers he represented. He called for a number of rights to be given to black mine workers, including:
❑ the removal of racial discrimination in the mining industry;

- equal pay for equal work for all mineworkers doing the same jobs as those reserved for whites;
- paternity leave for migrant workers so that they could see their families;
- similar pension benefits for black mineworkers as those given to whites;
- changes in working hours;
- representatives of miners on the Chamber of Mines Safety Committees; and
- the introduction of a bill of rights relating to the safety of mineworkers.

Cyril Ramaphosa was involved in organising the first legal strike by black mineworkers in South Africa, in September 1984. In November 1984, the Lebowa police arrested him and held him overnight on allegations of holding an illegal meeting. He was released without being charged. He was also instrumental in the formation of the Congress of South African Trade Unions (COSATU). This was a super-federation of trade unions, including the NUM and the Federation of South African Trade Unions (FOSATU). Ramaphosa was the convenor of the Rally of Unity held in Durban in December 1985 and delivered the keynote address. He was one of the main delegates representing COSATU when talks were held with the ANC and the South African Congress of Trade Unions in Lusaka, Zambia in 1986. In recent elections, Cyril Ramaphosa was elected Secretary-General of the African National Congress and commands the respect of all sectors of the South African community. His style of leadership is rational and his brilliant legal mind makes him the ideal person to manage the day-to-day running of the ANC's affairs.

CHAPTER 19

DESMOND MPILO TUTU (1931-)

Archbishop Desmond Tutu was born in Klerksdorp, Transvaal on 7 October 1931. He attended a number of mission schools at primary level and then the Madibane High School, formerly called the Bantu High School, Western Native Township. He went on to the Pretoria Bantu Normal College and obtained a Teacher's Diploma in 1953. He continued his studies and was awarded a BA degree a year later. For the next four years, he taught at the Munsieville High School.

Tutu left teaching in 1957 and entered St Peter's Theological College for training towards the priesthood. In 1960 he was ordained as a deacon, the following year he became a priest, working in the Benoni black location. He left for the United Kingdom in 1962 and settled in London. While in the British capital, he continued his studies and obtained a Bachelor's degree with Honours in 1965. In the following year, he completed a Masters Degree in Theology and returned to South Africa, visiting Israel on the way.

Tutu decided to continue teaching, this time as a Christian vocation, and was appointed to the Federal Theological Seminary at Alice, Cape. He left this seminary when it was taken over by the government, a step he did not agree with. He then began to lecture in the Department of Theology at Roma University in Lesotho. The year 1972 saw the family back in Britain, where Tutu was appointed to the post of Associate Director of the Theological Education Fund of the World Council of Churches. In 1975, he had to move back to South Africa when he was appointed Anglican Dean of Johannesburg. Less than a year later he was appointed Bishop of Lesotho, a post he held until 1978, when he was given the post of Secretary-General of the South African Council of Churches in Johannesburg. In 1978 he attended the Anglican Bishop's Conference in Britain. During the course of this conference, Bishop Tutu proposed a resolution, which was accepted, that all countries, not just South Africa, be condemned for their dismal human rights records.

In 1979, Tutu visited Denmark and during this visit he admonished that country for buying South African coal. This led to his being summoned to a meeting with the Minister of Justice and Co-operation and Development on his return home. He was asked to retract the statement made during his visit to Denmark, but refused. However, he expressed his willingness to participate in discussion with the government on fundamental reforms.

In May 1980 Tutu and a group of others, mostly clerics, were arrested in terms of the Riotous Assemblies Act. They had been involved in a march to protest against the detention of a Congregational Church minister, the Rev John Thorne. Two months later, all of them were convicted and sentenced to 50 days' imprisonment or a R50 fine. Tutu's passport was confiscated in March 1980, only a few days before he was to leave for a visit to Switzerland, but returned to him in January 1981. He then travelled to the United States and while there he met a number of important people, including Kurt Waldheim, then Secretary-General of the United Nations.

While in the USA, Tutu addressed the UN Special Committee Against Apartheid and is reported to have called for economic sanctions and disinvestment from South Africa. During another visit to Europe, Tutu met the Pope and held discussions with other leading churchmen. As soon as he returned to South Africa, his passport was once again withdrawn. In 1982 and 1983, he visited the United States, on the second occasion attending the 50th Anniversary of the birth of the American Human Rights Activist, Dr Martin Luther King Jr. In 1984 Tutu was awarded the Nobel Peace Prize. He became the Anglican Bishop of Johannesburg in 1985, at the same time relinquishing his post as Secretary-General of the South African Council of Churches.

He began to call for economic sanctions against South Africa in the hope that this non-violent form of pressure would make the government change its racial policies. However, when a number of killings by the 'necklace' method occurred in the townships, Tutu threatened to leave South Africa if this practice did not stop. He spoke against violence as a means of achieving political ends, especially black-on-black violence. In 1986, Bishop Tutu was made Archbishop of Cape Town. The Consecration took place in Cape Town's St George's Cathedral, scene of much human rights protest activity.

Archbishop Tutu has been the recipient of several international honours. He is the second South African to be awarded the Nobel Peace Prize. He has an honorary doctorate from the General Theological Seminary, USA (1978). He also holds five other honorary doctorates.

CHAPTER 20

ALLAN BOESAK (1946-)

Allan Boesak was born on 23 February 1946, in the small town of Kakamas, in the Northern Cape. In 1953 his father, a teacher by profession, died and the family moved to Somerset West. From a very early age, Allan Boesak took an active part in his church's affairs, even serving as a sexton at the age of 16.

His political awareness also came at a very early age, as did his disagreement with the socio-political system in South Africa. His anger at the apartheid system was first aroused when his family was forced to move in accordance with the Group Areas Act. He enrolled at the Bellville Theological Seminary and graduated in 1967. His first ministry was in Paarl, where he served for three years before going to the Kaupen Theological Institute, Holland, where he completed his doctorate in Theology.

On his return to South Africa, Dr Boesak was involved in founding the Alliance of Black Reformed Christians in Southern Africa, on 27 October 1981. He was elected its first Chairman. He was also a prominent member of the Broederkring, a group of influential persons in the Dutch Reformed Church. Upon being elected chairman of ABRESCA, Dr Boesak issued a statement which broke with DRC tradition. The statement included the following Creed (Gastrow 1987), rejecting the interpretation of the Reformed tradition which:

'(a) Subjected the word of God to a cultural or racist ideology;
(b) Confined the Lordship of Christ to a narrow "spiritual" reason;
(c) Denied Christian involvement in political matters;
(d) Demanded uncritical loyalty to the State which was regarded as divinely instituted; and
(e) Reaffirmed only the mystical unity of the church.'

The Conference of ABRECSA also affirmed the following as being in the Reformed tradition (ibid):

'(a) The word of God was supreme authority;
(b) Jesus Christ was the Lord of the whole of life;
(c) Christians bore responsibility for the world in its totality;
(d) Obedience to earthly authorities was only obedience in God; and
(e) Unity of the Church must be visible.'

The World Alliance of Reformed Churches, representing about 150 churches of Calvinist belief in over 76 countries, met in Ottawa, Canada, in

August 1982. The four South African reformed churches were also represented. Dr Boesak attended the Conference, at which he introduced a motion calling for apartheid to be declared a heresy and contrary to the teachings of Jesus Christ. The motion was adopted and the DRC and NHK were suspended from the Alliance and given conditions for re-admission. During this conference, Dr Boesak was elected President of the World Alliance of Reformed Churches. In September 1982, he was elected Assessor of the DRC Mission Church in Cape Town, having narrowly missed being elected to the post of Moderator, which went to the Rev I Mentor.

1983 was a critical year in Boesak's life. In January he was a member of a steering committee formed to establish the United Democratic Front (UDF), which was opposed to the tricameral parliamentary system. The UDF was launched at Mitchells Plain and Dr Boesak was elected its Patron. He set about establishing it as a powerful organisation, whose influence was felt both inside South Africa and internationally. In 1984, he was the first person to put his signature to a petition on which the UDF hoped to get one million people to signify their rejection of the tricameral parliament, which excluded blacks. This was known as the One Million Signature Campaign. In November 1984, Dr Boesak visited Australia, where he campaigned for that country to adopt a firmer stand against apartheid.

In 1985 he flew to Lusaka, Zambia, where he met both Oliver Tambo, then President of the ANC, and the then President of Zambia, Dr Kenneth Kaunda. On his return to South Africa he experienced some harassment by the authorities. He was arrested for allegedly attempting to enter a black township without the appropriate permit, but the charge was later dropped.

In August 1985, Dr Boesak planned a march on Pollsmoor Prison, Cape Town, in which he would be joined by thousands of people, to demand the release of Nelson Mandela. The march did not take place, as he was arrested and held in terms of Section 29 of the Internal Security Act. He was detained in Pretoria, later appeared in the Malmesbury Magistrate's Court on 20 September, and was released on R20 000 bail. Although one of the demands by the State was for the withdrawal of his passport while on bail, the court found him to be a 'man of high political morals and ideals' and ordered that his passport be returned to him.

Dr Boesak was one of a group of clerics who formed a delegation to the State President on 20 February 1986 to voice their concern at the deteriorating situation in Alexandra Township, Johannesburg. In March he attended the funeral of the assassinated Swedish Premier, Olaf Palme, in Stockholm. During this trip once again he held talks with Oliver Tambo and the new Swedish Prime Minister, Ingvar Carlsson.

Dr Boesak travelled extensively, visiting Thailand, Hong Kong, the United States and Switzerland, where he received an honorary degree from the University of Geneva. His beliefs are that the church has to involve itself politically and that faith in Jesus Christ means that one cannot remain distanced from injustice by merely being an onlooker. He suggests that apartheid had gone beyond an ideology and was being embraced as a pseudo-gospel, its apologists finding justification for its existence, particularly in the Afrikaans Reformed Churches.

Dr Boesak served on a number of committees and in various capacities, including that of Senior Vice-President of the South African Council of Churches. Recently he was elected Chairman of the Western Cape branch of the ANC.

CONCLUSION

The transition process in South Africa brings with it a number of important considerations, especially in relation to human rights. The development of an acceptable constitution, for instance, cannot be undertaken without the inclusion of some form of human rights charter or bill. If the society is to establish democratic structures, the issue of individual human rights becomes paramount, though group rights such as minority rights must be considered. Economic rights, religious rights and equality before the law are also very important facets of the human rights culture.

The human rights culture is relatively new to most South Africans. As such, it has to be spread by all influential institutions. These could include educational institutions, such as schools, universities and other teaching mediums such as correspondence colleges. Political organisations also have to learn and attempt to provide their members with some knowledge of human rights and civil liberties.

It must also be remembered that the human rights culture cannot be established overnight. During the years to come, human rights will have to be practised in order for one to become acquainted with its reality, rather than only its theoretical perspective. Another critical issue relates to educating the masses in the culture of human rights. The process of socialising the masses will not be an easy one and will depend upon many factors. One of them is the willingness of all concerned, particularly those in leadership positions, to spread the culture of human rights. This can be done through use of the press, television programmes, study forums and other such media.

With the current violence in South Africa it becomes even more pressing for the human rights culture to spread, thereby instilling precepts of tolerance for divergent opinions and beliefs. This can only be done successfully if there is strict adherence to the conditions stipulated in a bill of rights, which among other things must guarantee freedom of political choice.

APPENDICES

THE DRAFT BILL OF RIGHTS OF THE AFRICAN NATIONAL CONGRESS

A BILL OF RIGHTS FOR A DEMOCRATIC SOUTH AFRICA –
WORKING DRAFT FOR CONSULTATION
as prepared by the Constitutional Committee of the
African National Congress

Article 1 GENERAL

1 All south Africans are born free and equal in dignity and rights.

2 No individual or group shall receive privileges or be subjected to discrimination, domination or abuse on the grounds of race, colour, language, gender, creed, political or other opinion, birth or other status.

3 All men and women shall have equal protection under the law.

Article 2 PERSONAL RIGHTS

The Right to Life.

1 Every person has the right to life.

2 No-one shall be arbitrarily deprived of his or her life.

3 Capital punishment is abolished and no further executions shall take place.

The Right to Dignity

4 No-one shall be subjected to slavery, servitude or forced labour, provided that forced labour shall not include work normally required of someone carrying out a sentence of a court, nor military service or national service by a conscientious objector, nor services required in the case of calamity or serious emergency, nor any work which forms part of normal civil obligations.

5 The dignity of all persons shall be respected.

6 No-one shall be subjected to torture or cruel, inhuman or degrading treatment or punishment.

7 Everyone shall have the right to appropriate protection by law against violence, harassment or abuse, or the impairment of his or her dignity.

The Right to a Fair Trial

8 There shall be no detention without trial.

9 No persons shall be arrested or detained for any purpose other than that of

bringing them to trial on a criminal charge.

10 Arrests shall take place according to procedures laid down by law, and persons taken into custody shall immediately be informed of the charges against them, shall have access to a legal representative of their choice, and shall be brought before court within 48 hours or, where that would be a Sunday or a public holiday, on the first working day thereafter.

11 Bail shall be granted to awaiting-trial persons unless a court rules that in the interests of justice they should be kept in custody.

12 No-one shall be deprived of liberty or subjected to other punishment except after a fair trial in public by an independent court.

13 Trials shall take place within a reasonable time.

14 Everyone shall be presumed innocent until proved guilty.

15 No conduct shall be punished if it was not a criminal offence at the time of its occurrence, and no penalty shall be increased retrospectively.

16 No-one shall be punished twice for the same offence.

17 Accused persons shall be informed in writing of the nature of the allegations against them, and shall be given adequate time to prepare and conduct their defence.

18 Everything that is reasonable shall be done to ensure that accused persons understand the nature and the import of the charges against them and of the proceedings, that they are not prejudiced through illiteracy or lack of understanding, and that they receive a fair trial.

19 Accused persons shall have the right to challenge all evidence presented against them, to be defended by a legal practitioner of their choice, and if in custody, to have access to a legal practitioner at all reasonable times.

20 If a person is unable to pay for legal representation, and the interests of justice so require, the State shall provide or pay for a competent defence.

21 No persons shall be required to give evidence against themselves, nor, except in cases of domestic violence or abuse, shall persons be required to give evidence against their spouses, whether married by civil law or custom, their parents or their children.

22 No evidence obtained through torture or cruel, inhuman or degrading treatment shall be admissible in any proceedings.

23 Juveniles shall be separated from adult offenders.

The Right to Judicial Review

24 Any person adversely affected by an administrative or executive act shall have the right to have the matter reviewed by an independent court or tribunal on the grounds of abuse of authority, going beyond the powers granted by law, bad faith, or such gross unreasonableness in relation to the procedure or the decision as to amount to manifest injustice.

The Right to Home Life

25 No-one shall be deprived of or removed from his or her home on the grounds of race, colour, language, gender or creed.

26 The privacy of the home shall be respected, save that reasonable steps shall be permitted to prevent domestic violence or abuse.

27 People shall have the right to establish families, live together with partners of their choice and to marry.

28 Marriage shall be based upon the free consent of the partners, and spouses shall enjoy equal rights at and during the marriage and after its dissolution.

The Right to Privacy

29 No search or entry shall be permitted except for reasonable cause, as prescribed by law, and as would be acceptable in an open and democratic society.

30 Interference with private communications, spying on persons, and the compilation and keeping of secret files about them without their consent, shall not be permissible save as authorised by law in circumstances that would be acceptable in an open and democratic society.

The Right of Movement

31 Everyone shall have the right to move freely and reside in any part of the country, to receive a passport, travel abroad and to emigrate or return if he or she so wishes.

The Right to Conscience

32 The right to conscience shall be inviolate, and no-one shall be penalised for his or her beliefs.

Article 3 POLITICAL RIGHTS

1 South Africa shall be a multi-party democracy in which all men and women shall enjoy basic political rights on an equal basis.

2 Government at all levels shall be subject to the principles of accountability to the electorate.

3 Elections shall be conducted in accordance with an electoral law which shall make no distinction on the grounds of race, colour, language, gender or creed.

4 Elections shall be regular, free and fair and based on universal franchise and a common voters' roll.

5 All men and women entitled to vote shall be entitled to stand for and occupy any position or office in any organ of government or administration.

6 All citizens shall have the right to form and join political parties and to campaign for social, economic and political change, either directly or through freely chosen representatives.

Article 4 FREEDOM OF SPEECH, ASSEMBLY AND INFORMATION

1 There shall be freedom of thought, speech, expression and opinion, including a free press which shall respect the right to reply.

2 All men and women shall have the right to assemble peacefully and without arms, and to submit petitions for the redress of grievances and injustices.

3 All men and women shall be entitled to all the information necessary to enable them to make effective use of their rights as citizens or consumers.

Article 5 RIGHTS OF ASSOCIATION, RELIGION, LANGUAGE AND CULTURE

Freedom of Association

1 There shall be freedom of association, including the right to form and join trade unions, religious, social and cultural bodies, and to form and participate in non-governmental organisations.

Freedom of Religion

2 There shall be freedom to worship and tolerance of all religions, and no State or official religion shall be established.

3 The institutions of religion shall be separate from the State, but nothing in this Constitution shall prevent them from co-operating with the State with a view to furthering the objectives of this Constitution, nor from bearing witness and commenting on the actions of the State.

4 Places associated with religious observance shall be respected, and no-one shall be barred from entering them on grounds of race.

Language Rights

5 The languages of South Africa are Sindabele, Sepedi, Sesotho, Siswati, Setswana, Afrikaans, English, Tsongo (Shangaan), Venda, Xhosa and Zulu.

6 The State shall act positively to further the development of these languages, especially in education, literature and the media, and to prevent the use of any language or languages for the purpose of domination or division.

7 When it is reasonable to do so, one or more of these languages may be designated as the language to be used for defined purposes at the national level or in any region or area where it is widely used.

8 Subject to the availability of public and private resources, and limitations of reasonableness, primary and secondary education should wherever possible be offered in the language or languages of preference of the students or their parents.

9 The State shall promote respect for all the languages spoken in South Africa.

Creative Freedom

10 There shall be freedom of artistic activity and scientific enquiry, without censorship, subject only to such limitations as may be imposed by law in accordance with principles generally accepted in open and democratic societies.

The Right to Sporting, Recreational and Cultural Activities

11 Sporting, recreational and cultural activities shall be encouraged on a non-racial basis, drawing on the talents and creative capacities of all South Africans, and autonomous organisations may be established to achieve these objectives.

Article 6 WORKERS' RIGHTS

1 Workers shall have the right to form and join trade unions, and to regulate such unions without interference from the State.

2 Workers shall be free to join trade unions of their choice, subject only to the rules of such unions and to the principles of non-discrimination set out in this Constitution, and no worker shall be victimised on account of membership of a union.

3 The right to organise and to bargain collectively or any social, economic or other matter affecting workers' interests, shall be guaranteed.

4 In the furtherance of these rights, trade unions shall be entitled to reasonable access to the premises of enterprises, to receive such information as may be reasonably necessary, and to deduct union subscriptions where appropriate.

5 No law shall prevent representative trade unions from negotiating collective agreements binding on all workers covered by such agreements.

6 Workers shall have the right to strike under law in pursuance of their social and economic interests subject to reasonable limitations in respect of the interruption of services such as would endanger the life, health or personal safety of the community or any section of the population.

7 Workers shall have the right to peaceful picketing, subject only to such reasonable conditions as would be acceptable in a democratic society.

8 Trade unions shall have the right to participate in lawful political activities.

9 Trade unions shall have the right to form national federations and to affiliate to international federations.

10 Employers shall be under a duty to provide a safe, clean and dignified work environment, and to offer reasonable pay and holidays.

11 There shall be equal pay for equal work and equal access to employment.

12 The State shall make provision by way of legislation for compensation to be paid to workers injured in the course of their employment and for benefits to be paid to unemployed or retired workers.

13 Trade unions shall have the right to form national federations and to

affiliate to international federations.

Article 7 GENDER RIGHTS

1 Men and women shall enjoy equal rights in all areas of public and private life, including employment, education and within the family.

2 Discrimination on the grounds of gender, single parenthood, legitimacy of birth or sexual orientation shall be unlawful.

3 Positive action shall be undertaken to overcome the disabilities and disadvantages suffered on account of past gender discrimination.

4 The law shall provide remedies for sexual harassment, abuse and violence.

5 Educational institutions, the media, advertising and other social institutions shall be under a duty to discourage sexual and other types of stereotyping.

Article 8 DISABLED PERSONS

1 There shall be no discrimination against disabled persons.

2 Legislation shall provide for the progressive opening up of employment opportunities for disabled men and women, for the removal of obstacles to the enjoyment by them of public amenities and for their integration into all areas of life.

Article 9 CHILDREN

1 All children shall have the right to a name, to health, to security, education and equality of treatment.

2 The State shall, to the maximum of its available resources, seek to achieve progressively the full realisation of these rights.

3 No child shall suffer discrimination or enjoy privileges on the grounds of race, colour, gender, language, creed, legitimacy or the status of his or her parents.

4 In all proceedings concerning children, the primary consideration shall be the best interests of the child.

5 Children are entitled to be protected from economic exploitation and shall not be permitted to perform work that is likely to be hazardous or harmful to their education, health or moral well-being.

6 It shall be unlawful to oblige children to work or perform services for the employers of their parents or other family members.

Article 10 SOCIAL, EDUCATIONAL, ECONOMIC
AND WELFARE RIGHTS

General

1 All men and women have the right to enjoy basic social, educational, economic and welfare rights.

2 The State, shall, to the maximum of its available resources, undertake appropriate legislative and executive action in order to achieve the progressive realisation of basic social, educational, economic and welfare rights for the whole population.

3 Such State action shall establish standards and procedures whereby all men, women and children are guaranteed by law a progressively expanding floor of enforceable minimum rights, with special attention to nutrition, shelter, health care, education and income.

4 In order to achieve a common floor of rights for the whole country, resources may be diverted from richer to poorer areas, and timetables may be established for the phased extension of legislation and minimum standards from area to area.

5 The State may collaborate with non-governmental organisations and the private sector in achieving these goals, and may impose appropriate responsibilities on all social and economic bodies with a view to their materialisation.

6 In circumstances where persons are unable through lack of means to avail themselves of facilities provided by the State, the State shall, wherever it is reasonable to do so, give appropriate assistance.

Freedom from Hunger

7 In order to guarantee the right of freedom from hunger, the State shall ensure the introduction of minimum standards of nutrition throughout the country, with special emphasis on pre-school and school feeding.

The Right to Shelter

8 In order to guarantee the right to shelter, the State shall, in collaboration with private bodies where appropriate, dismantle compounds, single-sex hostels and other forms of accommodation associated with the migrant labour system, and embark upon and encourage an extensive programme of house-building.

9 The State shall take steps to ensure that energy, access to clean water and appropriate sewage and waste disposal are available to every home.

10 No eviction from homes or from land shall take place without the order of a competent court, which shall have regard to the availability of alternative accommodation.

The Right to Education

10 In order to guarantee the right to education, the State shall, in collaboration with non-governmental and private educational institutions where appropriate, ensure that:

there shall be free and compulsory primary education for all, with a school-leaving age of sixteen,

there shall be progressive expansion of access by all children as of right to secondary education,

there shall be progressive increase in access to pre-school institutions and institutes of vocational training and of higher learning,

there shall be increasingly extensive facilities to enable adults to overcome illiteracy and further their education.

11 Education shall be directed towards the full development of the human personality and a sense of personal dignity, and shall aim at strengthening respect for human rights and fundamental freedoms and promoting understanding, tolerance and friendship among all South Africans and between nations.

The Right to Health

12 In order to guarantee the right to protection of health, the State shall establish a comprehensive national health service linking health workers, community organisations, State institutions, private medical schemes and individual medical practitioners so as to provide hygiene education, preventive medicine and health care delivery to all.

The Right to Work

13 In order to guarantee increasing enjoyment of the right to work, the State shall, in collaboration where appropriate with private bodies and non-governmental institutions:

make technical and vocational training available to all, remove the barriers which keep large sections of the population out of technical, professional and managerial positions,

and promote public and other works with a view to reducing unemployment.

The Right to a Minimum Income and Welfare Rights

14 In order to guarantee the achievement of a minimum income for all, the State shall introduce a scheme of family benefits and old age pensions financed from general reserve.

15 In order to guarantee the enjoyment of basic social welfare rights, in particular unemployment benefits, compensation for injury, superannuation or retirement pensions, the State shall, in collaboration where appropriate with private bodies, establish a system of national insurance based upon contribu-

tions by employers, employees and other interested persons.

Article 11 THE ECONOMY, LAND AND PROPERTY

1 Legislation on economic matters shall be guided by the principle of encouraging collaboration between the State and the private, co-operative and family sectors with a view to reducing inequality, promoting growth and providing goods and services for the whole population.

2 All men and women and lawfully constituted bodies are entitled to the peaceful enjoyment of their possessions, including the right to acquire, own, or dispose of property in any part of the country without distinction based on race, colour, language, gender or creed.

3 All natural resources below and above the surface area of the land, including the air, and all forms of potential energy or minerals in the territorial waters, the continental shelf and the exclusive economic zone of South Africa, which are now owned by any person at the time of coming into force of this Constitution, shall belong to the State.

4 The State shall have the right to regulate the exploitation of natural resources, grant franchises and determine royalties, subject to payment of appropriate compensation in the event of interference with any lawfully vested interest.

5 The State may by legislation take steps to overcome the effects of past statutory discrimination in relation to enjoyment of property rights.

6 There shall be no forced removals of persons or communities from their homes or land on the basis of race, colour, language, gender or creed.

7 No persons or legal entities shall be deprived of their possessions except on grounds of public interest or public utility, including the achievement of the objectives of the Constitution.

8 Any such deprivation may be effected only by or pursuant to a law which shall provide for the nature and the extent of compensation to be paid.

9 Compensation shall be just, taking into account the need to establish an equitable balance between the public interest and the interest of those affected.

10 In the case of a dispute regarding the amount of compensation or its mode of payment, provision shall be made for recourse to a special independent tribunal, with an appeal to the courts.

11 The preceding provisions shall not be interpreted as in any way impeding the right of the State to adopt such measures as might be deemed necessary in any democratic society for the control, use or acquisition of property in accordance with the general interest, or to preserve the environment, or to regulate or curtail monopolies or to secure the payment of taxes or other contributions or penalties.

Article 12 ENVIRONMENTAL RIGHTS

1 The environment, including the land, the waters and the sky, are the common heritage of the people of South Africa and of all humanity.

2 All men and women shall have the right to a healthy and ecologically balanced environment and the duty to defend it.

3 In order to secure this right, the State, acting through appropriate agencies and organs shall conserve, protect and improve the environment, and in particular:

 i prevent and control pollution of the air and waters and degradation and erosion of the soil;

 ii have regard in local, regional and national planning to the maintenance or creation of balanced ecological and biological areas and to the prevention or minimising of harmful effects on the environment;

 iii promote the rational use of natural resources, safeguarding their capacity for renewal and ecological stability;

 iv ensure that long-term damage is not done to the environment by industrial or other forms of waste;

 v maintain, create and develop natural reserves, parks and recreational areas and classify and protect other sites and landscapes so as to ensure the preservation and protection of areas of outstanding cultural, historic and natural interest.

4. Legislation shall provide for co-operation between the State, non-governmental organisations, local communities and individuals in seeking to improve the environment and encourage ecologically sensible habits in daily life.

5 The law shall provide for appropriate penalties and reparation in the case of any direct and serious damage caused to the environment, and permit the interdiction by any interested person or by any agency established for the purpose of protecting the environment, of any public or private activity or undertaking which manifestly and unreasonably causes or threatens to cause irreparable damage to the environment.

Article 13 AFFIRMATIVE ACTION

1 Nothing in the Constitution shall prevent the enactment of legislation, or the adoption by any public or private body of special measures of a positive kind designed to procure the advancement and the opening up of opportunities, including access to education, skills, employment and land, and the general advancement in social, economic and cultural spheres, of men and women who in the past have been disadvantaged by discrimination.

2 No provision of the Bill of Rights shall be construed as derogating from or limiting in any way the general provisions of this Article.

Article 14 POSITIVE ACTION

1 In its activities and functioning, the State shall observe the principles of non-racialism and non-sexism, and encourage the same in all public and private bodies.

2 All benefits conferred and entitlements granted by the State shall be distributed on a non-racist and non-sexist basis.

3 The State and all public and private bodies shall be under a duty to prevent any form of incitement to racial, religious or linguistic hostility and to dismantle all structures and do away with all practices that compulsorily divide the population on grounds of race, colour, language, or creed.

4 With a view to achieving the above, the State may enact legislation to prohibit the circulation or possession of materials which incite racial, ethnic, religious, gender or linguistic hatred, which provoke violence, or which insult, degrade, defame or encourage abuse of any racial, ethnic, religious, gender or linguistic group.

5 All organs of the State at the national, regional and local levels shall pursue policies and programmes aimed at redressing the consequences of past discriminatory laws and practices, and at the creation of a genuine non-racial democracy in South Africa.

6 Such policies shall include the implementation of programmes aimed at achieving speedily the balanced structuring in non-racial form of the public service, defence and police forces and the prison service.

7 Without interfering with its independence, and with a view to ensuring that justice is manifestly seen to be done in a non-racial way and that the wisdom, experience and judicial skills of all South Africans are respected on the bench, the judiciary shall be transformed in such a way as to consist of men and women drawn from all sectors of South African society.

8 In taking steps to correct patterns or practices of discrimination, special attention shall be paid to rectifying the inequalities to which women in South Africa have been subjected, and to ensuring their full, equal, effective and dignified participation in the political, social, economic and cultural life of the nation.

9 Legislation may be enacted requiring non-governmental organisations and private bodies to conduct themselves in accordance with the above principles.

Article 15 LIMITATIONS

1 Nothing in the Constitution shall be interpreted as implying for any group or person the right to engage in any activity or perform any act aimed at the destruction of any of the rights and freedoms set forth in the Constitution, or at their limitation or suppression to a degree other than is authorised by the Constitution itself.

2 Nothing in this Constitution should be interpreted as impeding the right of the State to enact legislation regulating the manner in which fundamental rights and freedoms shall be exercised, or limiting such rights, provided that such regulation or limitation is such as might be deemed necessary in an open and democratic society.

3 Any restrictions permitted under the Constitution to fundamental rights and freedoms shall not be applied to or used as a cover for any purpose other than that for which they have been expressly or by necessary implication authorised.

4 Any law providing for any regulation or limitation of any fundamental right or freedom shall:

    i be of general application;

    ii not negate the essential content of the right, but simply qualify the way that is to be exercised or the circumstances in which derogation from the right is permitted;

    iii as far as practicable, identify the specific clauses of the Constitution relied upon for the limitation of the right and the specific clauses of the Constitution affected by the legislation;

    iv specify as precisely as possible the exact reach of the limitation and the circumstances in which is shall apply.

Article 16 ENFORCEMENT

General

1 The fundamental rights and freedoms contained in this Bill of Rights shall be guaranteed by the courts.

2 Provision shall be made for the establishment of a constitutional court.

3 The terms of the Bill of Rights shall be binding upon the State and organs of government at all levels, and where appropriate, on all social institutions and persons.

4 All persons who claim that rights guaranteed them by the Bill of Rights have been infringed or threatened, shall be entitled to apply to a competent court for an order for the declaration or enforcement of their rights, or for the restraining of any act which impedes or threatens such rights.

5 Any law or executive or administrative act which violates the terms of the Bill of Rights shall be invalid to the extent of such violation, save that the Court shall have the discretion in appropriate cases to put the relevant body or official to terms as to how and within what period to remedy the violation.

Human Rights Commission

6 Parliament shall have a special responsibility for ensuring that the basic social, educational, economic and welfare rights set out in this Bill of Rights

are respected.

7 Parliament shall establish by legislation a Human Rights Commission to promote observance of the Bill of Rights.

8 Such Commission shall have the right to establish agencies for investigating patterns of violation of any of the terms of the Bill of Rights and for receiving complaints and bringing proceedings in court where appropriate.

9 The Commission shall monitor proposed legislation with a view to reporting to Parliament on its impact on the realisation of the rights set out in the Bill of Rights.

Ombudsman

10 With a view to ensuring that all functions and duties under the Constitution are carried out in a fair way with due respect for the rights and sentiments of those affected, the office of Ombudsman shall be created.

11 The Ombudsman shall be independent in the carrying out of his or her functions and may open offices in different parts of the country.

12 The Ombudsman shall receive and investigate complaints from members of the public concerning abuse of power or unfair, insensitive, capricious, harsh, discourteous or unduly delayed treatment of any person by any office of government at national, regional or local level, or any attempts by such official to extort benefits or corruptly to receive favours.

13 In accordance with his or her findings, the Ombudsman may initiate legal proceedings, refer the matter for prosecution, negotiate a compromise, or make a report to the department or organ concerned containing recommendations with a view to remedying the improper conduct, preventing repetition, and, where appropriate, making amends, including compensation.

14 Recourse to the Human Rights Commission or to the Ombudsman shall not oust the jurisdiction of the courts to hear any matter.

APPENDIX B

DRAFT CHARTER OF
FUNDAMENTAL RIGHTS

ISSUED BY THE SOUTH AFRICAN GOVERNMENT
FEBRUARY 1993

Operation of Charter against the State

1 (1) Every person, including, where appropriate, every legal person and every entity or body or group of persons which can be the bearer of rights, shall have against the State the rights set out in this Charter.

(2) The rights which a person has against the State in terms of subsection (1) are fundamental rights, and the limitation or suspension of these rights shall be permissible only –

(a) under the common law or by way of a law of a competent legislature; and

(b) to the extent provided for in section 35 or 36 or where otherwise expressly authorised.

(3) The provisions of this Charter shall –

(a) bind all legislative, executive and judicial institutions, bodies and functionaries at central, regional and local government level; and

(b) apply to all laws whether made before or after the commencement of this Charter, and to all executive and administrative actions performed after such commencement.

Operation of Charter against Third Parties

2 (1) No provision of this Charter shall be construed so as to create or regulate legal relations other than those between the State and a person as contemplated in section 1.

(2) In the interpretation of any law regulating legal relations among persons *inter se*, the spirit, objects and purport of this Charter shall be taken into account.

(3) Where a person exercises or enjoys a right recognised by this Charter, such person shall do so in a manner which will not infringe the rights of any other person.

Human Dignity

3 The State shall in its legislative, executive and judicial acts respect and protect the human dignity of every person.

Protection of Life

4 (1) Every person shall have the right to life.

(2) No person shall be deprived of his or her life intentionally save in the execution of a death sentence imposed in accordance with section 6 of the International Covenant on Civil and Political Rights.

Physical and Mental Integrity

5 Every person shall have the right to physical and mental integrity.

Equality before the Law

6 (1) All persons shall be equal before the law and entitled to equal protection by the law.

(2) No person shall be favoured or prejudiced solely by reason of race, colour, language, sex, religion, ethnic origin, social class, birth, political or other convictions, or disabilities or other natural characteristics.

(3) A law shall be deemed not to be contrary to subsection (2) if such law provides for special measures for the sole purpose of furthering the development and advancement of specific communities, groups and individuals to enable them to develop and realise their natural talents and potential to the full and to exercise and to enjoy their fundamental rights on a basis of equality with, and with due regard to the interests of, other communities, groups and individuals.

Citizen's Rights

7 Every citizen shall have the right not to be –

(a) deprived of his or her citizenship;

(b) exiled or expelled from the Republic;

(c) prohibited from returning to the Republic;

(d) prevented from leaving the Republic, whether temporarily or permanently;

(e) denied a passport or deprived thereof.

Political Rights

8(1) Every citizen shall have the right to –

(a) form a political party;

(b) join a political party of his or her choosing or not to join a political party;

(c) participate or not to participate in the activities of a political party;

(d) give expression to his or her political convictions in a peaceful manner;

(e) make himself or herself available for nomination for and election to any legislative, executive or administrative office for which he or she qualifies.

(2) Subsection (1) shall not preclude the prohibition or regulation of par-

ticipation in politics by persons in the service of the State.

Freedom of Speech

9 (1) Every person shall have the right to freedom of speech and other forms of expression, and the right to obtain and disseminate information.

(2) Subsection (1) shall not preclude the registration and licensing of newspapers and other forms of communication.

Meetings, Demonstrations and Petitions

10 Every person shall have the right to assemble and demonstrate with others peacefully unarmed, and to draw up and present petitions.

11 (1) Every person shall have the right to profess and practise the religion of his choosing.

(2) Subsection (1) shall not preclude ministration to the forces, the public service and other state institutions, religious instruction or exercise in schools, and religious broadcasts by an entity instituted by or under any law.

Family

12 Every person shall have the right to the protection of the integrity of his or her family.

Children

13 (1) Every parent shall have the right to have his or her child live with him or her and to care for and bring up such child, unless the interests of the child require some other arrangement.

(2) Every child shall have the right –
(a) not to be compelled to perform work or to render services harmful to his or her physical or mental health, upbringing, education or moral or social development, or which amounts to economic exploitation;
(b) not to be compelled to perform work or to render services for the benefit of the employer of the parents of the child or any other person;
(c) to protection against physical or mental violence, injury, neglect or abuse, including sexual abuse.

(3) Every child in need of care shall have the right to medical treatment by medical personnel in the service of the State or at medical institutions managed by the State in so far as such medical treatment is provided or can be provided by the State with available personnel and facilities.

(4) This Charter shall not be construed so as to affect the powers of the Supreme Court as upper guardian of all minors.

Education and Training

14(1) Every pupil or student who is a citizen shall have the right of equal access to state or state-aided educational institutions.

(2) Every pupil who is a citizen shall have the right to religion-oriented education in so far as it is reasonably practicable.

(3) Every pupil who is a citizen shall have the right to tuition in his mother tongue, including the right to take his mother tongue as a subject, in so far as it is reasonably practicable.

(4) *(a)* Every state-aided tertiary educational institution shall have the right to determine the medium of instruction and the religious and general character of such educational institution.

(b) The parent community of every state or state-aided school shall have the right to determine the medium of instruction and the religious and general character of the school.

(5) *(a)* Every pupil who is a citizen shall have the right to at least primary education for which the State with due regard to its financial means shall be responsible.

(b) All pupils at a particular level in a state or state-aided school shall have the right to equal state assistance in respect of compulsory education at such level.

(c) Every person shall have the right to establish and operate a private educational institution.

Participation in the Economy

15 Every person shall have the right freely and on an equal footing to engage in economic enterprise, including the right to establish, manage and maintain commercial undertakings, to acquire property and means of production, and to offer and accept employment against remuneration.

Legal Competence

16 Every person shall have the right to perform juristic acts, and to acquire rights and incur obligations.

Freedom of Movement

17 Every citizen shall have the right –
(a) of freedom of movement and residence in the Republic;
(b) to work, to establish and operate any undertaking, to exercise any profession or trade and to carry on any other lawful activity in any part of the Republic.

Private Ownership

18 (1) Every person shall have the right, individually or with others, to acquire, possess, enjoy, use and dispose of, including disposal by way of testamentary disposition or intestate succession, any form of movable and immovable property.

(2) Subject to the provisions of subsection (3) no person shall be deprived

of his property otherwise than under a judgment or order of a court of law.

(3) Property may be expropriated for public purposes, subject to the payment within a reasonable time of an agreed compensation or, failing such an agreed compensation, of compensation in cash determined by a court of law according to the market value of the property.

(4) Every person shall have the right not to be subjected to taxes on property which will have a confiscatory effect or will make unreasonable inroads upon the enjoyment, use or value of such property.

Employees

19 (1) Every employee shall have the right –

(a) to form an employees' organisation, to join such an organisation or not to join such organisation, to participate or not to participate in the activities of such an organisation, or otherwise to associate or not to associate or to organise;

(b) to negotiate or bargain, collectively or individually;

(c) to take part in strikes and to withhold labour;

(d) not to be subjected to unfair labour practices including intimidation and victimisation;

(e) to work under safe, hygienic and healthy conditions;

(f) to work reasonable hours;

(g) to be given a reasonable opportunity for rest, recreation and holiday;

(h) to receive reasonable remuneration for his or her labour;

(i) to be protected in his or her physical and mental wellbeing.

(2) Subsection (1) shall not preclude the prohibition of strikes in strategic industries and essential services or by persons in the service of the State, or the levying of contributions for and the management of provident funds.

Employers

20 (1) Every employer shall have the right –

(a) to form an employers' organisation, to join such an organisation or not to join such organisation, to participate or not to participate in the activities of such an organisation, or otherwise to associate or not to associate or to organise;

(b) to offer employment and to engage employees according to his or her needs with due regard to the fitness, qualifications, level of training and competence of the employees;

(c) to require of an employee adequate service of an acceptable quality and to lock out labour;

(d) to terminate the services of an employee under the common law,

the contract of employment with the employee or legislation, as the case may be;

(e) to apply the principle of "no work, no pay";

(f) to manage his or her business with a view to its economic viability and continued existence;

(g) to make use of alternative labour when necessary to maintain production or service;

(h) not to be subjected to unfair labour practices, including intimidation and victimisation.

(2) Subsection (1) shall not preclude the prohibition of labour lockouts in strategic industries and essential services, or the levying of contributions for and the management of provident funds.

Social Security

21 (1) Every person shall have the right to safeguard his or her existence or the existence of his or her dependants in the best possible manner by means of pension, medical, assurance or other providence.

(2) The State shall not in any manner make any inroad upon the benefits of such providence.

(3) Every person shall have the right to claim available state assistance to provide for essential subsistence and medical needs where he or she is unable to provide for such needs because of physical or mental illness or disability and where there is no person who is legally liable or who can legally be compelled, to provide for such needs.

Free Association

22 (1) Every person shall have the right of free association.

(2) No person shall be prohibited or prevented from associating with any other person.

(3) No person shall be compelled to associate with any other person.

Personal Freedom

23 (1) Every person shall have the right to personal freedom.

(2) Subject to the provisions of Section 37 a person may be deprived of his of her freedom only in the following instances and only in accordance with the procedure prescribed by a law of a competent legislature –

(a) detention of a person for investigation and trial on the ground of a reasonable suspicion that he or she has committed an offence;

(b) detention of an accused for or during his or her trial or for sentencing;

(c) detention of a person after conviction under a sentence or by order of a court of law;

(d) detention of a child by order of a children's court;

(e) detention of a person because of non-compliance or alleged non-compliance with the terms of process issued by or under the authority of a court of law, or of a condition or order of a court of law regarding attendance at such court, bail with or without conditions, any sentence or punishment, or any related matter;

(f) detention of an accused released on bail and who is about to flee or of a witness evading service of a subpoena or who is about to flee;

(g) detention of a recalcitrant witness or of a witness who refuses to divulge information regarding an alleged offence;

(h) detention of a witness by order of a judge with a view to the protection of the witness or the proper administration of justice;

(i) detention of a person for the prevention of the spreading of infectious diseases constituting a threat to public health;

(j) detention of a mentally disordered or suspected mentally disordered person for observation or treatment;

(k) detention of a person alleged to be addicted to a narcotic substance or alcohol, for the purpose of an enquiry whether he is so addicted, or of a person who is so addicted, for the purpose of his rehabilitation;

(l) detention of a person in connection with his or her unauthorised or alleged unauthorised presence or sojourn in the Republic or for the purpose of his or her deportation;

(m) detention of a person for the purpose of extradition;

(n) detention of a person by order of a court of law in connection with civil proceedings.

Detainees

24 (1) Every person who is detained shall have the right –

(a) as soon as is reasonably possible to be informed in a language which he or she understands of the reason for his or her detention;

(b) to be detained under conditions consonant with human dignity, adequately to be fed by the State and, when necessary, to receive medical treatment at public expense;

(c) to be given a reasonable opportunity to communicate and consult with a legal practitioner and, when necessary, a medical practitioner of his or her choosing;

(d) to be given a reasonable opportunity to communicate with, and to be visited by, his or her spouse, family, next-of-kin and religious conseller, unless a court of law orders otherwise;

(e) to be released when the reason for detention falls away or, in the case of a person detained for a specific period, at the expiry of the

term of detention.

(2) During detention persons awaiting trial shall, in so far as it is practicable, be separated from convicted persons, and juveniles from adults.

Accused

25 (1) Every person arrested for the alleged commission of an offence shall have the right –

(a) as soon as is reasonably possible, to be informed in a language which he or she understands that he or she has the right to remain silent and that he or she is not obliged to make any statement, and to be warned of the consequences of making a statement;

(b) within a reasonable time, but not later than 48 hours or the first court day thereafter, after arrest, to be brought before a court of law, and to be charged or to be informed of the reason for his or her detention, failing which he or she shall be entitled to be released from detention;

(c) to be tried by a court of law within a reasonable time after arrest;

(d) upon good cause being shown, to be released from detention with or without bail.

(2) Any infringement of the rights of an accused mentioned in subsection (1) shall not result in the setting aside of the proceedings unless on appeal or review the court finds that justice has not been done.

Fair Trial

26 (1) Every accused shall have the right –

(a) to a public trial by a court of law;

(b) to be presumed innocent until the contrary is proved;

(c) to remain silent during plea proceedings or trial and not to testify during trial;

(d) where he or she is not assisted by a legal practitioner, to an explanation of the possible consequences of any applicable presumptions and of his or her election to exercise his or her right to remain silent or not to testify;

(e) to examine witnesses testifying against him or her, to testify himself or herself, to call witnesses and to offer other rebutting evidence;

(f) to be represented by a legal practitioner at own expense;

(g) to be informed by the presiding officer regarding –

(i) his or her right to be assisted by a legal practitioner; and

(ii) the institutions that he or she may approach for legal assistance,

and to be given a reasonable opportunity to attempt to obtain legal assistance;

(h) not to be sentenced to inhuman punishment;

(i) not to be convicted of an offence in respect of any act or omission which was not an offence at the time it was committed, and not to be sentenced to a more severe punishment than that which was applicable when the offence was committed;

(j) not to be convicted of any offence of which he or she previously has previously been convicted or acquitted on the merits;

(k) to have recourse by way of appeal or review to a higher court than the court of first instance;

(l) to be informed in a language which he or she understands of the reasons for conviction and sentence;

(m) to be tried in a language which he or she understands or, failing this, to have the proceedings interpreted to him or her;

(n) to be sentenced within a reasonable time after conviction.

(2) Any infringement of the rights of an accused referred to in subsection (1)*(d)* or *(g)* shall not result in the setting aside of the proceedings unless the court on appeal or review finds that justice has not been done.

Forced Labour

27 (1) Every person shall have the right not to be subjected to forced labour.

(2) For the purposes of subsection (1) 'forced labour' shall not include the following –

(a) the performance of labour by a person serving imprisonment;

(b) the performance of community or other service by a person in terms of a sentence or an order of court of law;

(c) the performance of compulsory military service;

(d) the performance of civilian service in the place of compulsory military service.

Litigation

28 (1) Every person shall have the right to have any dispute settled by a court of law.

(2) Every person shall have the right that the South African law, including the rules of the South African private international law, be applied in all proceedings before a court of law.

(3) Subsection (2) shall not prevent –

(a) judicial notice of the law of indigenous groups;

(b) the application in civil proceedings of the law of indigenous groups or the religious law of religious groups.

Rules of Natural Justice

29 Every person shall have the right –

(a) to have the rules of natural justice applied in administrative

proceedings where, on the ground of findings of fact or of fact and law, his or her rights or reasonable expectations are or may be infringed;

(b) that in such a case the reasons for any decision be furnished on demand to him or her.

Privacy

30 (1) Every person shall have the right to privacy.

(2) A person's right to privacy is infringed also by entering or entering upon his or her property or place of residence or employment, by searching him or her, by seizing his or her property or possessions and by intercepting or obtaining information about his or her correspondence or other forms of communication.

(3) The interception of, or the obtaining of information concerning, the correspondence or other forms of communication of a person shall be permissible only in so far as it is authorised by a law of a competent legislature for the purpose of preventing and combating foreign intelligence operations, the illegal trade or trafficking in narcotics and weapons, serious economic offences and the organised sexual exploitation of women and children.

Art and Science

31 Every person shall have the right to practise the arts and science.

Environmental Rights

32 Every person shall have the right not to be exposed to an environment which is dangerous or seriously detrimental to the health or well-being of man, and the right to conservation and protection of the environment.

Women's Rights

33 (1) All women shall be entitled to equal rights with men.

(2) No law shall in any matter relating to women discriminate, distinguish or restrict on the basis of sex if it has the effect of denying or limiting women's right to equality with men in the political, economic, social, cultural, civil or any other sphere.

(3) Without derogating from the generality of the foregoing every woman shall have the right –

(a) to be elected to any public office for which she qualifies;

(b) to receive equal remuneration with men for work of equal value;

(c) not to be discriminated against solely by reason of her marital status or pregnancy;

(d) to perform juristic acts, to acquire rights and incur obligations, and to acquire and dispose of property;

(e) to her physical and mental integrity and in particular to legal

protection against rape and sexual harassment.

(4) A law shall be deemed not to be in conflict with the right to equality before the law if the object of the said law is –

(a) to bring about equality between women and men;

(b) to protect women in certain types of work in the case of pregnancy or for other reasons inherent in their physical nature;

(c) to exempt women from compulsory military service, excluding service in a non-combatant or supporting capacity.

Culture and Language

34 (1) Every person shall have the right to use the language of his or her choosing and to participate in the cultural life of his or her choosing.

(2) Every person shall have the right of communication with the State in the official language of his or her choosing.

Limitation of Fundamental Rights

35 (1) A law referred to in section (2) *(a)* in terms of which a fundamental right is limited or the limitation thereof is authorised, shall be permissible only to the extent in which such limitation is reasonably necessary –

(a) by virtue of state security, the safety of the public, the public order and interest, good morals, public health, the administration of justice or public administration;

(b) to uphold the rights and freedoms of others;

(c) to prevent or combat disorder, violence, intimidation, or crime, or;

(d) to counter or deal with a threatening or actual natural disaster or the consequences thereof.

(2) The question whether the limitation of a fundamental right is reasonably necessary shall be justifiable by the Constitutional Court.

Suspension of Fundamental Rights

36 (1) A law referred to in section 1(2)*(a)* in terms of which a fundamental right is suspended or the suspension thereof is authorised, shall be of force only during a state of emergency in which –

(a) the continued existence of the State or the safety of the public in the Republic or in a part of the Republic is threatened by an actual or threatening war or invasion, an insurrection or general riotousness; and

(b) the suspension of that fundamental right is reasonably necessary to ensure the continued existence of the State or the safety of the public.

(2) The question whether a state of emergency as contemplated in sub-

section (1) exists, shall be justifiable by the Supreme Court.

Absolute Prohibitions

37 Notwithstanding anything contained in this Charter no law contemplated in section 18(2) *(a)* shall regulate or authorise –

(a) the physical or mental torture or inhuman treatment of persons;

(b) the creation of offences with retrospective effect;

(c) the indemnification of the State or a person in the service of the State for the unlawful killing or injuring of any person;

(d) the detention of any person in circumstances other than those authorised in the specific instances set out in section 23 for a period longer than 10 days without leave or an order of a court of law.

FUNDAMENTAL RIGHTS

PROPOSED IN THE CONSTITUTION OF THE
STATE OF KWAZULU/NATAL

NOTE

The proposed Constitution of the State of KwaZulu/Natal was adopted by the KwaZulu Legislative Assembly as a Resolution on the 1st December 1992.

Although not having a separate Bill of Rights, the inclusion of fundamental rights in the Resolution signifies the wide range of civil and other liberties envisaged by KwaZulu/Natal. This is not a final document and may be subject to change, as and when negotiations and other political processes of accommodation take place.

The extract ranges from Section 15 of the Resolution to Section 59.

FUNDAMENTAL RIGHTS

15 Individual and Collective Rights

Fundamental rights are recognised and shall be protected both in their individual as well as in their collective exercise, and they imply the right to establish institutions, adopt rules of conduct and regulate interests which are instrumental to the collective exercise of such rights. All powers established and recognised under this constitution shall protect and nourish the exercise of these rights and respect and foster their collective exercise.

16 Justiciability of Rights

All rights and freedoms recognised and guaranteed under this constitution shall be justiciable to the fullest practical and reasonable extent. In case of a violation of the rights and freedoms recognised and guaranteed under this constitution any aggrieved party shall be entitled to be heard by a court of record on the basis of urgency and, upon showing a *prima face* violation of rights, shall be granted preliminary relief pending the final disposition of the case.

17 Limits of the Exercise of the Rights

The law may impose reasonable restrictions on the exercise of the rights set forth in this constitution to protect the rights of others and for compelling reasons of public interest. However, in such a case, the law must respect the essential content of the rights, and the limitation on the exercise of the right must not have the practical effect of preventing or deterring the free exercise of the rights in their reasonable manifestations.

18 Physical and Psychological Integrity

(a) The physical and psychological integrity of any individual shall be inviolable. No one shall be authorised to inflict any type of violence on another individual or to take a life. Capital punishment and any form of physical or psychological torture and punishment shall not be allowed.

(b) No one shall be submitted to unusual or cruel punishment and all punishments shall aim at the personal and social rehabilitation of the person. During imprisonment juvenile delinquents shall be kept separate from other delinquents and so shall men from women. Failure by a public official to report any and all instances of physical or psychological violence on a person deprived of his or her liberty shall be a criminal offence.

19 Freedom of Communication

(a) All persons shall be free to express and communicate their thought in private and in public, in oral, written, visual or any other fashion, and to establish institutions for such a purpose. All forms of censorship or limitation on the contents of such communications shall be prohibited.

(b) Limitations on the contents of commercial speech may be imposed to guarantee the truth and the fairness of the representations made to consumers and to ensure fair competition, provided that there shall be no prohibition of comparative advertising.

(c) Limitations on the form of communication may be imposed as to time, place and manner so as to protect and respect the rights of others and compelling public interests, but not to the extent that the limitation on the forms communication becomes a limitation on the contents thereof.

(d) No one shall be compelled directly or indirectly to disclose or express his or her ideology, creed, religious belief, or political opinions.

20 Freedom of Religion

Religious freedoms are recognised and shall be guaranteed. Everyone shall have the right to profess and promote his or her religion or belief, and to establish institutions and organise activities for this purpose. The State of KwaZulu/Natal shall not take any action supporting or endorsing any particular religious belief or confession or conditioning the exercise of religious freedom to any requirement, and shall promote conditions for the equal and free exercise of all religions and beliefs in the State.

21 Liberty

(a) No one shall be deprived of his liberty without cause and due process of law. Unwarranted arrest and detention shall be allowed only on the basis of probable cause related to an offence punishable by imprisonment. Anyone arrested or detained shall be informed of his or her rights in a language that he or she understands, shall be informed of the reasons for the arrest and detention with an indication of the charges, and shall have a court hearing within twenty-four hours from the time of his or her arrest, after which the detention may continue only by court order based on factually corroborated allegations.

(b) Anyone detained or accused has the right to remain silent. Anyone detained or charged with an offence punishable by imprisonment has the right to consult counsel, and if he or she cannot afford one the court shall appoint one at government expense. There shall be a right to counsel in any and all proceedings in which the accused participates.

(c) Detention prior to sentencing shall be limited to cases established by law and shall not exceed three months.

(d) Anyone detained, arrested or condemned unlawfully shall have the right to be rehabilitated, to receive indemnification and other rights determined by law.

(e) Any government authority shall inform anyone who is the subject of an investigation for any reason.

(f) No one may be tried twice for the same conduct. No one shall be charged for a conduct which at the time was not an offence, nor shall a penalty be imposed exceeding that which was applicable at the time when the offence was committed. There shall be no analogical or retroactive interpretation of criminal law.

(g) Anyone has the right to a speedy, open and public trial and to confront his or her accusers at trial. All trials shall be based on the accusatory principle and shall be subject to the right to appeal on the grounds of error of law.

(h) No one shall be removed from the authority of the judge with jurisdiction over the specific offence at the time the offence was committed. There shall be no special or *post facto* judges. Any accused person has the right to be tried in an impartial, independent and competent court. Anyone shall be presumed not guilty until proven guilty.

22 Travel and Movement

Everyone shall have the right to travel, move and reside within or outside the State. No government policy forcing the relocation of people shall be allowed.

Any citizen of the Federal Republic of South Africa shall have the right to take domicile in the State.

23 Privacy

(a) Everyone shall have the right to the protection of privacy, of his or her personal life, of his or her domicile, and to protection of his or her personal dignity and reputation. All private communications and all aspects of private life shall be protected. Search and seizure may be allowed only on the basis of a warrant issued on the basis of corroborated allegations, and in the cases and with the guarantees established by the law. Personal search shall be allowed as an incident to a legitimate arrest and detention.

(b) Anyone has the right to access the information collected on him or her by the Government or by private data or information banks.

24 Freedom of the Media

Anyone has the right to publish and distribute printed materials. The press and the media of mass communication shall have the right to inform the public on matters of public interest provided that they do not publish erroneous information as a result of gross professional negligence or malice. The media have the duty to rectify all erroneous information they publish which damages the reputation of others.

25 Assembly and Association

Everyone has the right of peaceful assembly. No notice shall be required for assembly in a private place or in a place open to the public. For assembly in a public place prior notice shall be given to the competent authority which may prohibit the assembly only for reasonable apprehension of public security and safety. Everyone has the right to associate for any legal purpose. Associations pursuing directly or indirectly political purposes by means of military training or association operating in a para-military fashion shall be prohibited.

26 Family Rights

A man and a woman have the right to join in marriage in accordance with the rituals and with assumption of the obligations and privileges of their choice. However, both spouses shall have equal rights, obligations and dignity. Both parents shall have responsibility for the upbringing, formation and education of the children, even if born outside wedlock. The law shall ensure that comparable rights and social protection shall be extended to children born outside wedlock as they shall be recognised to be children born in wedlock. Both parents have the right and the duty to exercise joint custody of the children unless a court otherwise decides in the interest of the children and on the basis of the specific circumstances of the case. Both parents have the right and the duty to choose an acceptable formation and education for their children.

27 Procreative Freedom

All people who so desire shall enjoy the freedom of procreative choice, including the right to receive sexual education, to use contraception and terminate unwanted pregnancy when safe. Anyone who finds these practices objectionable shall have the right to protect his or her own sphere of interests from any of these practices and from the exposure thereto.

28 Cultures and Traditions

Everyone shall have the right to enjoy, practice, profess, maintain and promote any culture, language, tradition or religion.

29 Human Rights in the Constitution

All fundamental human rights and all those other rights which are inherent to fundamental human needs and aspirations as they evolve with the changes and growth of society, and as they will be recognisable on the basis of the principles underlying the provisions of this constitution, are hereby entrenched in this constitution and in their essential content shall not be modified by virtue of constitutional amendments.

ECONOMIC, SOCIAL AND POLITICAL RIGHTS

Economic Rights

30 Free Enterprise

The right to free economic initiative and enterprise shall be recognised, protected and encouraged by the State. The State shall assist small businesses and provide other incentives to encourage access to economic opportunities. Within the limits set forth by the law to protect the public interest each enterprise shall be free to choose and organise the means of the production as it best sees fit.

31 Contractual Autonomy

Within the limits set forth by the law to protect the public interest, the State shall recognise and protect the right of individuals to self regulate and organise their interests in economic and other matters by means of legally enforceable contracts and by establishing legal entities to carry out their purposes and objectives.

32 Commercial and Insolvency Law

The State shall promote uniformity of its commercial and insolvency laws with those of other states and countries.

33 Permits and Licensing Requirements

The State shall not subject human conduct to unreasonable or unnecessary licensing and permitting requirements. Permits and licences shall be issued on the basis of objective and reasonable standards and criteria.

34 Private Property

Private property shall be guaranteed and protected. Limitations on the use and enjoyment of private property may be imposed so as to satisfy social, environmental and collective needs. The right to convey one's own property by contract or inheritance shall be protected subject to the reasonable exercise of the State's power of taxation.

35 Expropriation

The State or another entity authorised by law may expropriate property for public necessity subject to the prompt payment of a fair market value compensation.

36 Property of the State and the Regions

The State and the Regions may own property as private or public property. Public property shall not be alienated or encumbered and is related to the exercise of public functions or is held by the State or the Regions in the public interest. The law shall set forth the principles for the acquisition, administration and declassification of public property. The General Assembly shall publish a yearly report on the property owned by the State and the Regions indicating their current and planned use and their maintenance and carrying costs.

37 Public Enterprise

No enterprise shall be acquired or conducted by the State or the Regions either as a monopoly or as a free competition enterprise, and no service shall be provided to the public unless so authorised by a law demonstrating a public need and the inadequacy of the private sector to satisfy such need with comparable efficiency and reliability. When these requirements no longer exist, the enterprise or the service shall be privatised.

38 Property of the Federal Republic of South Africa

All tangible and intangible properties of the Federal Republic of South Africa in the State of KwaZulu/Natal shall be subject to the same rules and limitations set forth in this constitution for the properties of the State.

39 Communal Property
Communal property is recognised and shall be protected. Communal property shall be administered and regulated by traditional and customary Rules.

40 Practices in Restraint of Trade
All monopolies and practices and agreements in restraint of trade and free market competition shall be prohibited.

41 Agriculture
The State of KwaZulu/Natal shall encourage agriculture, the socially just and responsible use and distribution of land and the access of citizens to land ownership. The State shall promote agricultural co-operation and assist farmers on a co-operative basis.

Social Rights

42 Right to Education
(a) All citizens shall have the right to receive a basic education and professional training. The law shall determine the period and the minimum educational requirements for compulsory education. The State shall support the citizen's aspiration to higher education by means of scholarship and by promoting the highest standards of excellence in education.
(b) Both private and public schools shall ensure open and equal access to educational opportunities. Parents shall be entitled to participate in the administration and operation of their children's schools.

43 Right to Work
Everyone shall have the right to access any job opportunity for which he or she is qualified. As a matter of priority, the State shall promote the full employment of all citizens. No one's employment shall be terminated for political reasons or in violation of his or her constitutionally protected rights. Everyone shall have the right to receive a fair compensation for his or her work, shall be entitled to at least one vacation day a week, to a period of paid vacations during the year and to severance payment upon termination. All workers shall be entitled to social security, pensions, invalidity and unemployment benefits as determined by law.

44 Protection of Women
The law shall extend special protection to women. The law shall guarantee maternity leave and provide assistance to mothers in the work force. Until

such time when the social status of women in the State has significantly improved, the law shall recognise special privileges for women in all programmes and measures aimed to ensure equal access to political, social and economic opportunities, shall establish and maintain a Ministry for Women's Affairs, and reserve a portion of the available public offices to women.

45 Senior Citizens
The law shall promote the economic sufficiency of senior citizens and provide social services to assist them in relation to their housing, care, health, cultural and leisure needs.

46 Youth
The law shall promote conditions for the free and effective participation by the youth in political, social, economic and cultural developments.

47 Schools
Everyone shall have the right to establish private schools. Private schools shall have the power to determine their own curricula and syllabi within the general parameters set forth by law for the purposes of recognition and equipollence of degrees.

48 Universities
All public universities and institutes of higher education in the State shall be entitled to regulate their organisation and operations within the general parameters set forth by law.

49 Health Care
All citizens shall have the right to receive medical attention and care in case of need. The law shall determine the implementation of this right. The law shall develop policies of prevention, treatment, rehabilitation and integration of those who are physically, sensorially and mentally handicapped, including those who are substance addicted.

50 Job Conditions
The law shall ensure safe job conditions and shall provide special protection for women, minors and untrained labour.

51 Housing
The law shall promote conditions to ensure that all citizens have the possibility of living in a dignifying habitation and shall facilitate the purchase of residences through credit facilitation and other programmes. All citizens have the right to receive shelter and shall have equal access to housing opportunities.

52 Research, Arts and Teaching

The freedom of scientific research, artistic expression in all its forms and teaching is recognised and shall be guaranteed.

53 Right to a Pleasant and Clean Environment

The State shall recognise the rights of present and future generations of citizens to live in and enjoy a pleasant and clean environment. The law shall determine the cases and the limits in which citizens may bring legal actions on behalf of the community against those who cause environmental damages.

54 Labour Rights

Everyone shall have the freedom to form and join trade unions and employers' associations. The State shall respect and protect the right to strike, but may limit its exercise in cases determined by the law for reasons of public security and safety. Labour organisations shall have the right to negotiate and execute collective bargaining agreements to be effective with force of law vis-a-vis the category of workers covered by their provisions. During these negotiations the labour organisation shall be represented on the basis of the number of their members. Trade unions shall have the right to conduct reasonable activities in the work place aimed at improving labour conditions. The State may impose requirements on the trade unions only to ensure that they are organised and operated with full internal democracy.

POLITICAL RIGHTS

55 Right to Vote

(a) All citizens of eighteen years or older shall have the right to vote. The vote shall be personal, secret, free and equal. The right to vote may be suspended by a judicial adjudication of incompetence, or by an irrevocable sentence for major crimes specified by the law.

(b) The law recognises, and the State shall facilitate, the exercise of the right to vote by citizens who are outside the State.

56 Right to Petition and to Initiate Legislation

Any citizen has the right to petition the General Assembly, the Regional Congresses and any branch or level of government. A citizen's legislative proposal signed by five hundred citizens may be submitted to the General Assembly.

57 Freedom of Information

Any citizen has the right to access and receive any information or document which is in the possession of the State or Regional governments or of any of the commissions or agencies established in this constitution, provided that such document or information is not privileged as established by law to protect privacy, commercial secrets or national and State security. During the process of judicial review of the government's decision to withhold information, the court shall have the power to examine *in camera* the information withheld.

58 Political Parties

The citizens of the State have the right to form political parties to participate in all levels of democratic life. No one shall be directly or indirectly compelled in any way to join in a political party or shall be penalised for not belonging to one. Political parties shall ensure internal democracy in their organisation and operations.

59 Media of Mass Communication

Anyone shall have the right to establish media of mass communication, including newspapers, cable, radio and television stations. The law shall regulate the rights of citizens and political parties to access media of mass communication under the control of the government or in situations of virtual hegemony or monopoly.

THE ORGANISATION OF AFRICAN UNITY'S AFRICAN CHARTER ON HUMAN AND PEOPLE'S RIGHTS

The African Charter on Human and People's Rights was adopted in 1981 and came into force in 1986.

PART I: HUMAN AND PEOPLE'S RIGHTS

Article 1

The member states of the OAU party to the present Charter shall recognise the rights, duties, and freedoms enshrined in this Charter and shall undertake to adopt legislative or other measures to give effect to them.

Article 2

Every individual shall be entitled to the enjoyment of the rights and freedoms recognised in the present Charter without distinction of any kind such as race, ethnic group, colour, sex, language, religion, political or any other opinion, national and social origin, fortune, birth, or other status.

Article 3

1 Every individual shall be equal before the law.
2 Every individual shall be entitled to equal protection of the law.

Article 4

Human beings are inviolable. Every human being shall be entitled to respect for his life and the integrity of his person. No one may be arbitrarily deprived of this right.

Article 5

Every individual shall have the right to the respect of the dignity inherent in a human being and to the recognition of his legal status. All forms of exploitation and degradation of man, particularly slavery, slave trade, torture, cruel, inhuman or degrading punishment and treatment shall be prohibited.

Article 6

Every individual shall have the right to liberty and to the security of his person. No one may be deprived of his freedom except for reasons and conditions previously laid down by law. In particular, no one may be arbitrarily arrested or detained.

Article 7

1 Every individual shall have the right to have his cause heard. This comprises:
   (a) the right to an appeal to competent national organs against acts violating his fundamental rights as recognised and guaranteed by conventions, laws, regulations, and customs in force;
   (b) the right to be presumed innocent until proved guilty by a competent court or tribunal;
   (c) the right to defence, including the right to be defended by counsel of his choice;
   (d) the right to be tried within a reasonable time by an impartial court or tribunal.
2 No one may be condemned for an act of omission which did not constitute a legally punishable offence at the time it was committed. No penalty may be inflicted for an offence for which no provision was made at the time it was committed. Punishment is personal and can be imposed only on the offender.

Article 8

Freedom of conscience, the profession and free practice of religion shall be guaranteed. No one may, subject to law and order, be submitted to measures restricting the exercise of these freedoms.

Article 9

1 Every individual shall have the right to receive information.
2 Every individual shall have the right to express and disseminate his opinions within the law.

Article 10

1 Every individual shall have the right to free association provided that he abides by the law.
2 Subject to the obligation of solidarity provided for in Article 29, no one may be compelled to join an association.

Article 11

Every individual shall have the right to assemble freely with others. The exercise of this right shall be subject only to necessary restrictions provided for by law, in particular those enacted in the interest of national security, the safety, health, ethics and rights and freedoms of others.

Article 12

1 Every individual shall have the right to freedom of movement and residence within the borders of a state provided he abides by the law.
2 Every individual shall have the right to leave any country including his own, and to return to his country. This right may only be subject to restrictions, provided for by law for the protection of national security, law and order, public health, or morality.
3 Every individual shall have the right, when persecuted, to seek and obtain asylum in other countries in accordance with the laws of those countries and international conventions.
4 A non-national legally admitted in a territory of a state party to the present Charter may only be expelled from it by virtue of a decision taken in accordance with the law.
5 The mass expulsion of non-nationals shall be prohibited. Mass expulsion shall be that which is aimed at national, racial, ethnic or religious groups.

Article 13

1 Every citizen shall have the right to participate freely in the government of his country, either directly or through freely chosen representatives in accordance with the provisions of the law.
2 Every citizen shall have the right of equal access to the public services of his country.
3 Every individual shall have the right of access to public property and services in strict equality of all persons before the law.

Article 14

The right to property shall be guaranteed. It may only be encroached upon in the interest of public need or in the general interest of the community and in accordance with the provisions of appropriate laws.

Article 15

Every individual shall have the right to work under equitable and satisfactory conditions, and shall receive equal pay for equal work.

Article 16

1 Every individual shall have the right to enjoy the best attainable state of physical and mental health.
2 States party to the present Charter shall take the necessary measures to

protect the health of their people and to ensure that they receive medical attention when they are sick.

Article 17

1 Every individual shall have the right to education.
2 Every individual may freely take part in the cultural life of his community.
3 The promotion and protection of morals and traditional values recognised by the community shall be the duty of the State.

Article 18

1 The family shall be the natural unit and basis of society. It shall be protected by the State which shall take care of its physical and moral health.
2 The State shall have the duty to assist the family which is the custodian of morals and traditional values recognised by the community.
3 The State shall ensure the elimination of every discrimination against women and also ensure the protection of the rights of the woman and the child as stipulated in international declarations and conventions.
4 The aged and the disabled shall also have the right to special measures of protection in keeping with their physical or moral needs.

Article 19

All peoples shall be equal; they shall enjoy the same respect and shall have the same rights. Nothing shall justify the domination of a people by another.

Article 20

1 All peoples shall have the right to existence. They shall have the unques-tionable and inalienable right to self-determination. They shall freely determine their political status and shall pursue their economic and social development according to the policy they have freely chosen.
2 Colonised or oppressed peoples shall have the right to free themselves from the bonds of domination by resorting to any means recognised by the international community.
3 All peoples shall have the right to the assistance of the States party to the present Charter in their liberation struggle against foreign domination, be it political, economic or cultural.

Article 21

1 All peoples shall freely dispose of their wealth and natural resources. This right shall be exercised in the exclusive interest of the people. In no case shall a people be deprived of it.
2 In case of spoliation the dispossessed people shall have the right to the lawful recovery of its property as well as to an adequate compensation.

3 The free disposal of wealth and natural resources shall be exercised without prejudice to the obligation of promoting international economic co-operation based on mutual respect, equitable exchange, and the principles of international law.

4 States party to the present Charter shall individually and collectively exercise the right to free disposal of their wealth and natural resources with a view to strengthening African unity and solidarity.

5 States party to the present Charter shall undertake to eliminate all forms of foreign economic exploitation particularly that practised by international monopolies so as to enable their peoples to fully benefit from the advantages derived from their national resources.

Article 22

1 All peoples shall have the right to their economic, social and cultural development with due regard to their freedom and identity and in equal enjoyment of the common heritage of mankind.

2 States shall have the duty, individually or collectively, to ensure the exercise of the right to development.

Article 23

1 All peoples shall have the right to national and international peace and security. The principles of solidarity and friendly relations implicitly affirmed by the Charter of the UN and reaffirmed by that of the OAU shall govern relations between states.

2 For the purpose of strengthening peace, solidarity and friendly relations, states party to the present Charter shall ensure that:

   (a) Any individual enjoying the right of asylum under Article 12 of the present Charter shall not engage in subversive activities against his country of origin or any other state party to the present Charter.

   (b) Their territories shall not be used as bases for subversive or terrorist activities against the people of any other state party to the present Charter.

Article 24

All people shall have the right to a generally satisfactory environment favourable to their development.

Article 25

States party to the present Charter shall have the duty to promote and ensure through teaching, education, and publication, the respect of the rights and freedoms contained in the present Charter, and to see to it that these freedoms and rights as well as corresponding obligations and duties are understood.

Article 26

States party to the present Charter shall have the duty to guarantee the independence of the Courts and shall allow the establishment and improvement of appropriate national institutions entrusted with the promotion and protection of the rights and freedoms guaranteed by the present Charter.

CHAPTER II: DUTIES

Article 27

1 Every individual shall have duties towards his family and society, the State, and other legally recognised communities and the international community.

2 The rights and freedoms of each individual shall be exercised with due regard to the rights of others, collective security, morality, and common interest.

Article 28

Every individual shall have the duty to respect and consider his fellow beings without discrimination, and to maintain relations aimed at promoting, safeguarding, and reinforcing mutual respect and tolerance.

Article 29

The individual shall also have the duty:

1 To preserve the harmonious development of the family and to work for the cohesion and respect of the family; to respect his parents at all times, to maintain them in case of need.

2 To serve his national community by placing his physical and intellectual abilities at its service.

3 Not to compromise the security of the State whose national or resident he is.

4 To preserve and strengthen social and national solidarity, particularly when the latter is threatened.

5 To preserve and strengthen the national independence and the territorial integrity of his country and to contribute to its defence in accordance with the law.

6 To work to the best of his abilities and competence, and to pay taxes imposed by law in the interest of the society.

7 To preserve and strengthen positive African cultural values in his relations with other members of the society, in the spirit of tolerance, dialogue, and consultation and, in general, to contribute to the promotion of the moral well-being of society.

8 To contribute to the best of his abilities, at all times and at all levels, to the promotion and achievement of African unity.

PART II: Measures of Safeguard

Chapter I: Establishment and Organisation of the African Commission on Human and People's Rights

Article 30

An African Commission on Human and People's Rights, hereinafter called 'the Commission' shall be established within the OAU to promote human and people's rights and ensure their protection in Africa.

Article 31

1 The Commission shall consist of 11 members chosen from amongst African personalities of the highest reputation, known for their high morality, integrity, impartiality, and competence in matters of human and people's rights; particular consideration being given to persons have legal experience.

2 The members of the Commission shall serve in their personal capacity.

Article 32

The Commission shall not include more than one national of the same State.

Article 33

The members of the Commission shall be elected by secret ballot by the Assembly of Heads of State and Government, from a list of persons nominated by the States parties to the present Charter.

Article 34

Each State party to the present Charter may not nominate more than two candidates. The candidates must have the nationality of one of the States parties to the present Charter. When two candidates are nominated by a State, one of them may not be a national of that State.

Article 35

1 The Secretary General of the Organization of African Unity shall invite States parties to the present Charter at least four months before the elections to nominate candidates.

2 The Secretary General of the Organization of African Unity shall make an alphabetical list of the persons thus nominated and communicate it to the Heads of State and Government at least one month before the elections.

Article 36

The members of the Commission shall be elected for a six year period and shall be eligible for re-election. However, the term of office of four of the members elected at the first election shall terminate after two years and the term of office of the three others, at the end of four years.

Article 37

Immediately after the first election, the Chairman of the Assembly of Heads of State and Government of the Organization of African Unity shall draw lots to decide the names of those members referred to in Article 36.

Article 38

After their election, the members of the Commission shall make a solemn declaration to discharge their duties impartially and faithfully.

Article 39

1 In case of death or resignation of a member of the Commission, the Chairman of the Organization shall immediately inform the Secretary General of the Organization of African Unity, who shall declare the seat vacant from the date of death or from the date on which the resignation takes effect.

2 If, in the unanimous opinion of other members of the Commission, a member has stopped discharging his duties for any reason other than a temporary absence, the Chairman of the Commission shall inform the Secretary General of the Organization of African Unity, who shall then declare the seat vacant.

3 In each of the cases anticipated above, the Assembly of Heads of State and Government shall replace the member whose seat became vacant for the remaining period of his term unless the period is less than six months.

Article 40

Every member of the Commission shall be in office until the date his successor assumes office.

Article 41

The Secretary General of the Organization of African Unity shall appoint the Secretary of the Commission. He shall also provide the staff and services necessary for the effective discharge of the duties of the Commission. The Organization of African Unity shall bear the costs of the staff and services.

Article 42

1 The Commission shall elect its Chairman and Vice Chairman for a two year

period. They shall be eligible for re-election.

2 The Commission shall lay down its rules of procedure.

3 Seven members shall form a quorum.

4 In case of an equality of votes, the Chairman shall have a casting vote.

5 The Secretary General may attend the meetings of the Commission. He shall neither participate in deliberations nor shall he be entitled to vote. The Chairman of the Commission may, however, invite him to speak.

Article 43

In discharging their duties, members of the Commission shall enjoy diplomatic privileges and immunities provided for in the General Convention on the Privileges and Immunities of the Organization of African Unity.

Article 44

Provision shall be made for the emoluments and allowances of the members of the Commission in the Regular Budget of the OAU.

Chapter II: Mandate of the Commission

Article 45

The functions of the Commission shall be:

1 To promote human and people's rights and in particular:

    (a) To collect documents, undertake studies and researches on African problems in the field of human and people's rights, organise seminars, symposia and conferences, disseminate information, encourage national and local institutions concerned with human and people's rights and, should the case arise, give its views or make recommendations to governments;

    (b) To formulate and lay down, principles and rules aimed at solving legal problems relating to human and people's rights and fundamental freedoms upon which African governments may base their legislations;

    (c) Co-operate with other African and international institutions concerned with the promotion and protection of human and people's rights.

2 Ensure the protection of human and people's rights under conditions laid down by the present Charter.

3 Interpret all the provisions of the present Charter at the request of a state party, an institution of the OAU, or an African organisation recognised by the OAU.

4 Perform any other tasks which may be entrusted to it by the Assembly of Heads of State and Government.

Chapter III: Procedure of the Commission

Article 46

If a state party to the present Charter has good reasons to believe that another state party to this Charter has violated the provisions of the Charter, it may draw, by written communication, the attention of that state to the matter. This communication shall also be addressed to the Secretary-General of the OAU and to the Chairman of the Commission. Within three months of the receipt of the communication the State to which the communication is addressed shall give the enquiring State written explanation or statement elucidating the matter. This should include as much as possible relevant information relating to the laws and rules of procedure applied and applicable and the redress already given or course of action available.

Article 48

If within three months from the date on which the original communication is received by the State to which it is addressed, the issue is not settled to the satisfaction of the two States involved through bilateral negotiation or by any other peaceful procedure, either State shall have the right to submit the matter to the Commission through the Chairman and shall notify the other State involved.

Article 49

Notwithstanding the provisions of Article 47, if a state party to the present Charter considers that another state party has violated the provisions of the Charter, it may refer the matter directly to the Commission by addressing a communication to the Chairman, to the Secretary-General of the OAU, and the State concerned.

Article 50

The Commission can only deal with a matter submitted to it after making sure that all local remedies, if they exist, have been exhausted, unless it is obvious to the Commission that the procedure of achieving these remedies would be unduly prolonged.

Article 51

1 The Commission may ask the states concerned to provide it with all relevant information.
2 When the Commission is considering the matter, states concerned may be represented before it and submit written or oral presentations.

Article 52

After having obtained from the States concerned and from other sources all the information it deems necessary and after having tried all appropriate means to reach an amicable solution based on the respect of human and people's rights, the Commission shall prepare, within a reasonable period of time from the notification referred to in Article 48, a report stating the facts and its findings. This report shall be sent to the states concerned and communicated to the Assembly of Heads of State and Government.

Article 53

While transmitting its report, the Commission may make to the Assembly of Heads of State and Government such recommendations as it deems useful.

Article 54

The Commission shall submit to each Ordinary Session of the Assembly of Heads of State and Government a report on its activities.

OTHER COMMUNICATIONS

Article 55

1 Before each session, the Secretary of the Commission shall make a list of the communications other than those of states party to the present Charter and transmit them to the members of the Commission, who shall indicate which communications should be considered by the Commission.
2 A communication shall be considered by the Commission if a simple majority of its members so decide.

Article 56

Communication relating to human and people's rights referred to in Article 55 received by the Commission, shall be considered if they:

1 Indicate their authors even if the latter request anonymity.
2 Are compatible with the Charter of the OAU or with the present Charter.
3 Are not written in disparaging or insulting language directed against the State concerned and its institutions or to the OAU.
4 Are not based exclusively on news disseminated through the mass media.
5 Are sent after exhausting local remedies, if any, unless it is obvious that this procedure is unduly prolonged.
6 Are submitted within a reasonable period from the time local remedies are exhausted or from the date the Commission is seized of the matter.
7 Do not deal with cases which have been settled by these States involved in accordance with the principles of the Charter of the UN, or the Charter of

the OAU, or the provisions of the present Charter.

Article 57

Prior to any substantive consideration, all communications shall be brought to the knowledge of the State concerned by the Chairman of the Commission.

Article 58

1 When it appears after deliberations of the Commission that one or more communications apparently relate to special cases which reveal the existence of a series of serious or massive violations of human and people's rights, the Commission shall draw the attention of the Assembly of Heads of State and Government to these special cases.
2 The Assembly of Heads of State and Government may then request the Commission to undertake an in-depth study of these cases and make a factual report, accompanied by its finding and recommendations.
3 A case of emergency duly noticed by the Commission shall be submitted by the latter to the Chairman of the Assembly of Heads of State and Government who may request an in-depth study.

Article 59

1 All measures taken within the provisions of the present Charter shall remain confidential until such a time as the Assembly of Heads of State and Government shall otherwise decide.
2 However, the report shall be published by the Chairman of the Commission upon the decision of the Assembly of Heads of State and Government.
3 The report on the activities of the Commission shall be published by its Chairman after it has been considered by the Assembly of Heads of State and Government.

Chapter IV: Applicable Principles

Article 60

The Commission shall draw inspiration from international law on human and people's rights, particularly from the provisions of various African instruments on human and people's rights, the Charter of the UN, the Charter of the OAU, the Universal Declaration of Human Rights, other instruments adopted by the UN, and by African countries in the field of human and people's rights as well as from the provisions of various instruments adopted within the Specialised Agencies of the UN of which the parties to the present Charter are members.

Article 61

The Commission shall also take into consideration, as subsidiary measures to determine the principles of law, other general or special international conventions, laying down rules expressly recognised by member states of the OAU, African practices consistent with international norms on human and people's rights, customs generally accepted as law, general principles of law recognised by African states, as well as legal precedents and doctrine.

Article 62

Each state party shall undertake to submit every two years, from the date the present Charter comes into force, a report on the legislative or other measures taken with a view to giving effect to the rights and freedoms recognised and guaranteed by the present Charter.

APPENDIX E

BILL OF RIGHTS FOR THE TRANSITIONAL PERIOD IN THE REPUBLIC OF SOUTH AFRICA

NOTE: *The following bill of rights is part of the transitional constitution agreed upon by the Multi-Party Forum at the World Trade Centre, in November, 1993. The whole of chapter three of the transitional constitution deals with the issue of human rights for all in the period commencing after the April, 1994, general election for a constituent assembly. The bill may be subject to changes during the transitional period.*

Fundamental Rights

Application

7. (1) This Chapter shall bind the legislative and executive organs of the State at all levels of government including all statutory bodies and functionaries.

(2) This Chapter shall apply to all law in force and all administrative decisions taken and acts performed during the period of operation of this Chapter.

(3) Juristic persons shall be entitled to the rights contained in this Chapter where, and to the extent that, the nature of the rights permits.

(4) *(a)* When an infringement of or threat to any right entrenched in this Chapter is alleged, any person referred to in paragraph (b) shall be entitled to apply to a competent court of law for appropriate relief, which may include a declaration of rights.

(b) An application referred to in paragraph (a) may be brought by –

(i) a person acting in his or her own interest;

(ii) an association acting in the interest of its members;

(iii) a person acting on behalf of another person who is not in a position to bring such application in his or her own name;

(iv) a person acting as a member of or in the interest of a group or class of persons; or

(v) a person acting in the public interest.

Equality

8. (1) Every person shall have the right to equality before the law and to equal protection of the law.

(2) No person shall be unfairly discriminated against, directly or indirectly, and, without derogating from the generality of this provision, on one or more of the following grounds in particular: race, gender, sex, ethnic or social origin, colour, sexual orientation, age, disability, religion, conscience, belief, culture or language.

(3) *(a)* This section shall not preclude measures designed to achieve the adequate protection and advancement of persons or groups or categories of persons disadvantaged by unfair discrimination in order to enable their full and equal enjoyment of all rights and freedoms.

(b) Every person or community dispossessed of rights in land before the commencement of this Constitution under any law which would have been inconsistent with the provisions of subsection (2) shall be entitled to claim restitution of such rights subject to and in accordance with Chapter ... (ie the relevant chapter).

(4) Prima facie proof of discrimination on any of the grounds specified in subsection (2) shall be presumed to be sufficient proof of unfair discrimination as contemplated in that subsection until the contrary is established.

Life

9. Every person shall have the right to life.

Human dignity

10. Every person shall have the right to respect for and protection of his of her dignity.

Freedom and security of the person

11. (1) Every person shall have the right to freedom and security of the person which shall include the right not to be detained without trial.

(2) No person shall be subject to torture of any kind, whether physical, mental or emotional, nor shall any person be subject to cruel, inhuman or degrading treatment or punishment.

Servitude and forced labour

12. No person shall be subject to servitude or forced labour.

Privacy

13. Every person shall have the right to his or her personal privacy which shall include the rights not to be subject to searches of his or her person, home or property, the seizure of private possessions or the violation of private communications.

Religion, belief and opinion

14. (1) Every person shall have the right to freedom of conscience, religion, thought, belief and opinion, which shall include academic freedom in institutions of higher learning.

(2) Without derogating from the generality of subsection (1), religious observances may be conducted at state or state-aided institutions under rules established by an appropriate authority for that purpose, provided that such observances are conducted on an equitable basis and attendance at them is free and voluntary.

Freedom of expression

15. (1) Every person shall have the right to freedom of speech and expression, which shall include freedom of the press and other media, and the freedom of artistic creativity and scientific research.

(2) All media financed by or under the control of the state shall be regulated in a manner which ensures impartiality and the expression of a diversity of opinion.

Assembly, demonstration and petition

16. Every person shall have the right to assemble and demonstrate with others peacefully and unarmed, and to present petitions.

Freedom of association

17. Every person shall have the right to freedom of association.

Freedom of movement

18. Every person shall have the right to freedom of movement anywhere within South Africa.

Residence

19. Every person shall have the right freely to choose his or her place of residence anywhere in South Africa.

Citizens' rights

20. Every citizen shall have the right to enter, remain in and leave South Africa, and no citizen shall be deprived of his or her citizenship.

Political rights

21. (1) Every citizen shall have the right –

(a) to form, to participate in the activities of and to recruit members for a political party;

(b) to campaign for a political party or cause; and

(c) freely to make political choices.

(2) Every citizen shall have the right to vote, to do so in secret and to stand for election to public office.

Access to court

22. Every person shall have the right to have justiciable disputes settled by a court of law or, where appropriate, another independent and impartial forum.

Access to information

23. Every person shall have the right to access to all information held by the state or any of its organs at any level of government in so far as such information is required for the protection or exercise of any of his or her rights.

Administrative justice

24. Every person shall have the right to –

(a) lawful administrative action where any of his or her rights or interests is affected or threatened;

(b) procedurally fair administrative action where any of his or her rights or legitimate expectations is affected or threatened;

(c) be furnished with reasons in writing for administrative action which affects any of his or her rights or interests unless the reasons for such action have been made public; and

(d) administrative action which is justifiable in relation to the reasons given for it where any of his or her rights is affected or threatened.

Detained, arrested and accused persons

25. (1) Every person who is detained, including every sentenced prisoner, shall have the right –

(a) to be informed promptly in a language which he or she understands of the reason for his or her detention;

(b) to be detained under conditions consonant with human dignity, which shall include at least the provision of adequate nutrition, reading material and medical treatment at state expense;

(c) to consult with a legal practitioner of his or her choice, to be informed of this right promptly and, where substantial injustice would otherwise result, to be provided with the services of a legal practitioner by the state;

(d) to be given the opportunity to communicate with, and to be visited by, his or her spouse or partner, next-of-kin, religious counselor and a medical practitioner of his or her choice; and

(e) to challenge the lawfulness of his or her detention in person before a court of law and to be released if such detention is unlawful.

(2) Every person arrested for the alleged commission of an offence shall, in addition to the rights which he or she has as a detained person, have the right –

(a) in a language which he or she understands, to be informed promptly that he or she has the right to remain silent and to be warned of the consequences of making any statement;

(b) as soon as it is reasonably possible, but not later than 48 hours after the arrest or the first court day thereafter, to be brought before an ordinary court of law and to be charged or to be informed of the reason for his or her further detention, failing which he or she shall be entitled to be released;

(c) not to be compelled to make a confession or admission which could be used in evidence against him or her; and

(d) to be released from detention with or without bail, unless the interests of justice require otherwise.

(3) Every accused person shall have the right to a fair trial, which shall include the right –

(a) to a public trial by an ordinary court of law within a reasonable time after having been charged;

(b) to be informed with sufficient particularity of the charge;

(c) to be presumed innocent and to remain silent during plea proceedings or trial and not to testify during trial;

(d) to adduce and challenge evidence, and not to be a compellable witness against himself or herself;

(e) to be represented by a legal practitioner of his or her choice or, where substantial injustice would otherwise result, to be provided with legal representation at state expense, and to be informed of these rights;

(f) not to be convicted of an offence in respect of any act or omission which was not an offence at the time it was committed, and not to be sentenced to a more severe punishment than that which was applicable when the offence was committed;

(g) not to be tried again for any offence of which he or she has previously been convicted or acquitted;

(h) to have recourse by way of appeal or review to a higher court than the court of first instance;

(i) to be tried in a language which he or she understands, or failing this, to have the proceedings interpreted to him or her; and

(j) to be sentenced within a reasonable time after conviction.

Economic activity

26. (1) Every person shall have the right freely to engage in economic activity

and to pursue a livelihood anywhere in South Africa.

(2) Subsection (1) shall not preclude measures designed to promote the protection or the improvement of the quality of life, economic growth, human development, social justice, basic conditions of employment, fair labour practices or equal opportunity for all, provided such measures are justifiable in an open and democratic society based on freedom and equality.

Labour Relations

27. (1) Every person shall have the right to fair labour practices.

(2) Workers shall have the right to form and join trade unions, and employers shall have the right to form and join employers' organisations.

(3) Workers and employers shall have the right to organise and bargain collectively.

(4) Workers shall have the right to strike for the purpose of collective bargaining.

(5) Employers' recourse to lock-out for the purpose of collective bargaining shall not be impaired subject to section 34(1).

Property rights

28. (1) Every person shall have the right to acquire and hold rights in property and, to the extent that the nature of the rights permits, to dispose of such rights.

(2) No deprivation of any rights in property shall be permitted otherwise than in accordance with a law.

(3) Where any rights in property are expropriated pursuant to a law referred to in subsection (2) such expropriation shall be permissible for public purposes only and shall be subject to the payment of agreed compensation or, failing agreement, the payment of such compensation and within such period as may be determined by a court of law as just and equitable, taking into account all relevant factors, including, in the case of determination of compensation, the use to which the property is being put, the history of its acquisition, its market value, the value of the investments in it by those affected and the interests of those affected.

Environment

29. Every person shall have the right to an environment which is not detrimental to his or her health or well-being.

Children

30. (1) Every child shall have the right –

      (a) to a name and nationality as from birth;

      (b) to parental care;

    (c) to security, basic nutrition and basic health and social services;

    (d) not to be subject to neglect or abuse; and

    (e) not to be subject to exploitative labour practices nor to be required or permitted to perform work which is hazardous or harmful to his or her education, health or well-being.

(2) Every child who is in detention shall, in addition to the rights which he or she has in terms of section 25, have the right to be detained under conditions and to be treated in a manner that takes account of his or her age.

(3) For the purpose of this section a child shall mean a person under the age of 18 years and in all matters concerning such child his or her best interests shall be paramount.

Language and culture

31. Every person shall have the right to use the language and to participate in the cultural life of his or her choice.

Customary law

32. (1) Every person who –

    (a) in pursuance of the right entrenched in section 17 belongs to a community which observes a system of customary law; or

    (b) of free and informed choice observes the rules and practices of a system of customary law and associates with other persons observing the same rules and practices,

shall, subject to section 7(2) and 34(2), have the right to the recognition of such customary law as the legal disposition governing the internal affairs of the community mentioned in paragraph (1) or regulating his or her interpersonal relations with the persons mentioned in paragraph (b), as the case may be.

(2) It shall be competent for any court of law applying a system of customary law as contemplated in subsection (1) and finding certain of its rules and practices to be in conflict with section 8, to determine, to the extent that its jurisdiction allows , conditions on and a time within which such rules and practices shall be brought in conformity with section 8.

(3) This section shall not preclude legislation designed to assist the development of customary law in accordance with the values embodied in the other provisions of this Chapter.

Education

33. Every person shall have the right –

    (a) to basic education and to equal access to educational institutions;

    (b) to instruction in the language of his or her choice where this is

reasonably practicable; and

(c) to establish, where practicable, educational institutions based on a common culture, language or religion, provided that there shall be no discrimination on the ground of race or colour.

Limitation

34. (1) The rights entrenched in this Chapter may be limited by law of general application provided that such limitation –

(a) shall be permissible only to the extent that it is –

(i) reasonable; and

(ii) justifiable in an open and democratic society based on freedom and equality; and

(b) shall not negate the essential content of the right in question,

and provided further that any limitation to –

(aa) a right entrenched in section 10, 11, 12, 14(1), 21, 25 or 30(1)(d) or (e) or (2); or

(bb) a right entrenched in section 15, 16, 17, 18, 23, or 24, in so far as such right relates to free and fair political activity,

shall, in addition to being reasonable as required in paragraph (a)(i), also be necessary.

(2) Save as provided for in subsection (1) or any other provision of the Chapter, no law, whether a rule of the common law, customary law or legislation, shall limit any right entrenched in this Chapter.

(3) The entrenchment of the rights in terms of this Chapter shall not be constructed as denying the existence of any other rights or freedoms recognised and conferred by common law, customary law or legislation to the extent that they are not inconsistent with the provisions of this Chapter.

(4) This Chapter shall not preclude measures designed to prohibit unfair discrimination by bodies and persons other than those bound in terms of section 7(1).

(5)*(a)* The provisions of a law in force at the commencement of this Chapter promoting fair employment practices, orderly and equitable collective bargaining and regulating industrial action shall remain of full force and effect until repealed or amended by the legislature.

(b) If a proposed enactment amending or repealing a law referred to in paragraph (a) deals with matter in respect of which the National Manpower Commission, referred to in section 24 of the Labour Relations Act 1956, or any other similar body which may replace the Commission, is competent in terms of a law then in force to consider and make recommendations, such proposed enactment shall not be introduced in Parliament unless the Commission or such other body

has been given an opportunity to consider the proposed enactment and to make recommendations with regard thereto.

State of emergency and suspension

35. (1) A state of emergency shall be proclaimed prospectively under an Act of Parliament and shall be declared only where the security of the Republic is threatened by war, invasion, general insurrection or disorder or at a time of natural disaster, and if the declaration of a state of emergency is necessary to restore peace or order.

(2) The declaration of a state of emergency and any action, whether a regulation or otherwise, taken in consequence of it, shall be of force for a period not more than 21 days unless it is extended for a period of no longer than three months or consecutive periods of no longer than three months or consecutive periods of no longer than three months at a time, by resolution of the National Assembly adopted by a majority of at least two-thirds of all its members.

(3) Any superior court shall be competent to enquire into the validity of a declaration of a state of emergency, any extension thereof, and any action, whether a regulation or otherwise, taken under such declaration.

(4) The rights entrenched in this Chapter may be suspended only in consequence of the declaration of a state of emergency, and only to the extent necessary to restore peace or order.

(5) Neither any law which provides for the declaration of a state of emergency, nor any action taken in consequence thereof, shall permit or authorise –

   (a) the creation of retrospective crimes;

   (b) the indemnification of the State or of persons acting under its authority for unlawful actions taken during the state of emergency; or

   (c) the suspension of this section, and sections 7, 8(2), 9, 10, 11(2), 12, 14, 27(1) and (2), 30(1)(d) and (e) and (2) and 34(1) and (2).

(6) The detention of a person under a state of emergency shall be subject to the following conditions:

   (a) an adult family member or friend of the detainee shall be notified of the detention as soon as is reasonably possible;

   (b) the names of all detainees and a reference to the measures in terms of which they are being detained shall be published in the Gazette within five days of their detention;

   (c) when the rights entrenched in sections 11 or 25 have been suspended –

      (i) the detention of a detainee shall, as soon as it is reasonably possible but not later than 10 days after his or her detention, be reviewed by a court of law, and the court shall order the release of the detainee if it is satisfied that the detention is not necessary to restore peace or order;

(ii) the detainee shall at any stage after the expiry of 10 days of a review in terms of subparagraph (i) be entitled to apply to a court of law for a further review of his or her detention, and the court shall order the release of the detainee if it is satisfied that the detention is no longer necessary to restore peace or order;

(d) the detainee shall be entitled to appear before the court in person, to be represented by legal counsel, and to make representations against his or her continued detention;

(e) the detainee shall be entitled at all reasonable times to have access to a legal representative of his or her choice;

(f) the detainee shall be entitled at all times to have access to a medical practitioner of his or her choice;

(g) the state shall for the purpose of a review referred to in paragraph (c)(i) or (ii) submit written reasons to justify the detention or further detention of the detainee to the courts, and shall furnish the detainee with such reasons not later than two days before the review.

(7) If a court of law, having found the grounds for a detainee's detention unjustified, orders his or her release, such a person shall not be detained again on the same grounds unless the state shows good cause to a court of law prior to such re-detention.

Interpretation

36. (1) In interpreting the provisions of this Chapter a court of law shall promote the values which underlie an open and democratic society based on freedom and equality and shall, where applicable, have regard to public international law applicable to the protection of the rights entrenched in this Chapter, and may have regard to comparable foreign case law.

(2) No law which limits any of the rights entrenched in this Chapter, shall be constitutionally invalid solely by reason of the fact that the wording used prima facie exceeds the limits imposed in this Chapter, provided such law is reasonably capable of a more restricted interpretation which does not exceed such limits, in which event the law shall be construed as having the said more restricted meaning.

(3) In the interpretation of any law and the application and development of the common law and customary law, a court shall have due regard to the spirit, purport and objects of this Chapter.

BIBLIOGRAPHY

BENDIX, S *Industrial Relations in South Africa*. Juta & Company Limited, Wetton, Cape Town. 1992.

BUSH, C *Gandhi*, Burke Publishing Company, London, Toronto, New York. 1988.

BUTLER, J *et al* (eds) *Democratic Liberalism in South Africa*. David Philip Publisher, Cape Town, Johannesburg. 1987.

CLARK, P *Abraham Lincoln*. Wayland Publishers, Hove, East Sussex. 1981.

DAVIES, R *et al The Struggle for South Africa* vol 1. ZED Books, London. 1984.

GASTROW, S *Who's Who in South African Politics*. Ravan Press, Johannesburg. 1987.

HARTENIAN, L *Benito Mussolini*. Chelsea Home Publishers, New York, Philadelphia. 1989.

MANDELA, N *The Struggle is My Life*. IDAF Publications Limited, London. 1990.

MARÉ, G & HAMILTON, G *An Appetite for Power: Buthelezi's Inkatha and South Africa*. Ravan Press, Johannesburg. 1987.

OATES, S B *Let the Trumpet Sound: The Life of Martin Luther King, Jn Search Press, London and Tunbridge Wells. 1982.*

ODENDAAL, A *Vukani Bantu! The Beginnings of Black Protest Politics in South Africa*. David Philip Publisher, Cape Town, Johannesburg. 1984.

RUBIN, B *Modern Dictators*. New American Library, New York, Scarborough. 1987.

SACHS A *Promoting Human Rights in a New South Africa*. Oxford University Press, Cape Town. 1990.

UWECHUE, R *Makers of Modern Africa: Profile in History*. Africa Books Limited, Hammersmith, London. 1991.

UWECHUE, R *Africa's Who's Who*. Africa Books Limited, Hammersmith. 1991.

VAN RENSBURG, A P *Contemporary Leaders of Africa*. HAUM, Cape Town. 1975.

WEPMAN, D *Adolf Hitler*. Chelsea Publishers, New York, Philadelphia. 1989.

WILLIAMS, G & HACKLAND, B *The Dictionary of Contemporary Politics of Southern Africa*. Routledge, London. 1988.

INDEX